negotiating postmodernism

negotiating postmodernism

WAYNE GABARDI

University of Minnesota Press
Minneapolis / London

Published by the University of Minnesota Press
111 Third Avenue South, Suite 290
Minneapolis, MN 55401-2520
http://www.upress.umn.edu

Library of Congress Cataloging-in-Publication Data

Gabardi, Wayne, 1955–
    Negotiating postmodernism / Wayne Gabardi.
        p.   cm.
    Includes bibliographical references and index.
    ISBN 0-8166-3000-3 (alk. paper) — ISBN 0-8166-3001-1 (pbk. : alk. paper)
    1. Postmodernism — Social aspects.   2. Postmodernism — Political aspects.   I. Title.
    HM449.G33 2000
    301'.01 — dc21   00-008310

Printed in the United States of America on acid-free paper

The University of Minnesota is an equal-opportunity educator and employer.

11 10 09 08 07 06 05 04 03 02 01   10 9 8 7 6 5 4 3 2 1

To my parents,

Daniel Gabardi

and

Jean Marchese Gabardi

It is more of a job to interpret the interpretations than to interpret things themselves, and there are more books about books than about any other subject. We do nothing but write glosses about each other.
    — Michel de Montaigne, "Of Experience"

I fear that the animals consider man as a being like themselves that has lost in a most dangerous way its sound animal common sense.
    — Friedrich Nietzsche, *The Gay Science*

Do I contradict myself?
Very well, then, I contradict myself,
I am large, I contain multitudes.
    — Walt Whitman, "Leaves of Grass"

Contents

Preface

This book is about the modern-postmodern debate and its implications for contemporary social theory, political philosophy, and democratic thought at the turn of the twenty-first century. Its underlying premise is that the first wave of the modern-postmodern debate, which was cast in the 1970s and early 1980s in terms of a polemical opposition between modern critical theorists and postmodern radical deconstructionists, was superseded in the late 1980s and 1990s by a second wave of development that resulted in the emergence of a "critical postmodernism." This new theoretical perspective, indebted to, yet different from, both critical theory and postmodern theory, is the subject matter of this study.

I examine the genesis, development, and social and political significance of critical postmodernism through an interdisciplinary approach and exposition that incorporates contemporary social theory, cultural studies, political philosophy, and democratic theory. I critically assess the relevant literatures that have contributed to and sustained this second wave of the modern-postmodern debate from this interdisciplinary stance. Thus I have attempted to provide a comprehensive overview and critique of the varied dimensions of the modern-postmodern debate and its legacy. The text ranges across a number of academic disciplines, intellectual discourses, thinkers, and issues.

This approach, which relies on a rather broad reach and a profile-and-critique format, provides the reader with a much fuller picture of the modern-postmodern debate than can be gleaned from more in-depth yet narrowly focused scholarly studies on specific thinkers, ideas, and theoretical conundrums. The weakness of this approach lies in its tendency to reduce the complexity and subtlety of specific thinkers, ideas, and theoretical conundrums to what I have judged to be the kernel or central issue most relevant to the modern-postmodern debate.

Yet this was necessary to achieve my goal of illuminating the fuller scope of the debate and its consequences for today. I believe that students and scholars whose lives and work are not intimately bound up with the fate of the modern-postmodern debate will greatly benefit from this approach. Once they have read this book, they can choose for themselves which thinkers, ideas, and issues to explore in more detail. As for critical postmodern scholars, while they may be somewhat frustrated with the profile-and-critique flow of the book, my hope is that they will focus on the major theoretical propositions, as well as the practical strategies and proposals I advance. For it is here that my own voice emerges out of the narrative re-creation of the modern-postmodern debate.

Thus there is more to this book than a comprehensive overview and critique of the modern-postmodern debate and its legacy. For embedded in its richly textured narrative are three interrelated theoretical propositions that I present, develop, and defend. These theoretical formulations structure the overall organization of the text and propel it forward. They are: (1) a thesis of contemporary social and cultural change I call "our late modern/postmodern transition"; (2) the idea of a critical postmodern political philosophy; and (3) the idea and strategies of a "critical postmodern democratic politics."

It is also important to point out that the central figure appearing throughout this book is French philosopher-historian Michel Foucault. The thought of the "final Foucault" and his unfinished work both inspired and guided the conceptualization, research, and writing of this study on critical postmodernism and democracy. I remain convinced that Foucault is the most protean, critical, insightful, and compelling voice to speak and give meaning to the nature of our present condition.

Postmodern thought reminds us that as subjects we are socially and culturally constituted by a complex web of enabling and constraining networks of desire, power, discourse, and knowledge. The modernist in me has attempted to shape the modern-postmodern debate in a certain direction. Yet the postmodernist in me realizes that I am carried along by a stronger current and can navigate my way only in a limited sense. Thus I acknowledge that our present condition is a complex intertwinement of late modern and postmodern forces pulling us in different directions.

This book is primarily for advanced students and professionals in social and political theory. It can be used to think about and teach issues in contemporary social and political theory. It is interdisciplinary and comprehensive. Its profile-and-critique format lends itself to classroom teaching. It advances and defends specific theoretical stances, moving beyond its descriptive and explanatory infrastructure. And it profiles practical strategies and alternatives for negotiating our present social and political condition.

My hope is that this exercise in political thinking both illuminates and validates the creative power of the modern-postmodern debate. The emergence of the idea of a critical postmodernism is due to the creative energy and intellectual force of this debate. Critical postmodernism is in turn relevant to the fate of democracy today.

Acknowledgments

I want to thank several people who helped me in the course of writing this book. They include colleagues, friends and family, students and scholars, my editor and editorial assistants. Let me begin by acknowledging the encouragement and support of all my colleagues in the political science department here at Idaho State University—David Adler, Sean Anderson, Mary Jane Burns, Rick Foster, Ralph Maughan, Mark McBeth, and Douglas Nilson. I want to especially thank Rick Foster for his exemplary stewardship of our department as chair and for his invaluable influence on my professional development as a teacher, scholar, and colleague. I also want to thank Cheryl Hardy, who as administrative assistant and secretary goes out of her way to maintain a superb working environment with great energy, efficiency, and patience. She also helped word process and format drafts of this book.

I further want to thank those students at Idaho State University, graduate and undergraduate, who have worked with me both in class and outside of class to wrestle with complex ideas and perspectives in social and political thinking. They helped me craft a book that is accessible to both scholars and high-caliber students.

Leslie Paul Thiele read and provided insightful comments on the different drafts of this work, including the final draft. I also want to thank those anonymous reviewers retained by the University of Minnesota Press who read earlier drafts of the book. I incorporated some of their recommendations into the final manuscript. Thanks are due to all of these reviewers for their critical acumen and sage advice.

Thanks to Carrie Mullen. my editor at the University of Minnesota Press. She was interested in the idea and the first few rough chapters and proceeded to move the long process forward with great energy, skill, and good advice. Thanks to Linda Lincoln for her thorough and meticulous copyediting, which made this book a better read. The University of Minnesota Press was my first choice when I pitched the project to various publishers. I am glad they moved on it and offered me a contract.

I especially want to thank my parents, Daniel Gabardi and Jean Marchese Gabardi, for their lifelong love, support, and understanding on my behalf. This book is dedicated to them. My sister, Lisa Gabardi, has been equally supportive and a good friend and confidant.

As for my wife, Janis Stitt, I want to acknowledge her profound influence on my life. As my best friend and soulmate, her intelligence, love, practical wisdom, tenacity, and consummate skill as a social worker have contributed to what I regard as a very fulfilled life.

Introduction
The Nature of Our Present

> *The solemnity with which everyone who engages in
> philosophical discourse reflects on his own time strikes me
> as a flaw. I can say so all the more firmly since it is
> something I have done myself; and since, in someone like
> Nietzsche, we find this incessantly — or, at least, insistently
> enough. I think we should have the modesty to say to
> ourselves that, on the one hand, the time we live in is not
> the unique or fundamental or irruptive point in history
> where everything is completed and begun again. We must
> also have the modesty to say, on the other hand, that —
> even without this solemnity — the time we live in is very
> interesting; it needs to be analyzed and broken down, and
> that we would do well to ask ourselves, "What is the nature
> of our present?"*
> — Michel Foucault, "Structuralism and Post-
> Structuralism: An Interview with Michel Foucault"

The Nature of Our Present

What is the nature of our present? When French philosopher Michel Foucault posed this question during an interview in 1983, he was rephrasing the question posed two hundred years ago by German philosopher Immanuel Kant: What is enlightenment?[1] Both thinkers pondered what it meant to be modern. When Kant posed his question, modernity was a dynamic idea bound up with the rationalist and progressive spirit of the eighteenth-century European Enlightenment. When Foucault posed his question, modernity had become a contested idea under critical scrutiny.

In raising this question, Foucault situated himself within a discourse that ignited and consumed the intellectual passions of European and North American philosophers, cultural analysts, and social and political theorists during the 1970s and 1980s. They wrestled with the question of modernity and pondered its fate as a philosophical idea, historical project, and sociological condition. Divided into warring camps, these thinkers were principally influenced by the doctrines of French "structuralism," "poststructuralism," and German "Frankfurt School" critical theory. The ensuing polemical encounters between postmodern radical deconstructionists and modern critical theorists gave shape to what became known as "the modern-postmodern debate."

This debate centered on the relationship between the competing ideas of *modernity* and *postmodernity*. These opposing concepts were invoked to capture the historical character, sociological condition, and philosophical nature of the present situation in advanced Western societies. Employing these concepts, critical theorists and postmodernists confronted each other in a highly polemical and polarizing manner. Critical theorists rejected the conviction among postmodernists that we are witnessing a radical break with the modern age and the advent of a new postmodern condition. They regarded the project of modernity as "unfinished." The debate forced us to choose — late modernity or postmodernity?

Postmodernism emerged in Paris in the late 1960s and early 1970s, the product of French philosophy and the intellectual doctrines of structuralism, poststructuralism, and deconstruction. The first wave of the modern-postmodern debate reached its high point in the early 1980s when French postmodernism was directly challenged by the modernist critical theorist Jürgen Habermas. In the wake of this confrontation, a discernible second wave emerged in the mid-1980s as intellectuals critical of both French postmodernism and German critical theory embarked on new critical reconstructive projects. The modern-postmodern debate was phrased less in terms of polarizing polemics and more in the way of constructive dialogue, accommodation, and attempted syntheses.

By the 1990s, the French passion for the ruthless deconstruction of everything modern and Habermas's German idealist quest to resurrect the modern Enlightenment project had spent their respective dystopian and utopian energies. The concepts of modernity and postmodernity were reassessed and reintroduced to one another in a manner that refocused attention on their continuities, rather than on their discontinuities. More precisely, the exploration and elucidation of their more complex intertwinement, as well as the critical reweighing of both critical theory and postmodern theory, largely defined the second wave of the modern-postmodern debate in the late 1980s and early 1990s.

Today, at the turn of the twenty-first century, we have moved beyond the great modern-postmodern debate. Yet its legacy is still very much with us. We have been left with a rich array of tools with which to return to Foucault's question and rethink the role of critical theory and postmodernism in analyzing the nature of our present. Indeed, it is my contention that in the aftermath of the modern-postmodern debate, a new type of critical social and political theoretical perspective has emerged that is indebted to, yet different from, both German critical theory and French postmodernism. It is a hybrid Americanized orientation that I call *critical postmodernism.* Its genesis, development, and political significance is the subject matter of this study.

The central thesis of this book is as follows. The great modern-postmodern debate of the 1970s and 1980s gave birth in the 1990s to critical postmodernism. In developing its intellectual outlook, critical postmodern thought has both incorporated and jettisoned aspects of modernist critical theory and postmodernism. The result is an emphasis on the intertwinement of modernity and postmodernity conceived of as sociocultural, philosophical, and political conditions. Critical postmodernism values the importance of both normative critique and political action (the strength of critical theory), and ontological critique, cultural analysis, and aesthetics (the strength of postmodern theory) in constructing a critical social and political theoretical perspective.

This thesis is developed and defended in the following manner. I answer Foucault's provocative question concerning the nature of our present by doing what Foucault did not do, that is, examining the current sociological condition of advanced Western societies. Foucault's approach was philosophical and historical, and he employed the tools of ontological critique and genealogy. My approach is first and foremost sociological. Only by identifying the cultural and social-structural developments of our time can we fully understand the emergence of postmodernism, the modern-postmodern debate, and critical postmodernism.

In the course of assessing the sociological condition of contemporary Western societies, I advance the thesis of a *late modern/postmodern transition.* Our present moment is best understood in terms of a complex tension and linkage between postmodern sociocultural changes and late modern political-economic institutional changes. A societal restructuring is under way, driven by a postmodern dynamic of high-tech, cultural change that has forced existing modern institutions to reorganize. The term *late modern/postmodern transition* refers to this dynamic of social change. The term *critical postmodernism* refers to that theoretical and ideological perspective best suited to make sense of this social condition.

I define critical postmodernism as the recent product of the modern-postmodern debate as it has developed in the intellectual field of political philosophy. I contend that a critical postmodern dialogue has been constructed around the work of philosophers Jürgen Habermas, Martin Heidegger, Hannah Arendt, and Michel Foucault. I work within this interpretive matrix and conclude that a critical postmodernism is best achieved by working through Foucault's unfinished project.

The ideas of a late modern/postmodern transition and critical postmodernism assess the nature of our present as both a sociological condition and a philosophical idea. Armed with these two ideas, I come to terms with the fate of democracy in our time. I proceed, again under the influence of Foucault, to develop a *critical postmodern democratic politics*. This leads me to critique our dominant mode of governance, as well as contemporary normative models of democracy. I profile several alternative *strategies of democracy* for our time that are again indebted to Foucault's thought. I conclude that the dynamics, structure, and discourse of Western democracy have shifted away from the modern model of liberal representative democracy and toward a new global-local dynamic of complexity and techno-oligarchy, as well as toward new modes of democratic resistance and self-governance.

Our Late Modern/Postmodern Transition

In part I of this book I accomplish two tasks. In chapter 1, I set the context for this study by developing a detailed account of the modern-postmodern debate. I define this debate in terms of two developmental waves. The first, which gained momentum in the 1970s and peaked in the mid-1980s, was cast in terms of a polemical opposition between French postmodernism and German critical theory. The second, which lasted from the mid-1980s to the mid-1990s, moved beyond the theme of modernity versus postmodernity and toward a critical postmodern dialogue.

In chapter 2, I pursue a sociological answer to Foucault's question on the nature of our present by examining competing "postmodern" and "late modern" models of contemporary society. While I agree with postmoderns such as Jean Baudrillard, Jean-François Lyotard, and Zygmunt Bauman that a postmodern social and cultural shift has occurred, I question their radical cultural and institutional accounts of this shift. Late modern social theorists such as Jürgen Habermas, David Harvey, and Anthony Giddens fail to grasp our postmodern social and cultural shift, but their models of a late modern institutional shift are more accurate than those of the postmoderns. I develop the idea of a late modern/postmodern transition that sees the present as a confluence of postmodern cultural and late modern structural changes. I demonstrate this thesis by drawing on the work of Edward Soja, Stewart Clegg, Scott Lash, and John Urry.

I define our present historical situation as a transitional time that is best understood as a complex interplay of postmodern social and cultural changes coupled with late modern economic and political institutional changes. Advanced Western societies have experienced a postmodern cultural shift in conjunction with changes in what has become a high-tech, global capitalism. Postmodern ways of life have proliferated in the wake of these changes. Yet at the institutional levels of advanced capitalism and the nation-state, we are still in the midst of a late modern shift driven by the forces of complex globalization. These cultural and structural changes have significantly altered our everyday lives. Daily activities are increasingly shaped by heightened levels of complexity and contingency.

Critical Postmodernism

This assessment of our current sociological condition informs my understanding of critical postmodernism. I conceive of critical postmodernism not only as a product of the modern-postmodern debate, but also as a theoretical and ideological response to our current late modern/postmodern transition and a practical tool for negotiating this transition. In part II, I develop the idea of a critical postmodernism along these lines.

I focus my analysis on the interpretive matrix that has exerted a significant influence over the modern-postmodern debate in political philosophy. This matrix has been shaped by Jürgen Habermas's critical modernist philosophy of communicative action, Martin Heidegger's postmodern ontology, Hannah Arendt's conception of political action, and Michel Foucault's postmodern histories and critical ontology of power/freedom. I negotiate this intellectual terrain with a central conviction and a guiding question. I am convinced that a viable political philosophy must explain how we relate to the world as existential beings (ontology), how we develop and defend a normative stance (critique), and how we negotiate the historical field of political action (*praxis*). Thus I pose the question: What is the relationship between ontological identity and difference, critical rationality, and human action in the context of our late modern/postmodern transition?

I begin my case for a critical postmodernism in chapter 3 by locating its identity in the idea of a *critical ontology.* I then explore the development of a dialogue between Habermas and Heidegger as one pathway toward a critical postmodernism. It features the work of philosophers and political theorists Fred Dallmayr, Richard Bernstein, and Stephen White. Although Habermas is a critical theorist working to reconstruct the Enlightenment project by building a new theory of rationality, and Heidegger is a critical ontologist concerned with concrete worldly existence and the experience of Being, they share an underlying theme of reconciliation. Therefore, political theorists have drawn on the sophisticated worldviews of these thinkers to help rebuild disintegrated solidarities through new models of intersubjective reconciliation, community, and democracy.

Those thinkers influenced by Arendt and Foucault have embarked on a different path. They embrace the very aspects of the human condition that Habermas and Heidegger radically tame or purge: subjectivity, power, and *virtù* (existential, aesthetic, and political virtuosity). Here I turn to the work of political theorists Bonnie Honig and Dana Villa, who have developed postmodern readings of Hannah Arendt. What emerges out of this encounter is a model of politics that combines ontological disclosiveness (the Heidegger influence) with a politics of existential *virtù* (the Nietzsche influence). I call this a "politics of disclosive *virtù.*"

I reach the conclusion that neither the Habermas-Heidegger dialogue on reconciliation nor the postmodern Arendtian thought project are viable paradigms for a critical postmodern political philosophy. I contend that they do not effectively resonate with our current late modern/postmodern transition and that we need to move beyond Habermas, Heidegger, and Arendt in favor of Michel Foucault as the better site upon which to construct a critical postmodernism for our time.

In chapter 4 I work through Foucault's unfinished project. By carefully examining his "final" and "unfinished" work, we can uncover the tools needed to articulate a critical postmodern political philosophy. Foucault's final work reveals a shift away from poststructuralism and post-modernism and toward a rethinking of the critical spirit of modernity. In the end, he left us with an intellectual constellation that was both a critique of modernity and a complex mixture of ancient, modern, and postmodern ideas and practices. I proceed to connect his ideas concerning the nature of our present, critical ontology, the power/freedom relationship, resistance, becoming an ethical subject, and the practice of government with my ideas of a late modern/postmodern transition and critical postmodernism.

My idea of a critical postmodernism is "perspectivist." That is, I believe we must take into account the multiple perspectives (worldviews and truth-claims) circulating today between cultures, subcultures, communities, lifestyles, and life-worlds. Thus I view our current reality in terms of the complexity of social and cultural spaces and environments. Engaging and translating our multicultural and multidimensional world intelligibly should occur from multiple vantage points. I further propose a framework of analysis that conceptualizes social, cultural, and political change in terms of four interrelated sets of explanatory variables: (1) biological evolution and the body field; (2) the reproduction of cultural practices; (3) organized social power networks; and (4) the reflexive or interpretive self.

Toward a Critical Postmodern Democratic Politics

Can critical postmodernism inform a democratic politics able to make a practical impact on individuals, groups, and institutions enmeshed in our late modern/postmodern transition? Are calls for greater democratization realistic in a time of postmodern change, increased social and technological complexity, and globalization? More importantly, what does democracy mean today? And what of its fate? Does democracy as we have known it have a future? These questions frame the intellectual organization and trajectory of part III of this book.

In chapter 5 I describe the current state of democracy. I begin by explaining the distinction between "politics" and "the political" and its relevance for political analysis. I further assert that today we find ourselves moving from a modern to a postmodern political condition. Influenced by Foucault's concept of governmentality, I develop a model of our current democratic government that I call "postmodern, neoliberal, techno-oligarchy." It is a mode of governance shaped by the forces of techno-oligarchic globalization, hyperreal media technologies, and new advanced liberal strategies. I then profile four normative models of democracy that have emerged in the past decade as alternatives to this existing government. They are communitarian, deliberative, agonistic, and associative models of democracy.

I critique and expose the limitations of these normative models, calling for greater sociological and political realism in contemporary democratic theorizing. Here I rely on the work of Italian political philosopher Danilo Zolo. His realist assessment of contemporary Western democracies as self-legitimizing, oligarchic, mass-media panopticons is similar to Foucault's view of modern governance. That is, politics today exists as a vast array of governing technologies, both micro and macro, that discipline and seduce both the body politic and individual subjects.

In chapter 6 I develop the idea of a critical postmodern democratic politics by calling for the revaluation of the idea of democracy. With Sheldon Wolin, I argue that democracy today should be reconceived as a "mode of being" rather than a "form of government." The contemporary *demos* operates in the form of local and microlevel strategies of creative resistance to modern government. A critical postmodern democratic politics perceives its task as advancing specific strategies of freedom and democracy in this context. Those "strategies of democracy" relevant to our present political condition are again indebted to the work of Foucault. They are (1) transgressive negation; (2) self-care; (3) performative action; (4) agonistic *praxis*; (5) the practice of *parrhesia* or "frank speech"; and (6) local resistance.

This critical postmodern democratic politics is different from a modern democratic politics. It does not appeal to a universal human nature, free will, natural rights, individualism, a common good, egalitarian justice, rational consensus, representation, or emancipatory action. Instead, it grasps our social condition as one of complex glocality, embracing a perspectival pluralism and creative engagement, revisioning civil society as a postmodern associational space, shifting from a work to a leisure ethic, and negotiating the power fields of our existing government by way of alternative global-local and microlevel democratic strategies. As an oppositional subculture, a critical postmodern democratic politics can help redefine and reshape the democratic experience as it unfolds in our late modern/postmodern times.

In conclusion, I reaffirm that our time is transitional, a passage from one set of circumstances to another. I further contend that negotiating our late modern/postmodern transition requires a kind of critical postmodern modesty reminiscent of Michel de Montaigne's Renaissance pre-scription for daily living. That is, we should cultivate an ethic that gen-erates a modest yet vigilant skepticism toward things. We also need to rethink the meaning of human freedom and association, of how we re-late our experience of our selves to the experience of others, both hu-man and nonhuman. And we need to continually remind ourselves that a democratic existence is concerned first and foremost with ordinary people as they struggle to create and sustain a free way of life. Together, these reflections embody an ethos that assigns meaning to the task of making sense of the nature of our present.

Part I

1 — The Modern-Postmodern Debate and Its Legacy

The debate is now no longer between ancients and moderns, but between moderns and postmoderns.
— David Couzens Hoy,
"Foucault: Modern or Postmodern?"

The First Wave: The Challenge of Postmodernism

The modern-postmodern debate took as its main point of reference the fate of the modern Enlightenment project, the eighteenth-century European vision of transforming the world in the name of rational progress. The Enlightenment was the high point of modernity, an era encompassing the Renaissance, the Protestant Reformation, and the Scientific Revolution through the American and French Revolutions to the flowering of socialism. It crystallized the modernist belief in human perfectibility through rationality. The Enlightenment ideal of the free rational individual living in a free rational society reflected an optimistic view of human nature and the prospects of human emancipation.[1]

Today we live in a time not anticipated by Enlightenment thinkers. Yet whether we live in a post-Enlightenment or postmodern period is open to debate. Modernists, hopeful that the consequences of modernization can be corrected, believe that the Enlightenment project should be defended. Postmodernists, skeptical of both the Enlightenment and modernization, champion new cultural movements and new models of social and political life.[2]

Postmodern cultural movements first emerged in the 1960s in painting, architecture, and literary criticism. Pop art challenged modernist art

3

by experimenting with new cultural forms and contents that embraced everyday life, radical eclecticism, subcultures, mass media, and consumerism.[3] Charles Jencks identified the development of Late-Modernism and Post-Modernism in architecture. Late-Modernism exhibited an exaggerated modernist, slick, high-tech style. Post-Modernism exhibited a new "double-coded" style (part modern, part something else) that embraced "neo-vernacular," "ad-hoc urbanist," and "straight revivalist" motifs.[4] And a postmodern literature emerged around two new models of language and textual interpretation: "structuralism" and "deconstruction."[5]

Two major developments in the Paris of the 1960s set the stage for the birth of postmodernism as a movement in philosophy and the social sciences. First, as mentioned, the influence of new linguistic theories in the humanities and social sciences gave rise to a new type of analysis known as structuralism. Second, the revolts of May 1968 resulted in the apocalyptic rebirth and dissolution of revolutionary politics. Many intellectuals on the Left abandoned Marx and socialism for Nietzsche and a new kind of postmodern politics.[6]

The roots of structuralism can be found in the language theory of Ferdinand de Saussure.[7] For Saussure, our encounter with the world is an encounter with linguistic signs or words whose meanings can only be fathomed by understanding their relational status within a language system. The identity of signs is defined in relation to the underlying rules of the symbolic system or "signifying chain." Therefore, the meaning of a signifier (a word or phrase) is to be found not in its representational relation to the signified (a subject or object), but in its differential relation to other signifiers.

French structuralists crafted methodologies that analyzed social and cultural phenomena as the product of deep-seated linguistic orders or codes. Both the individual self and social life were understood as operating like a language. Claude Lévi-Strauss in anthropology, Jacques Lacan in psychoanalysis, and Louis Althusser in Marxism all developed structuralist approaches. Social structures were reinterpreted as symbolic systems and the human agent was largely eliminated as a key explanatory factor in understanding the workings of culture and society.[8]

Structuralism soon gave rise to poststructuralism, an intellectual movement influenced by the thought of German existentialist philosophers Friedrich Nietzsche and Martin Heidegger, as well as the language theory of British analytic philosopher Ludwig Wittgenstein.[9] Poststructuralists rejected the idea that there are innate structures of mind or culture that can be identified and universally applied. They asserted that social linguistic networks called "discourses" are historically produced and context dependent. Where structuralists located "structure," poststructuralists found "difference." While discourses are organized systems of language that regulate experience, language itself is a contingent construct, an open-ended field of infinite sign substitutions.

Poststructuralism and postmodernism both challenged the very logic of Western thought. The poststructuralist view of language as a radically pluralized field of sign networks and of the self as a decentered, narrative construct informed the postmodern critique of Western modernity. While poststructuralism was largely a philosophical and literary movement, postmodernism emerged as a new cultural movement and an academic field of cultural studies.[10]

In its early and most radical phase, most evident in the work of Jacques Derrida, Gilles Deleuze, Félix Guattari, Jean-François Lyotard, and Michel Foucault, postmodernism leveled an assault on the fundamental premises of modernity. It rejected the Enlightenment belief in the unity of reason and progress, the idea that there is a rational purpose or teleology to history. It also rejected the notion that the individual is a free and rational agent capable of self-conscious reflection, that science and technology can rationally control and develop the natural and social worlds, and that liberty, equality, and democracy rest upon universal humanistic foundations. Every modern referent was on the chopping block and the guillotine fell quite frequently.

Georges Bataille's (1897–1962) studies on cultural taboos, eroticism, and the obscene influenced early French postmodernism.[11] His radical Dionysian ethic of transgression rested on the conviction that only through the pursuit of eroticism, madness, sadomasochism, religious profanation, intoxication, and revolution can we experience liberation from rigid identity structures. This strategy of self-overcoming through the deliberate cultivation of states of delirium fueled the fires of a radical aesthetics and a nihilistic politics of experience.

Gilles Deleuze's *Nietzsche and Philosophy* (1962) helped establish Nietzsche as the pivotal figure in early French postmodernism.[12] Rejecting both Marxism and psychoanalysis as not radical enough, he and psychiatrist Felix Guattari analyzed the social schizophrenic character of advanced capitalist society in terms of postmodern liberation rather than modern alienation.[13] The breakdown of meaning and identity that characterizes schizophrenia can be viewed as an opportunity for transforming disintegrated egos into radical postmodern desiring subjects. The "schizo-subject" is able to experience a "molecular revolution" whereby psychological meltdown becomes the condition for a radical reforging of human identity.

Philosopher Jean-François Lyotard's early postmodern career began with the book *Discourse, Figure* (1971). Radicalizing the insights of Nietzsche and Freud, Lyotard rejected the modern model of "discourse" (conceptual representation) for the postmodern model of "figure" (that oppositional dynamic working within discourse that ruptures the rules of conceptualization and that is evoked in visual perception, sexual desire, the unconscious, rhetoric, and the sublime). In *The Libidinal Economy* (1974), Lyotard put forth his own philosophy of desire, which replaced Marx with Nietzsche.[14]

Jacques Derrida, the father of deconstruction, critiqued what he regarded as the implicit premises of structuralist thought — the "metaphysics of presence" (that consciousness has an unmediated correspondence with reality) and the "transcendental signified" (the assumption of an originative cause or first principle).[15] Reality itself, understood as an infinitely reconstituting universe of language games or "texts," has no foundation, point of origin, or end point. Since human events and artifacts (texts) do not have a stable set of referents, they are open to multiple interpretations.[16] No one text has an intrinsic meaning because meaning is a function of its differential relationship to other texts. Thus we must grasp the world in terms of what Derrida described as *différance* — as a differential universe of symbolic relations whose meaning is always contingent, always beyond full comprehension and certainty.[17]

Deconstruction uprooted the suspect metaphysical foundations of Western civilization, revealing a succession of hegemonic cultural identities ("the Same") whose meaning and status were constructed at the expense of their binary opposite ("the Other"). These binary oppositions — same/other, male/female, mind/body, good/evil, civilized/barbarian — were in turn legitimized through strategies of inclusion and exclusion.[18] Deconstruction saw its task as the transformative disruption of unitary and dualistic thought constructs. This implied political interventions, not just critical interpretive analyses of texts. To deconstruct was not merely to dis-integrate, but to create new "inscriptions" that privileged multiplicity and ambiguity.[19]

Finally, Michel Foucault would write anti-Enlightenment histories or "archaeologies of knowledge" that challenged the very notions of modern rationality, individual agency, and humanism.[20] Archaeological analysis portrayed the world not as the product of rational-purposive human agency, but as the construct of "discursive formations" (language practices organized into cultural codes of discourse and institutional norms). Foucault was interested in excavating alternative interpretations of human culture and knowledge that had been hidden in the sedimented layers of Western history. "History," as it has been traditionally represented, consists of a series of grand legitimizing narratives of hegemonic discursive formations that have subjugated alternative modes of knowledge and experience. The histories that Foucault resurrected revealed discursive fields that were more discontinuous than continuous, more spatial than linear, and more radically pluralized and dispersed than teleologically centered and causally linked.

In his most ambitious archaeological study, *The Order of Things* (1966), Foucault examined the modern origins of the empirical social sciences and their principal creation and referent— "Man." The modern birth and mutation of Man as an epistemological object of knowledge and subject of humanist action, a subject-object duality, spanned four eras: (1) the Renaissance; (2) the classical period (1660–1800); (3) the modern period (1800–1950); and (4) the postmodern present. Foucault's analysis reversed the logic of modern humanism and then deconstructed it. Man was not the foundation of modern knowledge, but rather the product or effect of the institutionalization of scientific discourses needed to further propel Enlightenment modernization forward. Foucault's "death of Man" conclusion looked forward to the dissolution of modern humanism and a posthumanist cultural transition.[21]

Jane Flax best summed up the challenge of postmodernism by identifying eight modern convictions that it had thrown into doubt: (1) the existence of a stable or unified self; (2) that reason, best exemplified in science, can provide an objective, reliable, and universal foundation for knowledge; (3) that the knowledge acquired from the right use of reason will be "true"; (4) that reason has transcendental and universal qualities that exist independent of the self's contingent existence; (5) that the right use of reason will ensure autonomy and freedom; (6) that reason can effectively distinguish true knowledge from power; (7) that science is the paradigm for all true knowledge; and (8) that language is transparent in its representation of reality.[22]

Modernity versus Postmodernity

Sociologist Daniel Bell was one of the first to take up the challenge of postmodernism. In *The Cultural Contradictions of Capitalism* (1976) he identified a moral crisis in Western society bound up with the decline of Puritan bourgeois culture and the ascendence of a postmodern culture that he described in terms of an aesthetic relativism and a hedonistic individualism.[23] Yet the most formidable critic of postmodernism and defender of modernity has been German philosopher and heir to the Frankfurt School tradition of critical theory — Jürgen Habermas.

Critical theory is best understood in terms of two generational waves of development. The first developed in Germany in the 1930s with the establishment of the Frankfurt Institute for Social Research, reaching its crest in the late 1960s and early 1970s. This generation, which developed a neo-Marxist cultural analysis of modernity, included Max Horkheimer, Theodor Adorno, Erich Fromm, and Herbert Marcuse.[24] The current second generation is exemplified in the thought of Habermas and represents a significant shift from first-generation critical theory. Habermas has drawn more upon analytic language philosophy and is indebted more to Kant and cognitive psychology than to Marx and Freud. He views modernity in terms of a distorted dynamic of progress, rather than as decadence.[25]

The first wave of the modern-postmodern debate reached its high point when Habermas took on French thinkers directly in a series of twelve lectures on modernity and postmodernity published in 1985 as *The Philosophical Discourse of Modernity.* Here Habermas defended modern reason against postmodernism. He defined postmodernism as the latest manifestation of aesthetic modernism, which began with the Romantic revolt against the philosophy of Hegel.[26] He further identified Nietzsche as the father of postmodernism and argued that his heirs had taken two paths leading to dead ends.[27] The first, the radical critique of metaphysics by Heidegger and Derrida, is a regression back to the mysticism of Being.[28] The second, the radical aesthetic pathway of Bataille and Foucault, rejects modern reason and morality for an aesthetics that plunges us deeper into self-absorption.[29] He concluded that postmoderns have repeated the flawed Nietzschean and Heideggerean endeavors of destroying modern Western reason and linking radical deconstruction to simplistic accounts of modernization.[30]

Habermas's attempt to revitalize the Enlightenment project was based on the intellectual legitimacy of his theory of communicative action. Habermas argued that modernity failed to achieve the rational society because it rested on a model of rationality that was too dependent on the philosophy of consciousness and its grounding in the subject-object relation.[31] From Descartes and the British empiricists through Kant and Hegel to Nietzsche, Weber, the early Frankfurt School thinkers, and even French postmodernists, he argued, Western thought has been on the wrong path. Our models of knowledge, society, and human action have located cognitive, practical, and aesthetic forms of rationality primarily in the reflective individual. Habermas questioned the correspondence between rationality, reflective individuality, and subject-object consciousness.

He proceeded to rethink the foundations of Enlightenment reason by replacing modernist models of rationality based on the philosophy of self-consciousness with a linguistic model that located rationality in the very structures of human speech. Habermas redefined social action in terms of language and redefined language use in terms of intersubjective action. Social action was interpreted as communicative action and rationality as communicative rationality. In shifting from individual subjectivity to inter-subjective interaction, Habermas externalized and relocated human rationality and judgment as a sociological process of "discourse."

Habermas's reformulation of modern reason found its home in the logic and structure of human communication, in what he defined as the "universal pragmatics" of speech acts.[32] He asserted that all language communication presupposes an ideal communication community oriented toward mutual understanding. This assertion was further grounded in a part scientific, part transcendental ("quasi-transcendental") claim about the very structure of language itself. By developing procedures of normative discourse (to discuss the validity of norms or standards of judgment), we can progress from our diverse moral positions toward a general consensus. This involves decontextualizing the specific contents of moral claims and focusing on the formal conditions of speech. Thus Habermas's moral theory of "discourse ethics" employed argumentative procedures to test norm validity claims.[33]

Discourse ethics is designed to translate everyday moral intuitions and opinions into concepts that lay claim to universal validity. According to Habermas, everyday communication occurs against a pretheoretical background of common understanding. When this breaks down, we must appeal to discourse ethics to analyze the validity of the contested norm, to reestablish a background consensus, and to resume normal communication. Therefore, Habermas's discourse ethic claims to both rationally reconstruct the general presuppositions underlying all communication and provide a set of procedures for resolving moral disputes. The logic underlying this procedural ethic is that justice is the most fundamental human moral intuition, that impartiality is central to justice, that impartiality demands a fixed and formal procedure or set of rules in judging norm validity, and that modern moral argumentation and justification require moral principles that can be universalized.[34]

Modern culture, no longer subject to traditional, closed belief systems and absolute moral truths, must rely on norms that are rationally tested through critical argumentation. Yet the tragedy of modernity lies in its failure to achieve this rational culture. In explaining this failure, Habermas's research pointed to two major problems: (1) the development of a subject-centered model of reason into a dominant form of instrumental, economic rationality; and (2) the employment of this model in the social processes of modernization.[35] The result has been the systematic repression of intersubjective communication and democratic public life, the proliferation of technocratic modes of organization, and the periodic emergence of countercultural movements of Romantic revolt, of which postmodernism is the latest wave.

Thus the first wave of the modern-postmodern debate reached its culmination. By the mid-1980s, the battle lines between postmoderns and followers of Habermas had been drawn. At the same time, a second wave of the debate emerged. Critical of both Habermas's rationalist quest to resurrect the Enlightenment project and the neo-Nietzschean anarchism of French postmodernism, participants explored alternative paths and developed more constructive dialogues between the modern and the postmodern.

The Second Wave: Toward a Critical Postmodernism

By the 1990s we would find ourselves in the middle of the second wave of the modern-postmodern debate. By this time the first wave of radical French postmodernism had largely run its course. The ruthless deconstruction of everything modern gave way to new reconstructive endeavors. Distinctions were made between affirmative and nihilistic perspectives, and between theories promoting radical discontinuity and those that defined postmodernity as a transition rather than a radical rupture with modernity. This second wave spoke more readily to contemporary social, economic, and political concerns. And it was phrased less in terms of polarizing polemics and more in the way of dialogue, accommodation, and attempted syntheses. What began in the mid-1980s and gained momentum and maturation in the 1990s was a series of fusions or integrations of postmodernism with other critical theories of society, culture, and politics, ranging from Marxism to liberalism, feminism, critical theory, and radical ecology.

1) A major first step in this movement beyond the modern-postmodern impasse was achieved by political theorists Ernesto Laclau and Chantal Mouffe in their pathbreaking work *Hegemony and Socialist Strategy: Towards a Radical Democratic Politics* (1985). By constructing a critical dialogue between Marxism and postmodernism, they were able to produce a post-Marxist critical theory that incorporated postmodern philosophy and cultural insights and pointed the way toward a critical postmodernism. They deconstructed both the Marxist tradition and its core concepts, purging it of its grand Hegelian vision of historical progress, its labor model of society, the centrality of class analysis, and its outdated working-class model of revolution.[36] What remained standing was the concept of "hegemony." Their rethinking of this idea, formulated by Italian Marxist Antonio Gramsci, became the fundamental pivot of their postmodern, post-Marxist critical theory.[37]

Marxists have defined cultural hegemony as the ability of the dominant social class in a capitalist society to socialize the other classes into conforming to its political system and culture. Cultural traditions, practices, and institutions play an integral role in assimilating the working classes and oppositional countercultures. Laclau and Mouffe redefined cultural hegemony as a process of democratic struggle among diverse political actors who operated according to what they determined to be a new social logic of pluralization. "Radical democracy" replaced socialism. It was decentralist and participatory, associated with the new social movements of the 1970s and 1980s, and dedicated to a postmodern cultural politics of radical pluralism.[38]

In the language of poststructuralism and postmodernism, Laclau and Mouffe redefined society as a complex field of "discursive practices" organized around highly contested "nodal points" of power due to increased social and cultural pluralization. They concluded that "society" does not exist "as a sutured and self-defined totality." Society as a complex field of power relations and different identities is not reducible to a single determinant logic. Rather, a multiplicity of "articulatory practices" compete for hegemony "in a field criss-crossed with antagonisms."[39]

In other words, human beings socially construct their world through discourses. These discourses, always shifting and diverse, are still subject to hegemony as they are selectively organized around certain privileged power points in the social field. Laclau and Mouffe defined discourse sociologically as an ensemble of social relations. They further rejected the distinction between "discursive" (conceived of as ideology) and "non-discursive" (conceived of as material forces) activities. By affirming the material character of every discourse, they abandoned the Marxist economic base/cultural superstructure model for a more complex cultural materialist field theory of society.

2) A critical postmodern movement from within the liberal democratic tradition also emerged in the 1980s in the work of political theorist William Connolly and philosopher Richard Rorty. In *Political Theory and Modernity* (1989), Connolly modeled his interrogation of modern political thought on Nietzsche and Foucault.[40] Political theories from Hobbes to Marx were interpreted as stories that tell us more about the rational disciplining of the individual and society than about the existential exploration of human freedom. Focusing on the ontological issue of identity and difference, Connolly concluded that Western cultures have historically placed human identity on an absolutist foundation, moralized the relation between one's identity and others who are different in terms of good and evil, and sustained this fundamentalist ontology through institutions that legislate rigid moral codes. He further asserted that modern liberalism, the dominant political discourse in America, is infused with fundamentalist beliefs that need to be radically deconstructed.[41]

Rorty's critique of modern liberalism claimed that most liberals lack irony (John Rawls and Habermas) and most ironists are not liberal (Nietzsche, Heidegger, and French postmoderns). Thus what is needed is a new political philosophy of "liberal ironism." Let irony rule in the private realm, let solidarity and sensitivity to cruelty reign in the public realm, and acknowledge that both private and public life need to be understood against the background of existential contingency. This was the central theme of *Contingency, Irony, and Solidarity* (1989).[42]

Rorty crafted a new vocabulary for a postmodern liberal bourgeois political culture. He combined a postmodern epistemological and cultural relativism with an optimistic pragmatism to fashion a new rhetoric of Western liberalism more "poeticized" than "rationalized" or "scientized."[43] Truth is made, not discovered. It is an achievement attributable to cultural creativity shaped within a language community. This community, wherein reside our beliefs and values, is the product of time and circumstance. Therefore, the liberal community common to Western countries needs to jettison its outmoded Enlightenment philosophical foundations and adopt a postmodern voice relevant to our current circumstances.

Rorty reinvented or "redescribed" the liberal distinction between private and public life.[44] The result was a bifurcated political culture in which creative irony and liberal values could coexist. This combined a Nietzschean passion for self-creation and an ironic discourse in one's personal life with a public ethic of liberal outrage against cruelty. With irony restricted to the world of private persons and associations, and ideologies and metaphysical thinking purged from the public sphere, politics would be governed by a commonsense liberal concern for liberty, opportunity, fair play, and tolerance. We should look to philosophers and artists for models of self-creation.[45] Yet it is novelists, journalists, and ethnologists that bring home our obligations to others through their vivid empirical portrayals of human struggle and suffering.[46]

3) A postmodern feminism emerged in the 1970s in the work of French writers and philosophers Luce Irigaray, Hélène Cixous, and Julia Kristeva. Influenced by structuralism (Lacan) and deconstruction (Derrida), they developed the idea of "Woman-as-Other" as a radical critique of "phallogocentrism" (patriarchal thought organized according to masculine rules of language and styles of writing and rooted in male sexuality).[47] The deconstruction of patriarchal constructions of female identity opened the way toward redefining the feminine. This was achieved by rediscovering the unique ontology of the female body and expressing it in a new language and writing style.

Irigaray employed the "speculum," a mirrored gynecological instrument, as a metaphor to illustrate how men from Plato to Freud have constructed women as inferior mirror images of their own narcissistic speculations on the human condition.[48] Cixous claimed that masculine discourse and writing interprets reality through a conceptual grid that employs dichotomous, hierarchical oppositions. By contrast, feminine discourse and writing is more open, expressive, and pluralistic because female sexuality is more complex than male sexuality.[49] And Kristeva would call for a "semiotic revolution" in language that fundamentally challenged the patriarchal symbolic order, an order reproduced through the repressive mechanism of the Oedipus complex.[50]

Postmodern feminism's critique of patriarchal domination was unsettling for many modern feminists. Relativist and apolitical to many, it was perceived as a threat to feminism as an emancipatory movement. Its emphasis on radical difference proved to be a powerful weapon in the feminist arsenal. Yet in scrutinizing the ontological and epistemological underpinnings of patriarchal modernity, postmodern feminism called into question the universalistic premises of freedom, equality, and democracy.

The debates between modern and postmodern feminists resulted in a reconfigured relationship between the feminine, the modern, and the postmodern. This took postmodern feminism in different directions. While feminist thinkers such as Jane Flax, Judith Butler, and Susan Hekman advanced radical postmodern feminist perspectives, Jana Sawicki and Lois McNay sought a more balanced accommodation between postmodernism and critical theory.[51] However, what is most noticeable is that Michel Foucault has had the greatest influence on this second wave of postmodern feminism.[52] Indeed, as I consistently maintain throughout this study, it is Foucault who emerges from the modern-postmodern debate as the most protean, critical, insightful, and compelling voice to speak and give meaning to the nature of our present condition.

4) A reconstructed critical theory that incorporated postmodern theory was also developed in the 1990s by American critical theorists Douglas Kellner, Steven Best, and Ben Agger. However, Herbert Marcuse, not Jürgen Habermas, was their critical theorist of choice. In their opinion, Habermas largely renounced his radical credentials when he shifted from the neo-Marxist analysis of legitimacy in advanced capitalist societies to the ethics of discourse and the idea of a more deliberative model of liberal democracy driven by a Kantian emphasis on morality and law.[53]

Kellner and Best drew a distinction between the "extreme postmodern theories" of French thinkers Baudrillard, Lyotard, Deleuze, and Guattari and the "reconstructive postmodern theories" of Fredric Jameson, Laclau and Mouffe, and Flax.[54] Radical postmoderns reject modernity and thus the very idea of critical social theory. Reconstructive or critical postmoderns maintain that we are living in a transitional period that is "a borderline region between modernity and a new, as yet inadequately theorized, social situation."[55] They concluded that "in this transitional era, both modern and postmodern theories are helpful to theorize the continuities with the past and the novel, 'postmodern,' phenomena."[56] In American critical postmodern fashion, they incorporated and moved beyond German critical theory and French postmodernism to produce a "multidimensional and multiperspectival critical theory."[57]

Ben Agger has also maintained a distinction between a conformist "affirmative postmodernism" and "postmodernism as critical theory."[58] Affirmative postmodernism rejects all normative standards of judgment, denies history in favor of an "eternal present," falsely proclaims the "death of the subject," embraces consumerism, is antipolitical, and reduces everything to a symbolic, cultural explanation. Critical postmodernism preserves a continuity with "rebellious modernism," maintains a new cultural materialist conception of human rationality and subjectivity, adopts a multiperspective approach that avoids the twin extremes of absolutism and relativism, and sees politics everywhere, except in the formal political system.

5) A dialogue between postmodernism and ecological thought emerged as another product of the second wave of the modern-postmodern debate. This is best exemplified in Michael Zimmerman's *Contesting Earth's Future: Radical Ecology and Postmodernity* (1994). Deep ecology, social ecology, and ecofeminism, as well as critical postmodernism, are identified as being on the cutting edge of contemporary critical thought. Critical postmodernism is defined as "an intriguing intersection of modernity's emancipatory goals, postmodern theory's decentered subject, and radical ecology's vision of an increasingly nondomineering relationship between humans and nonhumans."[59] Furthermore, Zimmerman demonstrates how radical ecology and postmodern theory both develop a more in-depth critique of modernization: "its control obsession, its logic of identity, its anthropocentric humanism, and its dualism."[60]

6) Finally, a critical postmodern dialogue in political philosophy took shape around the work of philosophers Jürgen Habermas, Martin Heidegger, Hannah Arendt, and Michel Foucault. It pursued two alternative paths: the construction of a dialogue between Habermas's critical theory of communicative action and Heidegger's postmodern ontology,

and the development of a neo-Nietzschean democratic ethos culled from the thought of Arendt and Foucault. These developments toward a critical postmodern political philosophy are discussed in part 2 of this book.

This second wave of the modern-postmodern debate achieved an impressive momentum and maturation in the 1990s. All the work profiled here demonstrates a movement toward exploring constructive encounters between late modern and postmodern thought. This narrative exposition of six significant streams of contemporary critical thought provides empirical evidence of the central thesis informing this book: that the modern-postmodern debate of the 1970s and 1980s gave birth to critical postmodernism in the 1990s. It further provides the intellectual context from which a critical postmodern social theory (part I, chapter 2), political philosophy (part II), and analysis of democracy (part III) are advanced and interrelated.

2 — A Society in Transition

My own feeling is that while postmodern social theory is articulating real problems and posing important challenges to radical social theory and politics today, it is exaggerating the break, rupture, and alleged novelty in the contemporary socio-historical epoch and is downplaying, and even occluding, the continuities. Adopting a term of Max Horkheimer, I would prefer to speak of a "society in transition" rather than a completely new postmodern social formation.

— Douglas Kellner, "Postmodernism as Social Theory: Some Challenges and Problems"

Society and Theory Today

Postmodernity and late modernity are as much social and historical categories as they are philosophical concepts. As stated from the outset, if the nature of our present is to be properly understood, it must be assessed first and foremost as a social condition. Only by identifying and explaining the social-structural and cultural developments of our time can we fully understand the concepts of postmodernity and late modernity as philosophical ideas and political projects. Therefore we begin by comparing two different sociological accounts of the current condition of affluent Western societies.

The current state of social theory can be defined in terms of the oppositional relationship between modern and postmodern models of social and cultural change.[1] Most practicing sociologists remain committed to the modern agenda.[2] They interpret our current condition as a transition to late modernity that remains continuous with the paradigm of modernization. Thus it is premature to speak of a new historic period that embodies new types of social organization and social and cultural interaction. Despite all the talk of postmodernism, we are not living in a postmodern social condition.

Postmodern social theory conceptualizes postmodernity as a radically discontinuous event of social and cultural change. It represents a novel, historic shift in Western culture that has effectively disorganized modern social structures. Technological as well as cultural transformations have recast everyday life and our relationship to existing institutions, which have become hollowed-out shells. Postmodern social theorists have therefore raised serious questions concerning the status of both modern social theory and its principal referent — modern society.

The Postmodern Condition

It was French philosopher Jean-François Lyotard who coined the term "the postmodern condition." In *The Postmodern Condition: A Report on Knowledge* (1979), Lyotard argued that the great "metanarratives" or grand rationalist stories of Enlightenment modernity are now exhausted in the wake of current postmodern changes. Written primarily to examine the current relationship between the production of scientific knowledge and the legitimation of postindustrial state capitalism, Lyotard drew a distinction between modern scientific activity (as the verification of existing paradigms) and postmodern scientific activity (as the pursuit of irreconcilable anomalies).[3] Scientific theories, he maintained, although epistemologically verified and argumentatively justified, are ultimately validated through epic modernist stories or myths of rational humanistic progress.[4] The problem is that these grand stories of modern legitimation no longer work.

The shift from an old industrial to a new informational capitalism, and from a modern to a postmodern culture, has rendered the metanarratives of modernity obsolete. Today capitalism operates as a vast desiring machine whose orientation is toward ever accelerating novelty. Governmental legitimacy is largely the function of the dominant power frameworks and values of technology, consumption, and the mass media. As for the moral and social bonds of civil society, they have unraveled and have been dispersed into new radically pluralized social and cultural networks.[5] And modern humanist models of rationality and morality have disintegrated into highly localized and specific contexts of discourse and judgment.

As sociologist Zygmunt Bauman puts it, while modernity championed universality, homogeneity, monotony, and clarity, modernization produced radical plurality, variety, contingency, and ambivalence.[6] This postmodern condition has "re-enchanted" a world that modernity tried to "disenchant."[7] The modern culture that emerged out of the breakdown of the feudal social order was confident that reason, freed from the shackles of religion and metaphysics, could impose sufficient "structure" on the world. From Cartesian science to Marxian socialism, modernity exemplified the compulsive drive to rationally organize everything. Yet the modern imperative to will the world as a malleable object has been questioned.

The postmodern condition can be understood as a disruption of modern society and culture driven by the return of the repressed features of modernization. Enlightenment modernity underestimated the negative consequences of its universalist humanism, dualistic epistemology, instrumental rationality, individualist ethos, and technological hubris. Postmodernism has called into question these fundamental modern values, which continue to strive to legitimize knowledge, aesthetic expression, morality, and political authority.

Today we find ourselves in a new phase of capitalism no longer organized around the production principle. The modern model of Puritanism, productivism, and the capital-labor relationship has been effectively superseded by a new mode of postmodern consumption, postindustrial information and telecommunication technologies, strategies of globalization, and the capital-technology relationship. Society has reorganized itself around the pleasure principle of consumer freedom. Furthermore, this economy is driven more by the production and consumption of informational and symbolic goods than by manufactured and raw material goods.

The early work of French sociologist Jean Baudrillard focused on the workings of advanced consumer societies. He concluded that consumption, not production, is the motor force of contemporary social life.[8] However, consumption is defined not by the possession of material goods, but by a system of symbolic or sign relations. Consumer objects are part of an advertising system that constitutes a "code" or social classification system.[9] Social differentiation and status are functions of the symbolic or sign value of commodities as determined by this cultural code. The value of consumer objects as expressive symbols has overtaken their utilitarian use and economic exchange values.[10] Thus the consumer cultural code has become the central force driving a society that requires consumers, not citizens, for its continued reproduction.[11]

Our perception of reality has been further altered by the fast-paced production and consumption of symbols and images. Everyday life is saturated by these postmodern artifacts, rendering it more multidimensional and multiperspectival, and thus more complex. The microelectronic and information revolutions have created a social condition in which dematerialized images are more prevalent and influential than material objects.

Baudrillard described this phenomenon as the arrival of "the simulated society."[12] At the heart of this new postmodern society is mass-media communication. The TV screen is the nexus in which simulations of reality blend into a phantasmagoric kaleidoscope. The distinction between appearance and reality, signs and objects, is blurred. We live our daily lives in a world of "hyperreality." This is a condition in which symbols, signs, and words are divorced from direct experience and freely associate to create a parallel world disconnected from and more "real" than everyday life. Furthermore, the boundaries between entertainment, information, advertising, and politics collapse, or "implode," into a collage of radically juxtaposed and ever changing images. Content and meaning dissolve into pure aesthetic form and are consumed as such. The result is a world where experience is increasingly the effect of self-referential, microelectronic images.

Baudrillard would further contend that this condition has created a new postmodern silent majority that refuses to be represented. People are aware that the political system is self-legitimizing and that in the world of televisual democracy voters have been effectively replaced by their own simulated projection constructed by the mass media and public opinion assessors. The "people," a statistical simulation, have responded by adopting the posture of "hyperconformity." It is a political silence "which refuses to be spoken for in its name. And in this sense, far from being a form of alienation, it is an absolute weapon."[13]

Where Baudrillard would find a new kind of civic virtue in the refusal of politics, Lyotard would reenvision the public realm as a hyperpluralist space of experimental situations. For Lyotard, social and political life should be characterized as a complex and fluid constellation of language games.[14] People interact with one another in a web of linguistic moves and countermoves. These movements, however, are rule governed and policed in order to determine what can or cannot be said and thus to suppress diversity. The inherent variety of discourses has been channeled by existing power frameworks into conformist, consensus-oriented monocultures.

Lyotard's postmodern idea of justice endorsed the following values: the will to invent criteria, cultural diversity, the impossibility of a common framework for neutral and rational dialogue, and the pragmatic contextuality of all judgments. This translated into an aesthetic model of public space (indebted to Kant's *Critique of Judgment*), a fearless experimentalism (Nietzsche), and the acceptance of rhetorical criteria of judgment (the position of the ancient Sophists) in a deconstructed world of diverse language games (the influence of Wittgenstein). In his writings, Lyotard deployed this idea of justice in the form of a rhetorical strategy that he referred to as "paganism" and "dissensus."[15]

Lyotard envisioned a patchwork of postmodern discourse communities and contestive border zones, an archipelago of islands in a vast ocean. These postmodern cultures inhabit small oases and occupy transversal flows in a world of modern power structures and hegemonic discourses. In designating justice as multiplicity, Lyotard made difference the central principle of postmodern legitimacy and the liberation of "differends" (marginalized and excluded discourses) the task of a postmodern politics.[16]

For Bauman, postmodern living amounts to the obsessive and contradictory search for both greater aesthetic self-expression and community identification in a world of heightened complexity, contingency, and ambiguity. Increasingly freed from the normative constraints of modern cultural traditions and the structural constraints of modern social and political institutions, our social world is being pulled in more libertarian and more communitarian directions. The postmodern individual operates in a world shaped by the conflicting imperatives of aesthetic freedom and the search for community, which cannot be reconciled.[17] His prescription for this state of affairs is moral. We need a new postmodern "morality without an ethical code."[18] This involves a repersonalization of morality away from modern moral and legal codes and toward a rediscovery of "the moral impulse" — that instinctive, unspoken demand to take full responsibility for others without waiting for reciprocity.[19] Indebted to the moral philosophy of Emmanuel Levinas, Bauman contends that the experience of the moral relationship (being-for-the-Other) comes before the experience of Being (being-with-others).[20] Indeed, moral consciousness is born out of this awakening of being-for-the-Other. This amounts to a morality of unconditional acceptance, of loving others without a concern for being loved or recognized in return. It takes us beyond the ethics of both self-interest and reciprocal equality.

The present, concludes Bauman, is best grasped as a moral condition in which modern ethical codes are no longer effective in providing norms able to deal with rapid technological change, globalization, and radical cultural pluralization.[21] The modern humanist paradigm of a law-like, universally binding code, erected on the foundations of a common human nature, individual autonomy, and the sovereign constitutional nation-state, has been shattered. In its place is a world of dispersed and relativized ethical orientations. Postmodernism, more at home in this floating world, has radically reversed the modernist formula of self-actualization, opening up a space for rediscovering the proximity of otherness and the experience of difference.[22] Modern moralities have always been bound up with a legislative imperative, with the will to define and judge. By contrast, the postmodern moral imperative is interpretive, an existential ethic of caring in the face of the inherent contingency and ambiguity of the human condition.[23]

The Late Modern Condition

Social theorists who contend that our condition is late modern rather than postmodern offer accounts of the present that stress the theme of change within continuity, rather than radical rupture. They grasp our transition by working within the modernization paradigm. Thus despite their differences, Jürgen Habermas, David Harvey, and Anthony Giddens all agree that we are still operating within a modern world, albeit "late" or "radically reflexive." Making sense of this condition requires that we not abandon modern social theory, but rather reconstruct its dominant Marxian and Weberian sociological frameworks.

In the case of Jürgen Habermas, this involves overcoming Max Weber's pessimistic vision of late modernity as a bureaucratized "iron cage" society in which dehumanized individuals are devoid of the capacity for meaningful action. Weber's research led him to conclude that the driving force of modernization was to be found in the emergence of a formal-instrumental rationality that penetrated all spheres of human life.[24] The transformation of society into differentiated and rationalized value spheres and institutions unleashed a powerful organizational dynamic. The mastery of all things by rational calculation led to the growth of bureaucratic modes of organization that coordinated social action through the functionalist values and mechanisms of hierarchic efficiency. The result was a more productive and predictable, as well as a more streamlined and routinized, social order.

Habermas has also assessed the crisis of modernity as the overextension of instrumental rationality into all spheres of life. Modern social evolution, he contends, involves the constant renewal of an instrumental logic embedded in capitalist markets and bureaucratic organizations, as well as an interactionist-hermeneutic, cultural logic that reproduces norms of social integration.[25] These social systemic and cultural lifeworld logics work in tandem so that sufficient levels of both technological efficiency and action-motivating meaning are produced. The problem is that societal modernization has been on a distorted track whereby processes of cultural learning have been colonized by the instrumental logics of our capitalist and bureaucratic social and political systems. However, the predominance of means rationality can be reversed if we introduce an alternative form of communicative rationality into appropriate lifeworld and institutional settings. Weber was more pessimistic. He believed that instrumental rationalization would continue to shape Western culture and civilization.[26]

Habermas has identified three types of modern rationality that correspond to the worlds of objective, social, and subjective human relations.[27] Cognitive-instrumental reason is appropriate in the domain of science, technology, and social technologies. Communicative rationality is the appropriate mode of reason in the normative world of morality, politics, and law. Aesthetic rationality is appropriate in the expressive world of art and intimate relations. His goal is to change our culture from one dominated by instrumental values to one integrated by communicative values. Communicative interaction is sustained by the rational deliberative justification of values.[28] Habermas therefore maintains an Enlightenment epistemological faith in the knowability of universal norms that validate a common human nature. Although we are enmeshed in a daily world of particular contexts and concrete mores, we have a moral duty to organize our social and political life in accordance with the universal humanist rules of intersubjective communication. In this way, Habermas believes he has saved the Enlightenment project.

While Habermas has devoted his energies toward reconstructing the Enlightenment project in terms of an updated Weberian approach and a new language model of rationality, Marxist geographer and social theorist David Harvey has devoted his energies toward a renewal of the Enlightenment project through a new version of historical materialism. In *The Condition of Postmodernity* (1989), Harvey accepts the reality of a postmodern cultural shift. Yet postmodernity needs to be understood as a particular historical moment in the evolutionary dynamic of late capitalism traceable to the current restructuring of the global division of labor.[29] More precisely, postmodernism is the cultural effect of the political-economic reorganization of Fordist-Keynesian capitalism into what Harvey calls "post-Fordist flexible accumulation."[30]

Modernism as both a mode of aesthetic representation and an artistic movement emerged in the mid-nineteenth century in response to capitalist modernization.[31] It created new mediums of subjective expression and abstraction able to capture the modern experience of "creative destruction." This was most evident in surrealism, futurism, and abstract expressionism. The countercultural movements of the 1960s helped shape the environment out of which contemporary postmodernism emerged. It took the logic of modernism to the extreme point of a disjunctive nihilism and then repackaged it as a new mode of popular culture and hip consumerism.[32] Therefore, rather than representing a progressive cultural dynamic, postmodernism is judged by Harvey to be the seductive false consciousness of post-Fordist flexible capitalism.

Post-Fordism refers to a new period in the organization of capitalism, away from industrial mass production (Henry Ford's model) toward a postindustrial model of flexible globalization.[33] The capitalism of the 1980s and 1990s has been characterized by the increased global mobility of capital; the increased importance of knowledge and information technologies in the organization of "just-in-time" production; the weakness of labor unions and new temporary and subcontracted work contracts; and the disintegration of mass-consumption markets into more specialized consumer lifestyle niches. This allows for more flexible production and distribution systems, which in turn render significant sectors of the labor force redundant. A smaller, multipurpose labor force is needed and accommodated, while a larger peripheral labor pool is employed temporarily and part-time.

Harvey not only links the emergence of a post-Fordist global capitalism to postmodernism, but also situates this theory of contemporary social change within a much larger historical dynamic that has shaped the trajectory of modernity — "time-space compression."[34] Time and space are conceptualized as dynamic sources of social power shaped by distinct, historically situated social formations. Changes in social reproduction result in changes in cultural representations of time and space relations, which in turn reorder our everyday lives. These "processes so revolutionize the objective qualities of space and time that we are forced to alter, sometimes in quite radical ways, how we present the world to ourselves."[35] Social revolutions occur when spatial barriers are so overcome and time accelerates to such a point that the world radically shrinks in terms of human time-space connections.

Today we find ourselves in a period of rapid time-space compression brought on by the high-tech globalization of capitalist production. During intensified periods of time-space compression, aesthetic and cultural practices become the primary sites of struggle and sources of explanation as we find ourselves without stable cultural referents. Harvey identifies three major episodes of time-space compression (the 1840s, 1910–1914, and 1968–73), which ushered in a new mode of capitalist economic accumulation, as well as a new cultural form.[36] Postmodernism should therefore be analyzed as the new culture of post-Fordist capitalism.[37]

Harvey's response to the challenge of postmodern capitalism is a new model of historical materialism and the hope of a new unified, class politics. His idea of a "historical-geographic materialism" integrates a critical understanding of the historical production of social space, as well as postmodern explanations of cultural change within a traditional Marxist analysis of changes in the mode and relations of production. It is described as a new version of the Enlightenment project designed to demystify postmodernism and thus control its reactionary effects.[38]

Postmodernism has both distorted our understanding of the deeper, objective, socioeconomic processes of change under way today and worked in tandem with post-Fordist capitalism by endorsing a culture of image production, charismatic politics, a retreat into the self, and new types of libertarianism, localism, and tribalism.[39] Postmoderns, concludes Harvey, reject emancipatory mass movements as both repressive and illusory. Instead they champion a politics of radical resistance. Yet they offer no realistic strategies for genuinely marginalized groups to become empowered. While admitting to the fragmented character of contemporary politics — the result of postmodern capitalism — Harvey hopes for trends that will fuse these fragments into a new populist movement organized around social class inequality.[40]

Habermas's neo-Weberian analysis of modernization and neo-Kantian model of communicative action, as well as Harvey's neo-Marxist theories of time-space compression and post-Fordist capitalism, refuse to give up on modernity. Both Habermas and Harvey agree that we have entered a new period of modernization and they remain convinced that the world is still amenable to humanistic mastery. Yet in the recent work of British sociologist Anthony Giddens, we encounter an analysis of our current condition that claims to take us beyond both the Enlightenment project and the postmodern condition. Adopting the idea of "reflexive modernization," Giddens describes the nature of our present as one of "radicalized modernity."[41]

German sociologist Ulrich Beck invented the term "reflexive modernization" in the 1980s to distinguish between the old model of "simple modernization," which was driven by an economic-scientific paradigm of linear progress, and a new model of modernization based on risk assessment and management in response to those social and environmental problems systematically produced by industrial progress.[42] The adjective "reflexive" does not simply mean critical reflection, it means "self-confrontation."[43] Reflexive modernization means confronting the effects of simple modernization by calling into question the very foundations of Enlightenment modernity.

Giddens discerns three major social revolutions that have taken us beyond the "Promethean outlook" of the Enlightenment and into a new period of modernity. They are: (1) intensified globalization; (2) radicalized social reflexivity; and (3) the emergence of a "post-traditional," rather than a postmodern, society.[44] Intensified globalization refers to a new dynamic of global-local, time-space compression brought into being by new telecommunication technologies. Radicalized social reflexivity refers to the information revolution that allows individuals and institutions access to unprecedented amounts of knowledge and diverse perspectives on life. Giddens defines reflexivity as "the use of information about the conditions of activity as a means of regularly reordering and redefining what that activity is."[45] The idea of a post-traditional society or "de-traditionalization" refers to the eclipse of received traditions due to heightened reflexivity. Traditional as well as modern sources of authority, social roles, and expectations have come under question.

Yet these changes have not ushered in a new postmodern age. Rather, we are witness to the dissolution and purging of the modern "traditions" that sustained Enlightenment modernity. These include the authority of scientific expertise, the legitimacy of the nation-state social paradigm, bureaucratic organization, modern gender roles, the nature of work, the social welfare state, liberal representative democracy, and modern warfare. These core features of modernization are being replaced by an upgraded set of norms, organizational principles, social structures, and lifestyles. Both individuals and institutions are under intense pressure to reflexively reorganize their environments of action. The result of all this, contends Giddens, is the advent of a second modernity.

Giddens has identified a number of changes that characterize this new modernity. They include the pervasive influence of abstract expert systems (computers) and mediated experiences (mass-media communication) in everyday life. Our lives are also being reshaped by the global restructuring of local circumstances, "the interlacing of social events and social relations 'at distance' with local contextualities."[46] We are witnessing the loss of both Tradition and Nature as stable external givens that exist independent of human intervention.[47] And the increased importance of personal lifestyle choice has created a new kind of "life politics" concerned with issues of identity, health, the environment, the recovery of community, sexuality and intimacy, reproduction, and genetic engineering.[48]

While these changes are significant, Giddens rejects the claim that we are in a new period of postmodern social development. He further rejects most of what he believes to be the key features of postmodernism.[49] While postmodernism understands current changes in cultural terms, Giddens focuses on institutional changes in relation to changes in self-identity. Postmodernism also overemphasizes the centrifugal character of the present to the detriment or exclusion of centripetal forces creating new modes of global interdependence and cosmopolitan dialogue. As for the self, Giddens defends the idea of the individual as a rational agent and not a "site of intersecting forces." Finally, postmodernism judges truth claims and values in terms of local contextuality, rather than fully grasping the global-local nature of current changes. In sum, postmodernism in practice creates a more fragmented and violent world of relativism, nihilism, and multiple fundamentalisms.[50]

For Giddens, modernity is largely about the reflexive reorganization of time and space for the purpose of creating and sustaining larger and more sophisticated social structures and institutional orders. This colonization of space and time is achieved by separating time and space, emptying their relational content, and then recombining them across larger spans of space-time. Social relations are disembedded, or taken out of their local contexts, and then stretched and institutionally recombined to make modern societies possible. The two most powerful products of this process of modern "structuration" have been the Western inventions of the sovereign nation-state society and industrial capitalism.[51]

Under the current conditions of reflexive modernization, we are seeing the creation of a fully globalized capitalism, a high-tech postindustrial social order, the pluralization of political identities and allegiances beyond the nation-state, and an emergent planetary consciousness.[52] However, we can no longer make bold pronouncements concerning the emancipation of humanity through the aggressive production of scientific knowledge and its application through centralized social technologies. At the same time, we cannot return to the womb of premodern society and its traditional values. Nor can we seek refuge in a return to Nature. The entire world must face the consequences of radicalized modernity. Giddens urges us to be more cautious and more prudent, and to appreciate the high-consequence risks we confront.[53] Yet at the same time he realizes that it is inevitable that we will sweep away the debris of the old modernity only to launch ourselves into the new historic wave of reflexive globalization.

Postmodernity or Late Modernity?

Both postmodern and late modern social theorists are "radical" in the sense of attempting to get to the root of contemporary change. Yet they differ on how "radically" cultural experiences and meanings, social structures, institutional orders, and ideologies have been altered. Their models part company in their divergent views concerning the continued validity of the modern Enlightenment project, the kind of culture we live in, and how our institutions have changed. Yet at the same time, both postmodern and late modern social theories acknowledge the arrival of a new high-tech capitalism, a globalized time-space compression, the information revolution, increased social and self-reflexivity, the pervasive presence of mass-media communication, and the pluralization of cultural identities, lifestyles, and ideologies.

I agree with postmoderns that a postmodern cultural shift has occurred. Yet I question their cultural and institutional accounts of this shift in that they overplay the technological (Baudrillard), aesthetic (Lyotard), and moral (Bauman) nature of our transition. Conversely, I hold that late moderns or neomoderns like Habermas, Harvey, and Giddens fail to fully grasp our postmodern cultural shift, yet their accounts of institutional changes are more accurate than those of the postmoderns. I contend that our present condition is neither a radical rupture with modernity, nor a continuation of the Enlightenment project of modernization. Rather, it exhibits the features of what I call *our late modern/postmodern transition.*

Thus while Baudrillard, Lyotard, and Bauman locate some of the defining traits of our present condition and are justified in characterizing them as postmodern, they exaggerate the extent to which this condition is one of a radically new postmodern society. For example, Baudrillard argues that information and mass-media systems have so overproduced simulated artifacts and events that our society has become "hypersimulated."[54] Defined as a condition of social entropy, we live in a "fractal" world of fragmentation, flux, and chaos, devoid of meaning and value. While hypersimulated lifeworlds do exist, the claim that a full-blown hypersimulated society has come to pass is clearly an overstatement. We live, rather, in a late modern/postmodern society in which microelectronic simulations structure more complex, spatial, and globalized forms of mediated experience. This condition is "hyperreal" in the sense of the greater complexity and intensity of mediated experience. However, we do not live in a virtual-reality social vortex where hyperfragmented images are the only discernible reality.

Lyotard, too, offered an exaggerated account of contemporary society. Advanced Western societies were portrayed as totalitarian ("terroristic") entities riddled with postmodern cracks and fissures that allow for pockets of radical cultural expression and politics. However, postmodern sociocultural changes are not as anarchistic as Lyotard claimed, nor are our institutions as totalitarian. His "incredulity to metanarratives" extended to institutions as well. Therefore, in moving from one extreme (modern, totalizing metanarratives) to another (postmodern anarchism), Lyotard was unable to generate a well-developed analysis of late modern institutional changes. What we need to do is generate larger narrative and analytic frameworks that are not monolithic and destructive of difference, yet are sufficient to engage in institutional analysis.

Bauman's idea of postmodernity as the triumph of modernist culture over modern society, resulting in the disintegration and reorganization of modern social and political structures, remains a compelling account of the nature of our present. Yet his moral imperative of being-for-the-Other hijacks his sociological analysis in the direction of a radical postmodernism that abandons both society and politics for pure moral-existential relationships. Bauman's postmodern morality imposes an unrealistic set of demands on the individual, much like Immanuel Kant's modern abstract moral formula of the categorical imperative does.

While Kant's moral directive (to act as if the maxim of your action should be a universal law) is grounded in the autonomy of the individual will (that each person legislates moral law), and Bauman's moral impulse is activated through heteronomous experience (action that is determined by someone other than one's self), both moral postulates are categorical (applying to all human or rational beings) and imperative (how we ought to act).[55] The problem is that moral imperatives are not enough. They remain largely impotent without appropriate social, political, institutional, and technological supports. What is needed is a rebalancing of the relationship between these multiple imperatives.[56]

Habermas's solution is to change our derailed modern culture and institutions by introducing a new type of humanist rationality. He conceptualizes modern society as driven by two distinguishable logics: an instrumental-materialist logic (conceptualized as interdependent "social systems") and a logic of normative structures (the "learning processes" of the cultural lifeworld). To reverse the trend of the former social logic dominating the latter, Habermas has turned to language philosophy and the remedy of intersubjective communication. To achieve his vision of a communicatively rationalized society, Habermas advocates changes designed to wall off strategic power relations from what he regards as the principal realms of normative life — processes of socialization and the public sphere.

Yet rather than becoming more separate and distinct, the interchange between social systems and lifeworlds, between cultural value spheres, and between different types of discourses and rationalities has been rendered more complex and interdependent. The interaction that occurs in both the specialized worlds of experts and in everyday life involves a complex mix of context-dependent cognitive, normative, strategic, and aesthetic values and judgments that cannot be placed in their proper value sphere and logically analyzed. In short, Habermas's model of late modernity is far removed from our mass-mediated, aesthetically driven, de-differentiated, and hybridized postmodern culture.

Habermas's main problem is his model of rationality. Reasoning is indeed intersubjective and social, as he points out. Yet it is also equally embodied and driven by contextual forces that cannot be formalized into a logic of human action. Indeed, lifeworld experiences determine our rationalities. Habermas wants our experiences, the product of highly nuanced contextual environments, to be streamlined and channeled into a very formal, procedural model of rationality. The result is a linguistic model of rational intersubjectivity that is both too narrow and too demanding a medium for effective social integration and political action. In effect, it instrumentally colonizes the existential lifeworld. It denigrates the experiential complexity, diversity, and potency that gives life its more profound meaning. Habermas's concept of a just society entails purging human life of much of its worldly contents so that it can conform to the norms of rational discourse.[57]

If the Enlightenment project is outdated, then what about the Marxist project? Harvey's analysis of postmodernism reduces a more complex, multidimensional process of contemporary change to an economic crisis of overaccumulation in which excess capital and labor cannot be effectively absorbed by existing production systems. Yet I believe the driving force of our transition is as much techno-informational (postindustrial), as it is cultural (postmodern), as it is accumulative (Marxist). While acknowledging the influence of postmodern culture, Harvey still regards it as the superstructure of capitalist productive forces and relations.

I agree with Harvey when he asserts that understanding time and space as sources of social power is crucial to explaining modernity and postmodernity. However, his theory of time-space compression is too limited by its adherence to the traditional Marxian substructure (the socioeconomic order) and superstructure (the ideological-cultural order) model of modern social analysis. Furthermore, while structural inequality and social class continue to be significant factors in today's world, Marxists have been unable to articulate a convincing politics that resonates with mass publics. I believe that the most difficult task facing the Left is not just reinventing itself, but reinventing politics. If this were undertaken, it would lead us beyond Marxism.

This is precisely the position of Giddens. We have moved beyond the Enlightenment project, the socialist project, and bureaucratic, welfare-state liberalism. The telecommunications and information revolutions, globalization, and radicalized social reflexivity have given birth to an ultra-modern society. The era of the industrial nation-state society is behind us. Our world is connected by new communications and information networks, it is more global and local, it is more individuated and cosmopolitan, and it is far less traditional, yet it is more dangerous and unpredictable due to the scope and speed of reflexive modernization.

Giddens is convincing in his claim that we are still operating within the institutional confines of a modern world undergoing reflexive reorganization. Yet in developing this analysis without a commensurate analysis of cultural change, he is open to the same criticism he levels against postmoderns. Giddens fails to link cultural and institutional analysis. Devoid of a cultural analysis, his social theory cannot begin to fathom the nature of our postmodern shift. For while Western institutions are becoming more globalized, Western national cultures are changing into more complex and contested formations. Yet Giddens focuses on the prospects of a new humanistic cosmopolitanism.

Furthermore, like Habermas and Harvey, Giddens remains oblivious to the existence of the second wave of critical postmodernism. While acknowledging that a postmodern sensibility exists, he dismisses it with a flurry of oversimplified generalizations about Nietzsche and postmodernity. He thus fails to make distinctions between different postmodern thinkers and perspectives. He also does not indicate that postmoderns have initiated significant shifts and revisions in their work. Giddens therefore avoids most of what is significant and provocative about the current modern-postmodern debate.

His main focus is on individual transformation.[58] Giddens assumes that changes in the psyches and social habits of radically reflexive individuals have the potential to alter the trajectory of the juggernaut that is late modernity. Here he envisions a world free from the compulsions of productivism and consumerism, enriched by greater democratic cosmopolitan dialogue, guided by more ecologically informed planetary management values, and moving toward "post-military society," as well as a world that places "questions of life, finitude and death" prior to knowledge or control.[59] Giddens calls himself a "utopian realist."[60] Yet in the end his utopianism far outweighs his realism. His underlying premises, aspirations, and conclusions are as universal, humanistic, and utopian as the eighteenth-century Enlightenment ever was.[61]

Our Late Modern/Postmodern Transition

Geographer, urbanist, and social theorist Edward Soja contends that today "every contemporary individual and social formation is simultaneously modern and postmodern."[62] In our everyday lives we "combine aspects of the modern and the postmodern in our discourses and social practices."[63] He describes late moderns as those thinkers who "edge very close to postmodernism, but refuse to step over the border for fear that too much would be lost."[64]

I propose that we grasp the nature of our present as a *late modern/ postmodern transition*. Our present condition is best understood in terms of a complex tension and linkage between postmodern sociocultural changes and late modern political and economic institutional changes. Advanced Western societies have experienced a postmodern cultural shift in conjunction with changes in what is now a globalized, high-tech capitalism. Yet at the institutional levels of advanced capitalism and the modern nation-state, we are in the midst of a late modern shift driven by the forces of complex globalization and reflexive reorganization. The result of this is the undoing or "decentering" of the cultural boundaries associated with the modern nation-state society and their recentering around new global-local "nodal points" and "flows" increasingly mediated by postmodern cultures.[65]

This dynamic of change is driven by several processes: (1) the high-tech televisual, communication, information, and biological revolutions and their global extension; (2) increased cultural and organizational complexity and hybridization due to time-space compression; (3) the creation of a global field of flows and networks of people, technologies, markets, goods, images, and ideas connecting up diverse locales; (4) the expansion of the capitalist economy into a genuine world market; and (5) the emergence of a transitional, post–Cold War political world order.

Roland Robertson has described this dynamic of change in terms of the concept of "glocalization." The development of diverse, overlapping fields of global-local linkages has created a condition of globalized pan-locality, the "global institutionalization of the expectation and construction of local particularism."[66] This is due, in part, to an increase in the types of organization available, from administrative levels (transnational, international, macroregional, national, subnational-regional, municipal, local) to functional networks (corporations, international governmental and nongovernmental organizations, professional associations, and the Internet) to what anthropologist Arjun Appadurai calls deterritorialized, global spatial "scapes" (ethnoscapes, technoscapes, finanscapes, mediascapes, and ideoscapes).[67]

This condition of glocalization also represents a shift from a more territorialized learning process bound up with the nation-state society to one more fluid and translocal. Culture has become a much more mobile, human software employed to mix elements from diverse contexts. With cultural forms and practices more separate from geographic, institutional, and ascriptive embeddedness, we are witnessing what Jan Nederveen Pieterse refers to as postmodern "hybridization."[68] This intercultural syncretism is driven as much by non-Western influences as by Western culture. With the proliferation of hybrid cultural spaces and border crossings, cultural theorist and literary critic Homi Bhabha contends that culture today is increasingly a "transnational and translational enterprise." The very act of cultural enunciation has become more "disjunctive and multiaccentual." He writes:

> It is in the emergence of the interstices—the overlap and displacement of domains of difference—that the intersubjective and collective experiences of nationness, community interest, or cultural value are negotiated.[69]

What is undergirding this process of social and cultural change is a new circuitry of power. Today we find increased levels and intensities of power moving at rapid speeds through a rewired circuitry of spatial networks and flows. The high-tech revolutions in microelectronics, information processing, telecommunications, microbiology and medicine, and cultural production and consumption have dramatically increased the levels of reflexive knowledge in all aspects of life—social, individual, and institutional. This increase has been facilitated by a new circuitry of spatial flows that have reorganized key power points into new global-local networks. The combination of technological revolutions, global-local time-space compression, exponential information production, capitalist reorganization, and cultural postmodernization has created this new circuitry of power.

Influenced by the work of social theorists such as Edward Soja, Michael Mann, and Stewart Clegg, I agree with Mann that societies are "constituted of multiple overlapping and intersecting sociospatial networks of power."[70] Societies are complex, confederal achievements of power relations organized and disorganized into diverse authoritative and diffuse sociospatial networks. Today we are witnessing the reflexive reorganization of organized social power networks around new circuits.

Clegg's "circuits of power" model does a good job of explaining how contemporary social power networks operate. Employing "an imagery more redolent of the post-modern microelectronic age," Clegg conceptualizes society in terms of power moving through different circuits to constitute organizational fields of action.[71] Power moves through three main circuits: episodic, dispositional, and facilitative. Episodic power manifests itself in the actions and behaviors of particular individuals. Dispositional power shapes the structural and organizational conditions of individual episodic actions. Facilitative power is embedded in an organizational field and both enables and constrains the ability of agents to construct identities and achieve goals.[72]

Clegg defines the relational conditions that both constitute and reproduce these circuits of power as "organizational agency."[73] This involves the fixing of the field of strategic agents around "privileged nodal points" or "obligatory passage points."[74] Resulting power networks are shaped into formal institutions through the mechanisms of social integration ("relations of meaning and membership") and system integration ("material conditions and techniques of production and discipline").[75] Organizational power fields are subject to destabilization as strategic agents contest key nodal points of power and struggle to rewire the circuitry of power around alternative power conduits and flows.

Human identity and action are therefore organizational achievements. They are the result of stabilized power relations channeling the flow of episodic events across a terrain of specific locales. The fixing of power into an organizational field is the outcome of agents working "to transform their point of connection with some other agency or agencies into a necessary nodal point" or privileged power position.[76] This occurs within arenas of struggle between different agents mobilizing diverse types of identities, rules, interests, and resources. The translation of episodic agency into key nodal or obligatory passage points creates stabilized conduits of dispositional and facilitative power.

The resulting flow of power through these connected circuits is one of both integration and dis-integration. Organizations are always open to challenge through the redeployment of strategic agents or environmental pressures. Effective power networks coordinate social and systemic integration at key nodal points in the organizational field. Destabilizing this field depends on how well agents can short-circuit these key nodal points.

This model portrays power as multidimensional and as the current or energy of social action, as well as the apparatus through which it passes. Power further follows a circuitous course in its movement through episodic-strategic, integrative-dispositional, and facilitative levels and circuit switches.[77] Existing social relations, cultural identities, and agencies are reproduced at different nodal points in the organizational field with respect to both locale and power circuit. Thus some organized power networks are more open to change, others more congealed and reified.

Today organized power networks and their institutional orders are undergoing reflexive reorganization. The core institutional building blocks of modern society—the nation-state, representative mass democracy, the bureaucratic welfare state, and the multinational corporation—have been forced to increase their capacities for critical reflexivity in the wake of the high-tech, information revolutions and globalization. This involves transforming traditional organizational hierarchies that are vertically integrated and spatially concentrated into entities more vertically dis-integrated and spatially dispersed. Reflexively reorganized organizations have become information and communication systems rewired with new technologies and organizational designs.

We also live in a time of cultural postmodernization. Society has become a complex field of diverse and overlapping social spaces and networks, more local, global, and culturally pluralized. These postmodern spaces and networks foster new kinds of work, recreational consumption, intimacy, and associational life. These activities intersect, recombine, and reconnect in faster and more complex ways. Therefore, our postmodernized society is one of diverse social and cultural identities linked by multiple networks of work, recreational consumption, intimacy, and civic associations.

The most compelling sociological account of our late modern/postmodern transition can be found in Scott Lash and John Urry's *Economies of Signs and Space* (1994). Their analysis of social, economic, and cultural change in advanced societies is shaped by an intellectual strategy and vocabulary that incorporates and moves beyond Marxist, postindustrial, postmodern, and reflexive modernization social theories. They forge an approach that both recognizes and illuminates the more complex intertwinement of late modernity and postmodernity.[78]

It is their thesis that contemporary social reality is structured by a process they describe as the high-tech and institutional "disorganization" of capitalism into a globalized, information-based, and aesthetically saturated network of object (things) and subject (persons) flows.[79] Global information and telecommunication structures have enabled "aesthetic reflexivity" (i.e., postmodern culture) to flourish. The cultural sphere has become the motor force of change with the high-tech engines of advanced capitalism running on postmodern fuel.

Life in advanced societies today is therefore primarily shaped by transnational networks or flows circulating information and postmodern goods. This is occurring "not just in the proliferation of non-material objects which comprise a substantial aesthetic component (such as pop music, cinema, magazines, video, etc.), but also in the increasing component of sign-value or image in material objects."[80] Increased flows of people can be found in patterns of career change and job relocation, immigration, the globalization of service industries, migrant labor, travel and tourism, refugees, and the growth of transnational governmental (IGOs) and nongovernmental (INGOs) organizations.

Contemporary advanced societies are both postmodern and late modern. They are postmodern in that the objects circulating through these transnational flows and networks have a high aesthetic content while subjects have become more critically reflexive. The result is an "accelerating individualization process" in which more people have greater freedom to determine their life plans and lifestyles.[81] The combined effect of a postmodern cultural environment and greater individual reflexive individuality has produced a condition of expanding aesthetic reflexivity in the economy, consumer practices, social interactions, work, and leisure.[82]

This new cultural economy is late modern in its institutional realignment. The combined effect of new information and communication technologies, global-local time-space compression, and the disorganization of both modern capitalism and the nation-state has created a new global power structure of "economic governance."[83] This features highly deregulated capital markets, microelectronic information superhighways, the new decentralized network model of the transnational corporation, and new global cities. The key nodal point of this economic power structure is the "global city."[84] It is the brain of what Lash and Urry describe as the new cultural economy of "reflexive accumulation." The worldwide dispersal of production and consumption requires the greater concentration of knowledge and expert systems. World cities such as New York, Los Angeles, and Tokyo serve as command-and-control centers for global flows and oversee transnational zones largely beyond national governmental control.

For Edward Soja, Los Angeles is the postmodern megalopolis of our time.[85] Its five counties constitute a sprawling, multicultural archipelago that sits on the global cultural and economic fault lines of North,

South, East, and West. Los Angeles is a global, high-tech capitalist nodal point, with a downtown "corporate-financial citadel" and new high-tech outer cities. Its inner city and older central urban areas have been flooded with immigrants. The city's architecture and the mass media and culture industries of film, popular music, television, advertising, fashion, and theme parks give it its postmodern identity. Postmodern subcultures flourish in its decentered spatial landscape. Yet Los Angeles is also divided into fortified communities and zones of poverty and crime. Lacking a distinctive national identity, it is both global and tribal, a nexus of transnational cultural hybridization and at the same time fragmented into ethnic enclaves.

Lash and Urry refer to this dynamic of economic-cultural reorganization as "reflexive accumulation." They use this term "to enable us to capture how economic and symbolic processes are more than ever interlaced and interarticulated; that is, that the economy is increasingly culturally inflected and that culture is more and more economically inflected."[86] Economic production and consumption today are driven less by modern social structures that are national in scope than by global information and communication structures. These structures form the networked flows through which information, capital, postmodern cultural objects, and mobile subjects circulate. Reflexive accumulation is sustained by the centrality of information and symbolic processing ("discursive knowledge") in production and consumption, the rapid expansion of postindustrial services, and greater individual reflexivity.

Economic production systems today are framed and driven by three key components: (1) information-processing activities; (2) the accumulation of cultural capital or learning; and (3) flows of information.[87] Thus the United States has become a postindustrial information economy driven by design, research and development, symbolic analysis, and service employment.[88] New communities and economic districts have been built around small, horizontally integrated high-tech firms, research universities, and the financial, leisure, and tourism service industries. With unprecedented levels of information being channeled into production systems, and new forms of reflexive individuality and aesthetic reflexivity (postmodern culture) transforming goods and services, reflexive accumulation fuels the "culturalization of economic life."[89]

Postmodernization therefore refers to the restructuring of social space by global flows of aesthetically saturated (i.e., postmodern) goods and services. The global circulation of postmodern cultural objects by way of television, film, advertising, fashion, music, and the Internet provides the conditions and resources for greater aesthetic-reflexive individuation. These postmodern changes have in turn led to important alterations in our existing institutional arrangements and their power to shape our everyday life. Lash contends that a new set of organizational dynamics and trends is evident in the way: (1) "institutions are becoming more cultural in character"; (2) "cultural institutions (especially education, media, and science) have become increasingly central"; (3) "a substantial measure of the cultural artefacts that are disseminated through these institutions is postmodern"; and (4) "an increasing proportion of our social interactions and communicative interchanges are going on external to institutions."[90]

Finally, it must be acknowledged that this process of postmodern reflexive reorganization has its costs as well as its benefits. That is, it has its winners and losers. The winners include a smaller yet wealthier elite class of transnational capitalists and managers; a new middle class of information, telecommunication, and symbolic workers and postmodern consumers; and a smaller, high-tech upgraded, industrial working class. The losers include the downsized, downwardly mobile, industrial working class; middle-management white-collar workers; isolated minority populations living in urban ghettos; high-school educated and drop-out youth; migrant and immigrant workers in the informal economy; and the growing ranks of single women with children.[91]

Today we live in a world in which capitalism has become globalized, high-tech, and informationalized; our culture has been postmodernized; our modern social structures are in a state of reflexive reorganization; and unprecedented levels of reflexive knowledge are available to those individuals with the necessary high-tech and cultural resources, skills, and access. It is a world defined by several significant social, cultural, economic, and political trends. Taken together, they give a discernible identity to our late modern/postmodern transition. I would summarize these trends as follows:

1. A new phase of capitalism organized around leisure and consumption and fueled by postindustrial technologies and strategies of globalization.
2. The unprecedented transformation and expanded production of culture and the effective saturation of everyday social life with postmodern cultural practices and artifacts.

3. The restratification of advanced societies around five key socioeconomic status groups: a) a finance-knowledge-media elite; b) a postmodern middle class; c) an industrial working class reorganized by high-tech; d) a postindustrial service class; and e) an impoverished and marginalized underclass.

4. Social relations that are increasingly abstract and media driven, combined with the radical pluralization of social spaces and lifestyle choices.

5. The resurgence of ascriptive identities (race, gender, ethnicity, religion, lifestyle) as the basis of politics.

6. A strong skepticism toward modern emancipatory ideologies combined with a greater postmodern acceptance of the contingency of existence and moral polytheism, as well as the more pronounced presence of antimodern fundamentalisms.

7. The privileging of ontology (Being or existence understood as the lived experience of identity and difference) over epistemology (the method or grounds of knowledge as embodied in scientific reason) in interpreting reality.

8. The idea of the individual self as an assemblage of cultural practices shaped within a contextual field.

9. The erosion of the authority, as well as the social and political structures, of the nation-state society, coupled with the resurgence of local political cultures and the proliferation of transnational organizational networks.

10. A shift in the dynamics, structure, and discourse of Western democracy away from the modern liberal-representational, nation-state paradigm and toward a new global-local dynamic of increased complexity and techno-oligarchy, as well as new modes of democratic resistance and self-governance.

Part II

3 — The Idea of Critical Postmodernism

> *To the extent that modern reason is seen in Kantian terms*
> *and "worldliness" as an ontological or quasi-ontological*
> *concern, the intellectual dilemmas of our age can be*
> *highlighted or summarized under the labels of "life-world*
> *and critique" or "ontology and critique."*
> — Fred Dallmayr, *Between Freiburg and Frankfurt:*
> *Toward a Critical Ontology*

Critical Ontology

Critical postmodernism is a theoretical and ideological response to our current late modern/postmodern transition. It is an intellectual construct designed to serve three main purposes. It evokes a *philosophical ethos* or attitude that has taken shape in the wake of the modern-postmodern debate. It is also an *interpretive matrix* through which analytic frameworks (social and political theories) can be constructed to examine our present condition. Furthermore, it is a *practical tool* to be used in the political negotiation of our current social and cultural condition. The task of critical postmodernism is to give meaning to the nature of our present and to develop the practical tools we need to navigate our current sociohistoric transition.

Foucault believed it would be more useful to treat modernity and postmodernity as philosophical attitudes rather than as social and historical categories.[1] His reading of the modern-postmodern debate led him to conclude that its polemical focus of pitting modernity as a period of history against postmodernity as its sequel was counterproductive. I have argued that we should concern ourselves with the sociological status

43

of our present situation before we assess this condition philosophically (as a question of political philosophy) and politically (as a question of democracy).

Therefore, it is central to my unfolding argument that we grasp the nature of our present as a late modern/postmodern transition. Western modernization, which has championed the ideals of scientific reason, technological progress, legal-bureaucratic organization, and democratic humanism, today finds itself in the midst of a sociohistoric transition where new understandings of human identity, rationality, and action permeate the landscape. This has forced us to rethink the relationship between our existential situation, our normative standards, and our associational life. That is why I turn to political philosophy, for it concerns itself with the relationship between these three integral conditions.

Political philosophy has been and continues to be defined differently by its practitioners. For the critical ontologist, it is a mode of existential questioning concerned with the fundamental conditions of human collective life. For the critical theorist, it is an intellectual discipline concerned with generating emancipatory knowledge. For the critical actor, it is a repertory of performative actions. For the traditionalist, political philosophy is an enterprise of hermeneutic retrieval, the interpretive encounter with historical texts of political thought. For the modernist, political philosophy is about connecting theory and practice, critique and action. For the postmodernist, it is deconstructive intervention.

Yet a viable political philosophy must explain how we orient ourselves to the world as existential beings (ontology), how we develop and defend normative standards (critique), and how we negotiate the historical field of social and political life (action). Norms of critique and models of action are crucial to any political theory. However, unless we more fully understand how they are achievements of a more fundamental and complex existential infrastructure, our critical theories and political strategies are doomed to failure. We have too often developed ways of life and plans of action that have sought to master a reality we do not fully understand. Critical postmodernism locates its identity in the challenge of articulating a "critical ontology" that can inform new modes of critique and strategies of democratic action.

Ontology (*ont* = being and *logos* = reason or discourse) is that branch of philosophy that deals with the nature of existence. It is the study of the fundamental characteristics of worldly existence (being) and really existing things (beings). Giddens defines ontology in terms of the following existential questions: (1) the nature of existence and the identity of objects and events; (2) the question of human finitude whereby "human beings are part of nature yet set apart from it as sentient and reflexive creatures"; (3) the experience of otherness or "how individuals interpret the traits and actions of other individuals"; and (4) the question of self-identity or "the persistence of feelings of personhood in a continuous self and body."[2]

Epistemological or scientific thinking is the basis of what Bauman calls modern legislative reasoning. This intellectual strategy takes its cue from Descartes and Kant and their notion of modern philosophy as the guardian and legislator of human rationality. The goal of modern legislative reasoning is "the possibility of a *method*—that is, of a procedure that guarantees the validity of the result by the sheer fact that it has been scrupulously followed; and the principle that the findings at the end of the methodological procedure carry superior validity no nonmethodical effort can claim."[3] By contrast, ontological thinking is the basis of postmodern interpretive reasoning. It strives to reveal what Bauman describes as "the intrinsically pluralist nature of the world and its inevitable consequence: the ambivalence and contingency of human existence."[4]

Leslie Paul Thiele characterizes the activity of interpretive reasoning in political theory as follows:

> To say that political theory is an interpretive rather than strictly scientific enterprise is to say something about what political theorists perceive when they look at the world as well as how they perceive it. Interpretive theory seeks to gain understanding of political life through self-reflective study. It is validated not by experimental verification but by its meaningfulness, that is, by the resonance it produces with its self-interpretive audience. This resonance may be gauged by the extent to which a theory informs or illuminates experience.[5]

It is not an exaggeration to say that one of the major trends of our current late modern/postmodern transition is the resurgence of ontological-interpretive thinking.[6] Political philosopher Fred Dallmayr has described this trend in terms of "the tensional-transitional character of our time: its precarious location between modernity—which is basically an age of 'critique' (or critical reason)—and incipient modes of postmodernism centerstaging language and (post-critical) ontology."[7] He further observes that "members of my generation—and probably of the next few generations—find themselves enmeshed in the transitional status of our age and hence in the *agon* of ontology and critique, regardless of what avenues are chosen to 'resolve' the conflict."[8]

Dallmayr's philosophical negotiation of our late modern/postmodern transition occurs through his idea of "critical ontology." This intellectual strategy reexamines the very practice of rational critique (modern legislative reasoning) by pursuing the path of ontological questioning (postmodern interpretive reasoning). Dallmayr is influenced by two prominent German schools of thought: the "Freiburg School" of phenomenological ontology and the "Frankfurt School" of critical theory. Combining the insights of Martin Heidegger's ontological philosophy of worldly existence and Theodor Adorno's idea of "negative dialectics," he constructs a postmodern discourse of ontological critique for our time.[9]

Political theorist William Connolly has also embraced the idea of postmodern ontological critique. He is suspicious of ontology because it implies a *logos* and therefore "suggests a fundamental logic, principle, or design of being." Invoking Foucault's statement that "Nothing is fundamental," Connolly asserts that there is no one logic or inherent purpose to human existence because human experience demonstrates the diversity of being. Therefore, the human condition cannot be encapsulated by a fundamental "Law, Identity, or Purpose." Connolly coins the term "ont*a*logy" to replace ontology. Ont*a*logy holds that "the most fundamental thing about being is that it contains no such overriding logic or design."[10]

Applying ont*a*logy to the activity of political theory, Connolly arrives at the idea of "ontopolitical interpretation."[11] Implicit in every interpretation of political events is an ontology that "invokes a set of fundamentals about necessities and possibilities of human being."[12] Ontopolitical interpretation seeks out the ontology contained within a political interpretation, makes explicit its implicit assumptions, and then critiques the very notion of a fundamental logic of reality. While this strategy is a form of postmodern deconstruction, Connolly perceptively realizes that the tools of critical genealogy and deconstruction are insufficient to the tasks of ethical and political thought. Their disintegrative powers fuel too much ambiguity and "critical detachment." A strategy of "attachment" is needed, a "positive ontopolitical interpretation."[13] How does one accomplish this? Connolly explains his idea of a critical ontology as follows:

[Y]ou project ontopolitical presumptions explicitly into detailed interpretations of actuality, acknowledging that your implicit projections surely
exceed your explicit formulation of them and that your formulations exceed your capacity to demonstrate their truth. You challenge closure in
the matrix by affirming the contestable character of your own projections, by offering readings of contemporary life that compete with alternative accounts, and by moving back and forth between these two levels.[14]

This is, of course, easier said than done. Nonetheless, ontological questioning is the starting point of critical postmodern thinking. At the same
time, there is more to critical postmodernism than critical ontology.
Here we need to return to the task of political philosophy and to the
central defining question of this study: What is the nature of our present? Only when we do this do we arrive at my idea of a critical postmodernism. It is framed by the following question: What is the relationship between ontological identity, critical rationality, and political
action in the present context of our late modern/postmodern transition?

Between Habermas and Heidegger: A Dialogue on Reconciliation

The development of a dialogue between Jürgen Habermas's modern
theory of communicative action and Martin Heidegger's postmodern
ontology represents one pathway toward a critical postmodern political
philosophy. At first the idea of a Habermas-Heidegger dialogue seems
implausible. A modern theory of critical rationality and ethical action
conceived in the spirit of Kantian rationalism confronts an ontology that
privileges lifeworld experience over deliberation. Yet I contend that both
Habermas and Heidegger are philosophers of reconciliation. Although
operating at different levels of inquiry — Habermas at the epistemological and Heidegger at the ontological — both yearn for an unalienated
existence. While Habermas seeks harmony through rational communication, Heidegger urges us to return to the existential lifeworld to re-
learn how to care for Being. Habermas's idea of democracy as reflective
dialogue rests on a cognitive model of discourse. Heidegger arrives at
community through the experiential retrieval of Being. The source of reconciliation lies not in abstract rules and argumentative procedures, but
in man's (*Dasein's*) participation in Being's (*Sein's*) disclosure.[15]

The development of a Habermas-Heidegger dialogue can be found
in the work of political philosophers and theorists Fred Dallmayr, Richard

Bernstein, and Stephen White. All three have constructed dialogues between critical theory and postmodern thought that rely on both Habermas and Heidegger. What is needed in our transitional time, they contend, is not the aesthetic individualism of a Nietzsche or Foucault, but new models of intersubjective reconciliation, community, and democracy. While Dallmayr sides with Heidegger, and Bernstein with Habermas, White pursues a more balanced synthesis. Yet all three thinkers are innovators in critical postmodern political philosophy. They all explore the relationship between ontology, critique, and action in the context of our present time.

Dallmayr's exploration of a pathway between modernity and postmodernity in *Between Freiburg and Frankfurt: Toward a Critical Ontology* (1991) is framed around a critical encounter between the Enlightenment thinking of Kant and Habermas and the postmodern ontology of Heidegger. As Dallmayr explains, Heidegger's rethinking of Western philosophy led him to replace the individual thinking self (the *cogito*) with "being-in-the-world" (contextualized human existence) as the ground or framework within which human identity formation, critical reflection, and human action take place.[16] For Heidegger, the purpose of human existence or *Dasein* is the disclosure of Being (*Ereignis*). By this he meant the illumination of the "worldliness of the world" as a holistic field within which human experiences are situated, revealed, and concealed.

This understanding of worldly existence is the backdrop for any act of critical thinking and human action. The experience of Being reveals not only the basic structure of the world, but also our place in it. Our place in the world is shaped by the structural conditions of finitude and contingency. We are in a world without fundamental foundations. Heidegger defined this situation as "throwness." Ontological reflection reveals that we exist as "thrown" beings, conscious of our mortality and faced with the task of finding a home in the world. Furthermore, in our endeavor to find a home we should come to understand our selves not as subjective entities whose destiny is to will the world as a malleable object, but as "thrown" beings put here to create a clearing for Being in its different manifestations. In realizing this, we should come to the life-altering revelation that much of the historical trajectory of Western culture has been on the wrong track, one enslaved by metaphysics and technology. Combined, they have distorted our culture's perception of the world and set us on a course of destruction through our theoretical and technological objectification of both Nature and Man.

What should we then do? Heidegger called on his fellow Westerners to develop an ethic of "authenticity" in our everyday lives. This involves opening ourselves and others to the experience of Being. In living an authentic life, one shaped by an ontological consciousness, we can experience a new kind of freedom and community or "Being-with-others." This also involves confronting the pervasive "inauthenticity" in our daily lives with both resolve and care. Inauthenticity is a denial of Being characterized by our unreflective immersion in everyday routines, idle talk, and frenzied busybody activities. The challenge of being-with-others involves the cultivation of authentic action in a world shaped and driven by inauthentic activities.

Dallmayr's attempt to develop normative standards from this ontology is bolstered by the support of first-generation Frankfurt School critical theorist Theodor Adorno. Influenced by art and music, Adorno conceived the task of philosophy to be that of illuminating specific phenomena as well as larger clusters of reality through the construction of interpretive ideas and images. These intellectual "constellations" sought to preserve the concrete particularity of specific phenomena within a larger conceptual field, to generate a more contextual type of critique, and to transform philosophy into a more aesthetic, experimental, and cultural materialist enterprise.[17]

Adorno called his approach "negative dialectics" and used it to critique the kind of "identity thinking" dominant in Western thought.[18] Identity thinking seeks to achieve an exact correspondence between particular concrete phenomena and abstract conceptual categories. Yet this reduces real phenomena to a constricting conceptual logic. Seeking to preserve the difference between reality and conceptual thought, Adorno proposed the idea of "non-identity thinking." Dallmayr describes this as "the disentanglement of reflection from subjective-rationalist enclosure— a disentanglement opening reflection up to otherness and non-identity."[19]

Dallmayr further contends that one can discover "submerged affinities" between Heidegger and Adorno.[20] Both were among this century's most sophisticated critics of modern Enlightenment thought. They both rejected the idea of the individual subject as an autonomous, rational actor; they critiqued modern science and technology as aggressive instruments in the possessive mastery of the world; they believed that the ontological infrastructure of the human condition is the matrix from which critical thought and action emerge; and they illuminated the possessive and instrumental nature of Western thought. In using Adorno and Heidegger, Dallmayr redefines the relationship between the everyday experiential life-world and human reason. This involves moving away from the modernist formula whereby legislative reason appropriates and organizes the life-world toward a postmodern formula whereby the life-world informs a more disclosive type of human reasoning.

This idea of a postmodern critical ontology places Dallmayr in opposition to the modernist critical theory of Habermas, which is deontological, cognitivist, formalistic, and universalist.[21] Dallmayr regards this model of rationality as a "truncated version of reason" narrowly tailored to meet the criteria of both empirical science and argumentative speech.[22] The result is a systematic devaluation of the ontological context from which reason emerges. As with Kant, Habermas's reconstruction of Enlightenment reason yields an abstract, formalistic rationality purged of the substantive content and diversity of lived human experience.

In Habermas's view, turning from modern epistemology to postmodern ontology to justify ethical and political life is an abandonment of the Enlightenment for a premodern worldview. The strength of scientific knowledge lies in its distance from the traditions, prejudices, and contingencies of the life-world. In "Discourse Ethics" and "Morality and Ethical Life" in *Moral Consciousness and Communicative Action* (1983), Habermas decouples norms from the substance of life-world contexts to determine their logical validity.[23] This is achieved through procedures of universalization designed to strip away all particulars to arrive at the "abstract core" of human nature and "a priori" structure of human speech.[24] Here Habermas distinguishes between moral questions of "rightness" or "justice" and substantive ethical questions concerning "the good life."

In Dallmayr's view, the political community cannot be sustained through a rationalist morality. Nor is democracy about rational justification and deliberative argumentation. It is about the negotiation of different and shared life-world experiences. Habermas's model of a universal humanist culture dedicated to a procedural-deliberative political ethic amounts to a cognitive-instrumental streamlining of the experiential life-world. Dallmayr reminds Habermas that reason, while universal in its claims, is always contextual in its existence. He urges him "to replace or supplement formal analysis with non-possessive and substantive types of reasoning" and treat "the life-world as a substantive experiential domain."[25]

For Dallmayr, the central task of politics is the creation and maintenance of authentic communities. The authentic community is one in which different people can live together under conditions of ontological reflection and disclosure. Critical ontology seeks to illuminate the deeper existential basis or "worldliness" of human collective life as manifested in the diversity of human identities, norms of critique, and forms of community and public life.

Richard Bernstein defines the present as a complex blending of modern and postmodern elements that has ushered in a "new modern/postmodern constellation." Negotiating this transitional time requires a new kind of pragmatism with Habermas at its core, flanked by the classical American pragmatists (Charles Sanders Peirce, William James, and John Dewey), the cultural hermeneutic philosophy of Hans-Georg Gadamer, and Hannah Arendt. Bernstein's assessment of the modern-postmodern debate and its aftermath is best summed up in the following tasks that he undertakes: (1) to make explicit the insufficiently thematized political ethic of postmodern thought; (2) to critique this stance as untenable due to its abandonment of rational critique and political action for radical otherness and indeterminate, abstract skepticism; and (3) to offer an alternative theory of practical intersubjectivity.[26]

He describes his philosophy as a "nonfoundational pragmatic humanism." It is defined by "the themes of anti-foundationalism, fallibilism, the social character of the self and the regulative idea of a critical community, contingency, and pluralism."[27] Bernstein accurately locates Habermas between the abstract morality of Kant and the communitarian ethical ideal (*Sittlichkeit*) of Hegel, yet closer to Kant. His strategy is to move Habermas closer to Hegel by way of the pragmatists, Gadamer, and Arendt.

Bernstein takes postmoderns to task for failing to affirm and justify normative values. It is his judgment that Heidegger's thinking reveals a stark, polarized view of the world understood in terms of the phenomenon of *Gestell* (technological control) and *poiesis* (poetic illumination) while excluding *phronesis* (practical wisdom) and *praxis* (human action).[28] As for deconstruction, its subversion of political theories and ideologies, which are characterized as fundamentally metaphysical, makes taking a stand impossible. It undermines both rational critique and political action.[29] For Bernstein, postmodernism translates into ethical and political relativism. In a postmodern world, it is aesthetic taste that makes one set of values better than another. Yet jettisoning rational justification as the basis of ethical and political life is tantamount to endorsing criteria of power and charisma. Thus it is a slippery slope from radical contingency and irony (the position of Richard Rorty) to power politics and nihilism.[30]

As for Stephen White, he stakes out a middle ground to accommodate both Habermasians and Heideggereans. Modernists like Habermas conceptualize language in terms of its "action-coordinating" capacity, whereas postmoderns focus on language's "world-disclosing" character. And while modernists emphasize connecting rational critique and political action, postmoderns emphasize the imperative to "bear witness to otherness."[31] White undertakes a series of modern-postmodern balancing acts to make postmoderns more politically responsible and modernists more attentive to worldliness and finitude. The result combines Habermas's intersubjective understanding of action, Heidegger's idea of the "nearness of Being" (*Nahe*), the feminist idea of "attentive care," and a more complex pluralist idea of justice indebted to the thought of Lyotard and Michael Walzer.

Heidegger left us an "ambiguous legacy," argues White, combining brilliant insights into the ontological fabric of the human condition with an "inability to reconstruct adequately the responsibility to act."[32] However, one can find in Heidegger a solution to the modern-postmodern tension in his idea of *Nahe*, or the "nearness of Being." This is described as the face-to-face experience of community that inspires a collective relearning of human existence and finitude.[33] White explores the affinities between Heidegger's idea of *Nahe*, Lyotard's idea of the postmodern as the sublime experience of everyday life, and feminist ethical theories of care to craft what he calls an "alternative experience of everyday life" or a "bearable lightness of care."[34]

The political implication of this ethical sensibility is "a new pluralist reconceptualization of justice" that "would respect the responsibility to act in a normatively justifiable way as well as the responsibility to otherness."[35] Criteria of judgment that inform our notions of justice should ideally emerge out of "the seam between the aesthetic and the moral."[36] White further steers a middle course between Carol Gilligan's notion of a female morality or "ethics of care" and Habermas's idea of morality as a function of cognitive development and language use.[37] In the end, White returns to Habermas and shifts the focus of normative justification from his more formal analytic-linguistic analysis to that of a more cultural hermeneutic strategy of justification. White writes:

> If one is persistently pressed to say why the criteria of normative justification ought to be understood in a certain way, one is forced to contextualize that judgment progressively up to the most general and comprehensive level of narrative about one's culture. And at this level, what we have is not simply another, slightly bigger, narrative than all the others floating around in our culture. Rather, we have a narrative that is recounted to those with whom we radically disagree, with the intention of showing them that they could freely recognize themselves as having a place within it, could find some sense of affirmation with it.[38]

A Bearable Negotiation?

Taken together, Dallmayr, Bernstein, and White offer us an innovative pathway beyond the modern-postmodern debate. Yet the question remains: Is this the pathway we should be pursuing? That is, how effective is the Habermas-Heidegger dialogue as a philosophical ethos, interpretive matrix, and practical tool in negotiating our late modern/postmodern transition?

Dallmayr's strength lies in his ontological and interpretive approach to grasping the relationship between the everyday life-world and the cultivation of rationality and normative critique. Yet thinking within the orbit of Heidegger and Adorno generates rather weak theories of political action. Heideggeran ideas such as *Andenken* (meditative thinking) and *Gelassenheit* (releasement from possessive individualism) urge us to face the threat of *Gestell* (the "enframing" of technological thinking now projected globally) by searching for an "abode" or "dwelling place" in which to live in a simple, sublime, and nonpossessive way. The overwhelming power of the modern technological way of life is countered with meditative attentiveness and communitarian empathy. Human action is defined as "letting be" (to let Being appear).

Dallmayr, like Heidegger, remains within the realm of ontological reflection and does not make connections between critical ontology (concerned with revisioning the human condition and the nature of the political) and the realm of politics (concerned with specific, concrete practices and policies). Political action, as conceived in terms of intentional and coordinated acts in which techniques of power are employed to accomplish certain goals, is part of the problem rather than part of the solution. Heidegger condemned this as the motor force of modernization's utilitarian juggernaut. He proposed an *aletheia* (bringing forth or revealing) model of action that linked human freedom to an anticipatory stance that patiently prepared the way for rare moments of ontological revelation.

This approach, with its ontological emphasis on worldly revelation and an ethic of releasement toward technology and possessive mastery, lacks a critical sociological analysis of our present condition, as well as a politics that resonates with the dynamics of this social condition. The velocity, complexity, and scope of postmodern cultural and late modern institutional changes have destabilized once stable modern notions of self-identity, rationality, society, and political action. Ontological reflection oriented toward the disclosure of Being is designed to stabilize and cure us of our ontological insecurity by searching for a safe place, a conception of the world, self, and community that we can call home. Yet to realize this homecoming, we must distance ourselves from the major social trends of our late modern/postmodern transition. We must, in effect, disengage from contemporary society in search of a "Zen-like" community or space of disclosure. Thus we must also reject several key elements of democratic political life—power, subjective action, and *virtù* (existential, aesthetic, and political virtuosity). Dallmayr rearticulates Heidegger's preference for a pristine simplicity in a world of late-modern complexity. He remains true to Heidegger by resisting the temptation to deploy his critical ontology as a tool for a new pragmatic politics. Yet it comes at a cost. We gain an ontological ethics at the expense of a sociology and a politics.

Bernstein maintains that a postmodern ontology is not enough to make sense of our present time. We need a new pragmatic political ethic that connects more directly with moral, social, and political problems. Yet his ideal of "practical intersubjectivity" inherits the strengths and weaknesses of Habermas's project. He makes Habermas more relevant to the substantive task of building a democratic humanist community. Yet like Habermas, Bernstein advances a modern philosophical worldview, while largely ignoring the fact that we live in a postmodern society and culture. His belief in the moral imperative of humanist dialogue underestimates the reality of contemporary social complexity and cultural diversity.

As Martin Matustik points out in his study of Habermas, Søren Kierkegaard, and Vaclav Havel, Habermas's social and political philosophy of communication is missing the "existing individual" because it privileges generic, moral deliberation and social integration over qualitative self-realization and existential expression.[39] Thus Habermas absorbs existential questions into sociolinguistic questions. Radical self-choice, relating questions of identity to specific settings, and choosing a "way of life" cannot be realized through logical analysis or pacified by universal ethical principles. For Matustik, human communication is as much about expressing one's existential identity as it is about reaching a common understanding.

As for White's "bearable lightness of care," his turning to feminist thought is a move in the right direction. The attention given by feminists to issues of intimacy, care, communication, friendship, and family, as well as their critiques of patriarchial conceptions of public life and citizenship, forces us to rethink the nature of public and private life. Yet White's reading of feminist thought is motivated by his desire to seek a common ground between feminists who espouse sexual difference and those who regard feminism as the most recent wave of modern humanism.[40] Furthermore, he fits this reading of feminist accounts of "care" into a larger philosophy of reconciliation framed by Habermas and Heidegger. The path toward an "agonistic feminism," evident in the work of Bonnie Honig and Chantal Mouffe, is not taken.[41]

How bearable, then, is this idea of a politics of lighter care? If one is in the camp of intersubjective reconciliation, one that includes Habermas and Heidegger, then White's negotiated settlement is bearable. Yet if one is in the camp of agonistic difference and resistance, the camp of Nietzsche, Arendt, Lyotard, and Foucault, then White does us an injustice. This is most evident in White's judgment that Foucault produced no significant insights into ethical and political issues.[42]

White, like Dallmayr and Bernstein, does not confront the power question. He fails to acknowledge Foucault's central insight that power is built into the very structure of human existence. Yet more than this, the Habermas-Heidegger dialogue seeks to radically tame or eliminate power, subjectivity, and *virtù* from the human condition, as well as from politics. This shift from subjectivity to intersubjectivity ends up distorting these integral features of human existence. In search of a political ethic of reconciliation, the Habermas-Heidegger dialogue faces significant criticism from its chief rival — the Nietzschean alternative of a post-modern aesthetic democratic politics.

The Politics of Disclosive *Virtù*:
The Postmodernism in Hannah Arendt

Hannah Arendt (1906–1975) was one of the greatest political philoso-phers of the twentieth century. Her reinterpretation of the Western tra-dition of political philosophy, reconstruction of the concept of political action, existential ontology of the human condition, and phenomenol-ogy of totalitarianism stand out as her most significant achievements.[43] Arendt's original and protean thinking continues to exert a major influ-ence on contemporary political theorists. While Bonnie Honig has high-lighted the Nietzschean dimension in Arendt's thinking, Dana Villa has focused on the influence of Heidegger and the idea of politics as onto-logical disclosure. Taken together, they provide sustenance for the de-velopment of a postmodern model of democratic politics that can be described as a "politics of disclosive *virtù*."

Honig observes that the dominant mode of thinking that has shaped the intellectual tradition of political theory has been the construction of models designed to facilitate "the displacement of politics" as a phe-nomenon of "dissonance, resistance, conflict, or struggle."[44] This way of thinking, what she calls "virtue" theorizing, continues to exert a domi-nant influence on political theory today as evident in liberal, republican, and communitarian models of democracy and in the work of Rawls, Habermas, and Sandel. Prevailing virtue theories "confine politics (con-ceptually and territorially) to the juridical, administrative, or regulative task of stabilizing moral and political subjects, building consensus, main-taining agreements, or consolidating communities and identities."[45] Virtue theories of politics (what I call theories of reconciliation) "assume that the world and the self are not resistant to, but only enabled and com-pleted by, their favored conceptions of order and subjectivity."[46]

In contrast to this perceived hegemony of virtue theories of politics, Honig draws on Nietzsche and Arendt to develop a contrasting perspec-tive she calls "the politics of *virtù*." *Virtù* theorists define politics in terms of dissonance, struggle, and the "remainders" of virtue thought projects. They "seek to secure the perpetuity of political contest."[47] Honig's choice of *virtù* over virtue theories of politics rests on her definition of demo-cratic politics. The politics of *virtù* is more democratic because it proliferates the sites of subjectivity and action, while virtue theories constrict and suppress the conflictual or agonistic heart of politics.[48] The active promotion of diverse and often irreconcilable pluralities is what democracy is all about, not stable identities, institutional fittedness, a shared conception of justice, or ontological homecoming.

In equating freedom with creative action, decoupling human action from moral codes and ethical systems, and defining it in terms of performative rather than purposive-rational criteria, Nietzsche and Arendt laid the groundwork for a *virtù* theory of politics.[49] Nietzsche's model of radical existential questioning and artistic self-reinvention and Arendt's model of political action led them to reject much of modern liberalism and Marxism. The result was an existential model of civic republicanism that combined Nietzsche's view of politics as radical deconstruction ("a revaluation of all values") with Arendt's view of politics as those exceptional actions that illuminate a greater public world.

Arendt was influenced by Aristotle because of the distinction he drew between private and public life and because he regarded politics as one of the highest of human activities insofar as it was dedicated to excellence in public deliberation. Yet while Aristotle enobled politics as a self-sufficient activity, he ultimately subsumed it under the formula of "the good life" as the communitarian modeling of character. Aristotle's distinction between production (necessity) and action (freedom) collapsed into a naturalistic teleological functionalism that rendered politics instrumental, a means to the goal of community well-being.[50]

This led Arendt to construct a model of political action as an activity of public disclosure that drew upon aesthetic interpretations of politics as performative. Like Machiavelli, Arendt defined political action in terms of *virtù*, not virtue. And like Machiavelli and Nietzsche, she judged human action in terms of agonistic contest and heroic glory. Action was primarily existential rather than moral, performative rather than deliberative. Yet aware of the dangers of thinking political action in terms of performance, Arendt turned to Kant's analysis of aesthetic judgment. Political judgment involves taste judgments of performative activity. Yet unlike Nietzsche, who located aesthetic judgment in the actor rather than the audience, Arendt followed Kant and located judgment in the audience's ability to judge the worth of public acts. Arendt appealed to the common sense of a common world. She placed Nietzsche's existential actor in a democratic, public arena of judgment where an informed audience judged action in terms of uniquely political criteria.[51]

Arendtian action, unlike Habermas's idea of communicative action, is therefore based more on an existential and aesthetic ethos of publicity than on rational moral deliberation. The self's passion for distinction and virtuosity is central to her vision of political action.[52] Yet the risks of this type of action must be balanced and stabilized by an account of authority that seeks to preserve and augment a viable public world. In Arendt's judgment, it is the civic republican tradition that best ensures the core ingredients — action, power, and plurality — of a lasting and vigorous political order. Republican governments rest on an "action augmenting form of authority" that sustains a reverence for both beginnings (foundation) and political conflict.[53]

While acknowledging Arendt's Nietzschean dimension, Dana Villa regards Heidegger as the principal influence on Arendt's thought. In Villa's reading, Arendt was profoundly affected by Heidegger's deconstruction of Western thought in *Being and Time* (1927). It led her to develop a disclosive, ontological conception of freedom and a phenomenological model of political action.[54] She defined human action as a type of freedom that both illuminates the world as a public space of appearances and gives greater meaning to this world through extraordinary acts. The Western moral imperative to master the world through a rationalist, technique-oriented, will-to-power has concealed rather than revealed the possibilities of worldly freedom. The result of this is the modern condition of "worldlessness," the loss of a common public world.

Villa maintains that Arendt's famous distinction between the human activities of labor, work, and action is best understood through Heidegger's distinction between authentic and inauthentic disclosure.[55] Human laboring is a nondisclosive activity bound up with the necessary, biological functions of self and species preservation. The world of work, the production of fabricated artifacts, is a "dimmed down" mode of limited disclosiveness that provides us with a permanent, uniquely human home. Arendt equates action with authentic disclosure. Human action illuminates ontological freedom and the experience of a shared common world through existential public acts.

The tragedy of modernity for Arendt was that its one-dimensional drive for global technological control was rooted in an "existential resentment" of authentic disclosure.[56] Indebted to Heidegger's interpretation of modernity as technological "enframing" (*Gestell*), Arendt regarded modernization as a process of "world alienation" in which human activity is enslaved by automated technological processes resulting in the triumph of a robotic existence over a worldly, active life. She pessimistically concluded that political action as the disclosure of worldly freedom has disappeared. It has been replaced with predictable and modifiable behavior. Mass technopolitics has triumphed in the form of varied malignant and benign totalitarianisms, ranging from Nazism to public administration.

Arendt's deconstruction of Western philosophy and political philosophy ("the tradition") was greatly influenced by Heidegger. Yet Arendt concluded that neither Nietzsche, nor Heidegger ever fully overcame the Western tradition of "productionist metaphysics." Both turned away from praxis or action only to retreat into *poiesis* or poetic thinking as an aesthetic enterprise of fabrication.[57] Arendt in effect repoliticized Nietzsche and Heidegger in order to recover and rearticulate the ideal of an authentic *praxis* in the "dark times" of twentieth-century late modernity.[58]

Arendt's reconceptualization of political action served as a standard by which to judge the world of human affairs and illuminate those rare moments when genuine action clears a public space of disclosure. This intellectual project was both heroic and tragic. Arendt spent her life affirming novel forms of public action against the background of a late modernity that did not value her brand of existential politics. Arendt's political actors had no stage upon which to perform. As out-of-work actors, they lived by taking everyday jobs and waiting for the opportunity to momentarily shine in larger-than-life performances on a fragmented, dimmed-down stage. Villa writes that Arendt's "faith in action" should be viewed as signifying "both loss and hope." Public spaces and "islands of freedom" do emerge for brief historic moments, yet "only to submerge once again."[59]

Honig further reminds us that Arendt's notion of heroic action and authority are out of step with the present. Her rigid distinctions between public and private life, everyday and authentic life, and social and political life, are unrealistic constructs that do not effectively connect with contemporary social, cultural, and political life. These distinctions were designed to provide a stable backdrop for political action and a dam against the private socialization of the public realm.[60] Honig rightly argues that in today's world, "public-private realm cross-fertilizations abound" and define the terrain of politics.[61] Arendt's characterization of the private sphere as the realm of natural, stable human functions should be understood as a foundational myth. Honig correctly asserts that the private realm is in many ways the "unnatural" product of human power relationships. Many human activities have been legitimized as "private" and "natural" due to the authority of tradition.[62]

Arendt's belief that political action has fallen victim to the rise of a new hybrid social realm needs to be reversed. Politics today is sustained by the interpenetration of public and private life. Arendt's notion of action translates as a Nietzschean politics of greatness and not a democratic politics of everyday life. Postmodernism, in essentially inverting Arendt, who inverted Heidegger, has championed a postexistential ethos of everyday life. Postmodernism illuminates the struggles, contingencies, and ambivalences of everyday life in a distinctly antiheroic way. Arendt's politics of action is rarely found in today's more postmodern world. Politics is more local and the product of contingent or situational circumstances, interwoven in a complex mosaic of social power networks and intercultural relations.

Therefore, I believe that the case can be made that it is not Arendt's concept of action but rather Michel Foucault's concept of resistance that better fits our current late modern/postmodern transition. The path beyond Arendt to Foucault, intimated in both Honig's and Villa's accounts of Arendt's thought, needs to be taken.[63] Returning to Villa's concluding remarks on Arendt's critique of modernity, he writes:

> An unlikely constellation appears when we view Arendt's emphasis upon agonism, plurality, and performance against the backdrop of her more Heideggerean thoughts concerning the destruction of the common world. Seen through this lens, Arendt's theory of political action, so clearly at odds with a Foucauldian politics of everyday life, links up with Foucault's concept of resistance. For where the space of action is usurped (as both Arendt and Foucault argue it is), action in the strict sense is no longer possible. Resistance becomes the primary vehicle of spontaneity and agonistic subjectivity, a kind of successor concept to action.[64]

Beyond Arendt to Foucault

I believe that the move beyond Habermas and Heidegger and toward a model of democratic *virtù* is the right one to make. Yet this further requires us to move beyond an Arendt-inspired politics of disclosive *virtù* toward a Foucault-inspired reweaving of aesthetics, ethics, and politics. The idea of a political philosophy that links critical ontology to an ethos of democratic *virtù* is best achieved by working through Michel Foucault's unfinished project.

My choice of Foucault as the site upon which to construct a critical postmodern political philosophy rests on two key convictions. First, Foucault's thinking better resonates with our late modern/postmodern transition. His understanding of society as a complex circulatory system made up of dense networks and spatial fields of power, knowledge, desire, and identity fits our current social condition. Clegg regards Foucault's reconceptualization of power as the principal influence on his circuits of power model.[65] Furthermore, one can make important connections between Foucault's historical studies and current issues regarding scientific expertise, social administrative power, technologies of government, self-identity, sexuality, and lifestyle politics. In short, Foucault's research better informs the issues facing individuals today, living as many of us do enmeshed in the hybridized, public-private social worlds of late modern/postmodern societies.

Second, it is my view that politics has always been intertwined with ethics and aesthetics. It has always been a strategic power game infused with moral concerns and matters of style. And it always will be intertwined with these activities. The real question involves the proper mix of politics, ethics, and aesthetics in the struggle to advance a democratic politics. Here I value Foucault's "mix" as a more relevant formulation for our time than that of Habermas, Heidegger, and Arendt.

I share William Connolly's doubts concerning "the quest for transparency" evident in Habermas's idea of a communicatively rationalized society and the Heideggerean pursuit of ontological attunement. As Connolly says, they believe that "the gaps between body and identity, desire and intrinsic purpose, knowledge and being" can be narrowed to the point that a reflective moral consensus or close attunement to a "higher direction in being" can be achieved.[66] Connolly sees their ideals as contributing to "the extension of disciplinary society," the reduction of politics to "collective action in concert or as communal realization," and the domestication of both desire and "the experience of contingency in life."[67]

Connolly is struck by Habermas's "persistent silence about the body, which is simultaneously the text upon which the script of society is written and the fugitive source from which springs desires, resistances, and thought exceeding that script."[68] He surmises that if Habermas did develop a theory of embodiment, it would undermine his ideal of discourse based on impartiality and universality. As for the quest for onto-logical attunement, Connolly concludes that "it remains deeply con-testable whether any pastoral hermeneutics responds to an immanent purpose in being or transcendentalizes a contingent organization of life by treating it *as if* it expresses communion with being."[69] He further re-marks that proponents of "the communion perspective" are "effective in conveying what we have lost, ineffective in showing why we should seek to return that lost world today."[70] They have been "unable to inspire general confidence that there is an intrinsic order of being generally avail-able to us."[71]

It is Connolly's judgment that "the most distinctive and salient fea-ture" of our present time is "the globalization of contingency."[72] He char-acterizes this condition as "the perverse correlation between the drive of dominant states to master contingency in their internal and external en-vironments and the corollary production of dangerous global possibili-ties that outstrip the capacity of any single state or the interstate system to control them."[73] This is evident "in the rupture in contemporary ex-periences of state sovereignty, global ecology, the internationalization of market relations, and speed in politics."[74]

While modernists like Habermas respond to the globalization of con-tingency with new techniques of rationality, and advocates of ontological attunement seek a safe abode from the juggernaut of globalized moder-nity, Connolly calls on us to radicalize the experience of contingency and channel this volatile energy into an ethos of postmodern pluraliza-tion. This self-described "Foucauldian ethical sensibility" rests upon the following imperatives:

1. Genealogical analyses that reveal the contingent basis of truth and identity claims and disrupt established dualities.
2. The "active cultivation of the capacity to subdue resentment" and "to affirm the ambiguity of life without transcendental guar-antees."
3. Generosity in interpreting how individuals construct their iden-tities through difference.
4. Experimentation in the forging of new social relations.[75]

Connolly translates this critical postmodern ethic into a politics ded-icated to the "pluralization of pluralism." American pluralism "remains too stingy, cramped, and defensive for the world we now inhabit."[76] The conventional pluralist imagination is confined to the modern territorial nation-state, to the liberal model of the normal individual as an autonomous moral agent with self-evident motivations and interests, to a middle-class politics of individual rights and instrumental interest groups, and to "monotheistic or monosecular conceptions of morality." In response to high-tech globalization and cultural postmodernization, liberal pluralism has become ossified and reactionary. This fundamentalized liberalism must be radically pluralized.[77]

Postmodern pluralization cultivates what Connolly describes as an "ethos of critical responsiveness." It seeks to disrupt and actively contest the congealed "operational standards of identity, nature, reason, territory, sovereignty, and justice" that make up liberal pluralism.[78] This involves fostering the pluralization of cultural and political identities as well as the logic of the territorial state. Postmodern pluralism is focused less on governance or interests than on the reconstitution of cultural life. It focuses its energies on the micropolitics of the self-identity and difference; on "the politics of disturbance through which sedimented identities and moralities are rendered more alert to the deleterious effects of their naturalizations upon difference"; on radicalizing "the experience of contingency in the formation and maintenance of identities and things"; and on the "politics of nonstatist, cross-national movements."[79]

Equally in search of a more radical democratic politics, political theorist Jeffrey Isaac maintains that the "rebellious politics" inspired by Arendt and Albert Camus is more relevant for our present time than the one influenced by Foucault. He identifies several important similarities between Arendt, Camus, and Foucault. They all shared the desire to problematize conventional politics, were indebted to Nietzsche, were suspicious of "general intellectuals" who speak in terms of universal human emancipation, favored civil society rather than the state as the site of political action, and were "inspired by those who exist at the political margins of normal society."[80]

Nonetheless, their differences outweigh their similarities and Foucault comes up short. Isaac maintains that while Foucault deconstructed modern freedom, Arendt and Camus reconstructed it. Furthermore, Foucault was too Nietzschean; Arendt and Camus took their Nietzsche in smaller doses and filtered his thought through democratic humanism. While Foucault avoided the language of human rights, Arendt and Camus embraced it. While Foucault advocated radical difference. Arendt and Camus realized "the importance of concordances in politics." Finally, Foucault's "ethical agnosticism" short-circuited any attempt to develop a viable democratic theory beyond anarchistic disruption and individualized strategies of resistance. In short, concludes Isaac, why "labor over Foucault's cryptic remarks" when thinkers like Arendt and Camus show us the way toward "rebellious political agency" with greater intellectual clarity and real-world relevance?[81]

I would argue that the limitations of Arendt's political thought are more profound than Foucault's. Arendt's rigid distinctions between labor, work, and action, between social life and political life, and between private and public life, cannot be sustained empirically. Her strict definition of political action — as self-contained public deeds and speech of authentic disclosure — defines it practically out of existence in order to preserve its purity. For Arendt, political action does not involve governmental concerns of administration, representation, or legitimation, nor does it include socioeconomic and cultural lifestyle issues. Yet it is precisely these issues that are in the foreground of public life today, clamoring for disclosure.

Isaac is quite correct to connect Arendtian action with the Central European dissident movements such as Charter 77 in Czechoslovakia and Poland's Solidarity, with Vaclav Havel and Adam Michnik.[82] Yet Foucault also crafted his own brand of "rebellious politics." In the 1960s he advocated "transgression" against the limits imposed on us by the modern culture of Enlightenment reason. In the 1970s he engaged in radical protest for prison reform. In the late 1970s and early 1980s he developed the idea of an "aesthetics of existence" as the basis of a political ethic of creative resistance.[83] And contrary to characterizations of Foucault as retreating into the pursuit of stoic autonomy and aesthetic self-absorption, he remained active in liberation movements and human rights causes related to gay and lesbian freedom, Soviet and East European dissidents, Iran, and Poland's Solidarity. While unwilling to elaborate a theory of human rights, Foucault was involved in the politics of human rights.[84]

Isaac fails to examine the significant shift that occurred in Foucault's work in the late 1970s before his death. Here he reconceived his genealogical approach and altered his intellectual agenda to develop a new model of ethical action, an investigation into the origins and developments of modern government and resistance, and a renewed interest in the Enlightenment themes of critique and emancipation as they relate to our present situation. The result was a new idea of freedom. Isaac acknowledges this in a footnote, yet he does not pursue the implications of Foucault's final and unfinished work.[85] If he did, I believe it would under-mine his case against Foucault.

For Isaac, Arendt remains the political philosopher of our time. Yet I contend that her time has passed. Foucault, I believe, is the critical post-modern philosopher of our time. I question Habermas's neo-Enlight-enment project of communicative rationalization, the Heideggerean per-spective of ontological attunement, and Arendt's heroic model of existential republicanism. Yet at the same time, I believe that Connolly's critical ontology remains too fixed on radical contingency, downplaying the dialectical interplay between complexity and contingency.

Our current late modern/postmodern transition is best understood in terms of increased complexity. As environments become more com-plex due to the rapidity of both technological and cultural changes, we see an exponential proliferation of variables. These variables form com-plex, rapidly changing interdependencies that increase the turbulence of environments. Contingency or aperiodic behavior appears more fre-quently, thereby rendering stability and predictable activity more diffi-cult to achieve. Thus the more complex the world becomes, the more contingency becomes an integral factor in making sense of it.

This interplay between complexity and contingency is a defining theme of Foucault's work. Foucault's defining passion was the struggle—per-sonally, intellectually, and politically—to understand and experience freedom (and the lack thereof). It led him to develop a concept of free-dom different from modern humanist and radical postmodern accounts. Foucault came to the realization that human freedom is constructed out of the tensional negotiation of existential contingency and individual autonomy, enmeshed as we are in complex, spatial fields of social power.

The space in which we live today is a complex field of highly plural-ized, heterogenous, intersecting, and overlapping flows and networks of power, knowledge, desire, and identity. Foucault characterized this space as "heterotopian."[86] I define this condition as one of "complexity." For Foucault, negotiating this postmodern, spatial environment required a rethinking of the relationship between the self, others, and power; an understanding of freedom that called for a reweaving of ethics, aesthetics, and politics; and a conception of politics understood in terms of "gov-ernmentality" and "resistance." He was headed in the right direction, yet the case for Foucault still remains to be made.

4 — Foucault's Presence

> *I carefully guard against making the law. Rather, I concern myself with determining problems, unleashing them, revealing them within the framework of such complexity as to shut the mouth of prophets and legislators: all of those who speak for others and above others.*
> — Michel Foucault, *Remarks on Marx*

> *There is a kind of Sisyphean optimism in the later Foucault.*
> — Colin Gordon, "Government Rationality: An Introduction"

Unfinished Work

When Michel Foucault died in Paris on the afternoon of June 25, 1984, he was the world's most famous intellectual, France's most important philosopher, and a cult figure in America. His intellectual work had a multidisciplinary influence on the humanities and social sciences from history, philosophy, and literary criticism, to sociology, cultural studies, and political science. In *The Passion of Michel Foucault* (1993), James Miller describes a Foucault driven by the tragic, neo-Nietzschean quest for transgressive intensity.[1] In the more balanced *The Lives of Michel Foucault* (1993), David Macey portrays Foucault as a more complex, multidimensional person who "lived many lives."[2] The last chapter of Macey's biography is titled "An Unfinished Life." This chapter on Foucault could be titled "Unfinished Work."

Foucault was a philosopher-historian whose sphinxlike intellect posed more riddles than it solved.[3] He never declared himself a structuralist, a poststructuralist, or a postmodern.[4] Yet this was the terrain he traversed. Foucault's corpus of work has been most often dissected in terms of three analytic shifts. In this reading, the early "archaeology of knowledge" period (1961–69) gave way to the "genealogy of power" period (1971–76), which in turn gave way to the "aesthetic-ethical subjectivity" period (1980–84).[5]

I interpret Foucault differently. I distinguish between his early archaeological and middle genealogical works, which yield the thesis of power/knowledge, a "later" Foucault who develops a new model of ethical agency, and an "unfinished" Foucault who was in the process of articulating a critical ontology of freedom and developing a new mode of political analysis. He conceptualized "government" as a complex array of normative social technologies, networks, strategies, and tactics coordinated by the state, which regulated self-identity and social conduct.

Foucault's early and middle periods are defined by: (1) his archaeological and genealogical methodological innovations; (2) his theory of discourse; (3) his critique of Enlightenment rationality; (4) his thesis of disciplinary power; (5) his power/knowledge analytic framework; and (6) the subject matter of his histories — mental illness, clinical medicine, the human sciences, prisons, and sexuality. Connecting all of these themes is the conviction that "thought" and "experience" are the products of historically shaped regimes of power. Disciplines of expert knowledge as well as everyday mores are determined by rules of discourse embedded in power relations over which we have very limited control.

Foucault's shift from archaeological discourse analysis to genealogical power analysis was more of a methodological progression than a change in philosophical assumptions. His early histories of the 1960s — *Madness and Civilization, The Birth of the Clinic,* and *The Order of Things* — portrayed the birth of the modern human sciences as the product of a new humanist "regime of truth."[6] These "disciplines of knowledge" were analyzed by Foucault as "discourses" (language practices) and "epistemes" (scientific conceptual frameworks) used to justify and facilitate the deployment of a new host of moral-legal norms and social regulatory practices.

Following *The Archaeology of Knowledge* (1971), Foucault developed a genealogical research agenda in order to investigate those power relations that determined the rules of discourse.[7] The key texts of this period include "Nietzsche, Genealogy, History," *Discipline and Punish: The Birth of the Prison, The History of Sexuality, Volume I: An Introduction,* and *Power/Knowledge: Selected Interviews and Other Writings, 1972–1977.*[8] His power/knowledge social theory unearthed the existence of a novel form of modern "disciplinary power." He defined it as a circuitry of microstrategic relations and specific procedures deployed as a scientific-legal complex of social normalization.

The vicious circularity of Foucault's power/knowledge grid allowed no space for freedom. The subject was an effect of power, the product of "subjectification," a "docile body." To seek knowledge or truth was to participate in a discourse linked to power networks that produced the techniques that determined what it meant to be an individual subject. Foucault realized he had thought his way into a disciplinary matrix. A critical space needed to be carved out to justify the very oppositional discourses and practices that made up his dissident lifestyle.

Thus in the late 1970s and 1980s he focused on the themes of critique, government, and ethical agency. This took shape out of his examination of ancient Greco-Roman sexual and ethical practices, his rethinking of Kant's idea of critical philosophy, and his historical inquiry into how disciplinary power practices were linked to technologies of government. The "final Foucault" (1978 to 1984) includes his lectures at the College de France, the University of California at Berkeley, Stanford University, and the University of Vermont; the essay "What Is Enlightenment?"; numerous interviews; and his final major works *The Use of Pleasure* and *The Care of the Self.*[9]

The Foucault that emerges from this reading of his work is a critical thinker who straddled the modern and the postmodern. He rejected the Enlightenment but not enlightenment, and critiqued modernity while recasting its critical ethos. Foucault was a skeptic and a contextualist who privileged the experiential nexus of power and freedom. The historical topics he chose were motivated by his persistent problematization of present ways of life among expert and deviant populations and the institutional orders that legitimized their existence. His methodologies were constructed specifically for these histories. Implicit in these histories was a logic of revolt that deliberately inserted countermyths and dramatic examples into otherwise cool, detached, scholarly studies. Foucault's "heroes" ranged from deviant artists to outcast social groups, misfits, ancient pagan Cynics, and the plebian struggles of ordinary people.

I further believe that the "final" and "unfinished" work of Michel Foucault provides us with the tools needed to construct a critical postmodernism. His ideas concerning critical ontology, the nature of our present, becoming an ethical subject, the power/freedom relationship, and the practice of government connect with my ideas of a late modern/postmodern transition and critical postmodernism. They speak to the need to rethink the relationship between our social condition, our moral conduct, our selves, and where we are at politically.

The Practice of Critique: Genealogy and Critical Ontology

What emerged from Foucault's later work on the self, ethics, critique, and government was a novel idea of freedom informed by a mode of historical-ontological critique. He described this work as contributing to "a historical ontology of ourselves."[10] It had two key objectives: (1) to explore and critique the limits of the present; and (2) to act upon this critique by seizing hold of the present and transfiguring it.[11] For Foucault, this meant transforming oneself into an ethical agent and fashioning a distinct style of existence. This involved the practice of liberty, which meant exercising freedom as a fundamental ontological condition in the form of critique (to think critically), resistance (to fight against), and art (to create).

Like Nietzsche and Weber, Foucault devoted most of his time and energy to exploring the circumstances that have shaped Western individuals into self-regulating subjects. Nietzsche's assessment of Christianity as a slave morality and late modernity as a period of nihilism, Weber's analysis of the modern Protestant work ethic, and Foucault's account of disciplinary power offer us powerful stories of how Western identities have been produced.

Foucault believed that the circumstances of our present "have been made, they can be unmade, as long as we know how it was that they were made."[12] He adopted a view of history as a murky abyss into which we descend with an eye for anomalies, a task that is "gray, meticulous, and documentary."[13] This approach was most indebted to Nietzsche's technique of genealogical critique. His investigations into the emergence of Western morality, rationality, and the sovereign individual were informed by the conviction that human values, worldviews, and identities are the product of specific historic power contexts. Thus there is no single, universal morality or rationality valid for all human beings.

Historical genealogy and critical ontology were the tools Foucault used to examine modernity. He attacked the positivist view of scientific knowledge and its claim that we can obtain objective and universal knowledge of the world. He also sought to discredit the liberal construct of the autonomous subject possessed of innate, natural rights and existing in a dualistic relationship to society. Foucault accomplished this by reconceiving Enlightenment liberalism as a specific modern regime of power that controlled people through a novel form of disciplinary power. The jewel in the crown of Enlightenment liberalism — the rational, autonomous, intentional agent — was decentered and devalued by Foucault as the social construct of disciplinary power.

Foucault's work described the existence of distinct types of modern Western social power that were intimately intertwined with specific kinds of scientific knowledge, administrative techniques, normative criteria, and models of individual identity. He described these power practices as "power/knowledge," "disciplinary power," and "biopower."[14] Power/knowledge refers to the dominance of knowledge-based modes of power. The key sites of contemporary knowledge production, the sciences and professions, are the primary forces behind the production and deployment of power formations. Disciplinary power describes how modern power/knowledge circuits and matrices produce "normalized" individuals. This is achieved through the coordination of legal and moral norms with detailed, highly structured, and supervised training techniques and assignments. Biopower describes how modern power/knowledge circuits and matrices seek to control human biological processes and functions as well as populations.

As John Ransom explains, Foucault employed two different types of genealogy in his investigations of modernity. The first type of "historical genealogy" was oriented toward explaining how modern cultural artifacts are the product of determinate power contexts. The second type of "political genealogy" was oriented toward opening up spaces of resistance and freedom within dominant power/knowledge circuits and matrices.[15]

Historical genealogies unsettle the past and thus disrupt the present by showing how specific ideas, institutions, moral codes, and ways of life are constructed out of contingent circumstances and "battle lines" between conflicting forces. The historical emergence of these cultural artifacts is the result of "a cobbled patchwork of heterogeneous elements" that become stabilized into a determinate power formation.[16] Stabilized power points, often the result of haphazard events, accidental convergences, and strategic struggles, become power/knowledge circuits that in turn grow into dominant social organizations and moral systems. Thus historical genealogies force us "to become aware of unquestioned assumptions, thoughtless gestures, seemingly legitimate institutions, and unexamined modes of thought by revealing their contingent and (sometimes) violent foundations."[17]

Yet Ransom reminds us that these genealogies do not instruct us "to move beyond unsettling our practices to propose (for example) new kinds of power relations to replace disciplines."[18] The most they can do is compare and contrast different ways of life. It is by adopting the strategy of political genealogy that we look toward "the creation of new power-knowledge circuits that can compete with and supplant old ones."[19] This can be accomplished in one of two ways. The first is to respond to a present problem by writing a history "that makes possible and even propels the formation of a community of action that will address the issue at hand."[20] The second way Foucault described as the "insurrection of subjugated knowledges."[21] Here the genealogist takes seriously the claims of different types of knowledge that have been discredited and marginalized by dominant power/knowledge formations. These local, popular, and fragmented types of knowledge "are not integrated into any power-knowledge circuit."[22] Thus they can be integrated into oppositional strategies that seek to challenge or replace specific matrices of power/knowledge.

Foucault's political genealogies opened the door to the idea of a critical ontology of freedom, an idea most fully articulated in the essay "What Is Enlightenment?" (1984). Here he disconnected enlightenment, understood as the practice of thinking critically, from the Enlightenment project. What connects us to the Enlightenment, argued Foucault, is "not faithfulness to doctrinal elements, but rather the permanent reactivation of an attitude — that is, of a philosophical ethos that could be described as a permanent critique of our historical era."[23] What we need to do is develop a critical ethos tailored to our present condition.

Thus Foucault defined enlightenment or critique negatively. It is an "exit" — as an "exit," a "way out."[24] Critique involves first and foremost the escape from disciplinary control. It is the tool we use to discover exit points in power/knowledge networks. This further implies a freedom from the modern Enlightenment project and its search for universal truths about the individual subject that are translated into humanist moral and legal codes. Indeed, it was Foucault's conviction that if we are to free ourselves from the constraints of a highly disciplined society, we must equally free ourselves from our heavy reliance on religion, science, and law to guide and shape our lives.

What Foucault valued in Kant's original essay on the Enlightenment was his emphasis on the critical thinker's relationship to the present.[25] Kant seems to be saying that to achieve "intellectual maturity," we must grasp how the present situation influences our thoughts and actions. To "know thyself" is to know what is going on now. Foucault, however, questioned Kant's specific answer to the question of how our obligation to critical thought should proceed. He rejected Kant's belief that freedom involves intellectually following self-chosen ethical principles while outwardly conforming to existing social norms and political authorities.[26]

For Foucault, intellectual maturity meant to "care for thyself" by transforming oneself into an ethical subject in direct relation to existing social norms and political power formations. This tenet moved Foucault away from Kant's modern ethical imperative of critical thinking and closer toward Baudelaire's modernist aesthetic imperative of self-transfiguration.[27] For Baudelaire, the artist's relationship to the present involves actively cultivating a rich experiential life and using the knowledge gained to shape the self into a work of art. Foucault, however, expanded Baudelaire's formula into the ideal of every person conceiving of his or her life as a project of creative expression and experimentation. This informed his idea of a "critical ontology of ourselves." We should strive to freely shape our self-identities by exploring, testing, and challenging both the forms and the contents of present-day social, cultural, and political environments of experience and action.

Therefore, Foucault concluded that critique is "no longer going to be practiced in the search for formal structures with universal value, but rather as a historical investigation into the events that have led us to constitute ourselves and to recognize ourselves as subjects of what we are doing, thinking, saying."[28] We reflect on how we have been shaped (disciplined) with respect to both our identities and our available courses of action. We then critique existing modes of conduct to test their limits and invent new norms.

A critical ontology of ourselves applies alternative modes of being and norms to the personal/political test of pushing the horizons of present-day cultural practices. These alternative ways of life evolve from both genealogical research and personal lifestyle experimentation. In doing this, we confront what Foucault called "the paradox of the relations of capacity to power."[29] That is, we must struggle to disconnect the growth of capabilities for self-determination from "the intensification of power relations," thereby creating a space of freedom.[30] It was in struggling with this relationship between power and freedom that Foucault developed his notions of "resistance" and "self-care."

He concluded his essay on enlightenment by defining critical ontology as a philosophical attitude or ethos, not "a theory, a doctrine, or even as a permanent body of knowledge that is accumulating."[31] It requires the willingness to conduct "diverse inquiries," engage in experimentation, and pursue "very specific transformations." This involves "putting historico-critical reflection to the test of concrete practices."[32] And above all, wrote Foucault, critical ontology should be conceived as "a patient labor giving form to our impatience for liberty."[33]

Points of Resistance: The Circuitry of Power/Freedom

Out of these investigations into the evolution of modern power/knowledge, disciplinary power, and biopower emerged a new understanding of the workings of social power. Foucault maintained that social power is largely generated and sustained out of a "microphysics" of incessant, small, discrete, everyday incidents of human interaction. These interactive practices are "capillary," strategic, and ever shifting. They are also highly productive — the energy and circuitry of human identities and organizations. Social structures, institutions, centralized states, and government policies are the products of relatively stabilized and built-up microlevel social dynamics.

The translation of these microworlds of modern social power relations into macrolevel social and political orders is achieved through "technologies of power." It is here that specific types of scientific knowledge, social norms, behavioral codes, and administrative techniques come together to form stable circuits and matrices of power/knowledge. These circuits and matrices have been stitched together to create the modern sovereign entity of the nation-state society. Thus, for Foucault, the very visible and politically legitimate mode of sovereign state power is the tip of a vast iceberg. The modern state juts up from an infrastructural social terrain of disciplinary power circuits and matrices.

In his own words, Foucault defined power as a "multiplicity of force relations" that "have a directly productive role." Power is "a complex strategical situation in a particular society." It is not defined in terms of "repression or law." It is not "a general system of domination" or "a group of institutions and mechanisms." It is "not something that is acquired, seized, or shared, something that one holds onto or allows to slip away." Power is not a "binary and all-encompassing opposition between rulers and ruled."[34] It is rather more cellular, decentralized, and horizontal.

Yet there is another feature of social power that is integral to its existence and functioning— the phenomenon of "resistance." Networks of power relations are permeated with multiple "points, knots, or focuses of resistance" that "are spread over time and space at varying densities" and that "are inscribed in the latter (power) as an irreducible opposite."[35] Foucault would write:

> These points of resistance are present everywhere in the power network. Hence there is no single locus of great Refusal, no soul of revolt, source of all rebellions, or pure law of the revolutionary. Instead there is a plurality of resistances, each of them a special case: resistances that are possible, necessary, improbable; others that are spontaneous, savage, solitary, concerted, rampant, or violent; still others that are quick to compromise, interested, or sacrificial; by definition, they can only exist in the strategic field of power relations.[36]

> Just as the network of power relations ends by forming a dense web that passes through apparatuses and institutions, without being exactly localized in them, so too the swarm of points of resistance traverses social stratification and individual unities. And it is doubtless the strategic codification of these points of resistance that makes a revolution possible, somewhat similar to the way in which the state relies on the institutional integration of power relationships.[37]

While power is omnipresent, it is not omnipotent. For present throughout power circuits and networks is a multiplicity of points of resistance that have the potential to alter existing power relations. Every power relation contains within it an element that cannot be controlled, integrated, or fully assimilated. This element, or cluster of elements, creates a tension within the social power environment. It is this tensional effect within the power relation that opens up the possibility of changing this relation. For Foucault, the tensional phenomenon of resistance is the most basic expression of concrete freedom. It is the instance in which evidence of strain and stress within the power formation opens up a space for a reversal or release from its control.

What makes resistance possible is the very nature of power itself. For the very power techniques and matrices that seek to achieve control over individuals and environments of action can be employed by subjects to resist this control, and in jujitsu-like fashion carve out a space of freedom. Foucault maintained that the body itself possesses certain resistant capacities. And individual resistance does not preclude the formation of communities of resistance. Disciplinary power isolates and trains bodies. Resistance contests the isolating matrices of disciplinary power.

In "The Subject and Power" (1982), Foucault proposed "taking forms of resistance against different forms of power as a starting point."[38] He defined resistance as struggles that: (1) are "transversal," not limited to one particular society or nation; (2) whose objective is the effects of power; (3) are "immediate," focused on local instances of power; (4) are against the "government of individualization," which both constrains free action and isolates individuals from community life; (5) are against "the privileges of knowledge" or expertise; and (6) are primarily concerned with the question "Who are we?" — that is, with ontological identity and difference.[39]

Foucault further maintained that resistance struggles are concerned with attacking "not so much 'such or such' institution of power, or group, or elite, or class, but rather a technique, a form of power."[40] Today, he concluded, "the struggle against the form of subjection — against the submission of subjectivity — is becoming more and more important, even though the struggles against the forms of domination and exploitation have not disappeared."[41]

As Anthony Giddens contends in *Modernity and Self-Identity* (1991), a new type of "life politics" or "lifestyle politics" has emerged whose "ethos of self-growth signals major social transitions in late modernity as a whole."[42] Its focus is upon "the issue 'how should we live?' in a post-traditional order and against the backdrop of existential questions."[43] While emancipatory politics "is concerned to reduce or eliminate exploitation, inequality, and oppression,"[44] lifestyle politics is concerned with issues of the body, self-identity, lifestyle choice, cultural difference, and the limits of scientific/technological innovation.

Foucault conceived of a politics of resistance struggles precisely in relation to these late modern/postmodern lifestyle issues. He opted for a politics of resistance in part because emancipation was too strongly linked to the Enlightenment political tradition, to the liberal humanist teleology of progress, and to the Marxist ideology of revolutionary trans-formation. He decoupled critique from the fashioning of utopian pro-jects of a liberated existence. Critique was specific rather than general-izable, oriented toward local context-dependent strategies rather than society-wide structural changes.

Andrew Cutrofello concludes that Foucault regarded any generaliz-able theory of human emancipation as a normative straitjacket. How-ever, his "care of the self" ethic did inform a general strategy of critical resistance.[45] The idea of an ethics of resistance that developed out of his analysis of the power/resistance relationship involved forging a "disci-pline of resistance" against a specific "disciplinary matrix" of domina-tion. The fashioning of a resistant type of power through strategically chosen practices of self-transformation requires an ethos of disciplined freedom. Thus while unwilling to endorse a Kantian categorical imper-ative, Foucault articulated a general strategic imperative to resist disci-plinary control.

Resistance was the first and most important step on the road toward freedom. Foucault located the most primal expression of concrete free-dom in those moments of disentanglement or release from disciplinary control. Yet he did not give us a road map or a programmatic agenda. He rather gave us tools to use as we see fit. Where, then, does this leave us? Let me suggest the following set of propositions. Where there is power, there is resistance. Where there is resistance, there is critique. Where there is critique, there is the possibility of self-transformation. Where there is self-transformation, there is the possibility of social and political change. Where there is social and political change, there is power. Where there is power, there is resistance.

The Practice of Freedom: Reweaving Ethics, Aesthetics, and Politics

In Foucault's final work, most evident in *The Use of Pleasure* (1984) and *The Care of the Self* (1984), a shift occurred from the analysis of disci-pline techniques (whereby a body is trained to discipline itself by power/knowledge regimes) to "practices of the self" (whereby ethical practices of self-transformation are employed by the self on the self to create a reflexive agent). In these two works, his research on ancient Greek and Roman sexual and ethical mores was not undertaken for antiquarian interests. Nor was Foucault interested in resurrecting Greco-Roman mores under present-day conditions. He was intrigued, rather, by how these ancient cultures thought about sexual and ethical issues and how they approached the organization of their sexual and ethical lives. Foucault also wanted to illuminate the difference between Greco-Roman and Christian-modern ethics in order to lay the groundwork for a new way of thinking about freedom.

He distinguished between "code morality" and "practices of the self."[46] Code morality, characteristic of Christian and modern ethics, emphasizes duty to common rules of behavior enforced by a common set of laws. Ancient Greek ethics, by contrast, emphasized the "arts of existence" (aesthetic techniques, methods, and exercises) and *askesis* (the disciplined organization of these techniques into a distinctive style of life).[47] This approach to the organization of an ethical life was defined by Foucault as "those intentional and voluntary actions by which men not only set themselves rules of conduct, but also seek to transform themselves, to change themselves in their singular being, and to make their life into an *oeuvre* that carries certain aesthetic values and meets certain stylistic criteria."[48] He valued this model because he had concluded that "the idea of a morality as obedience to a code of rules is now disappearing, has already disappeared. To this absence of a morality, one responds, or must respond, with a research which is that of an aesthetics of existence."[49]

Based on his research into ancient Greek ethics, Foucault identified four interrelated modes of ethical practice that formed the basis of both a framework of ethical analysis and a model of freedom. They were ethical substance, a mode of subjectivation, ethical work, and *telos*.[50] Ethical substance refers to that aspect or part of an individual's behavior that is determined to be the main focus or "the prime material of his (or her) moral conduct." The mode of subjectivation is the form with which the different parts or aspects of one's self are arranged. It is the model that fashions or molds one's self into a distinctive style of existence. Foucault's own mode of subjectivation fused aesthetics and politics into a model of creative resistance, making one's life into a work of art formed out of social and political struggle. Ethical work involves the means, the methods, and the techniques by which we change ourselves into an ethical subject. *Telos* involves committing oneself to a certain mode of being and striving to consciously place one's everyday actions within a pattern of conduct.

Taken together, these ethical practices inform a conception of selfhood in which a person takes an active role in shaping his or her identity, rather than conforming to existing external standards and systems of power/knowledge. The self is an assemblage of practices rather than an innate entity. While both disciplined bodies and active ethical subjects are forged within the same power environments, the active reflexive self appropriates practices of conduct from power/knowledge formations without being dependent on their disciplinary codes. Foucault based this activity principally on an aesthetic model because it was his conviction that art is the most potent medium of radical reflexivity and resistance. Art is a potentially explosive transformative force. By linking it to the pursuit of an ethical life, Foucault was able to stabilize and channel its energy into a relationship where "self-care" and "responsibility for the other" inform and enhance the aesthetic drive.

The interview "The Ethic of Care for the Self as a Practice of Freedom" (1984) illuminates how in his final work Foucault was reweaving ethics, aesthetics, and politics by making connections between power, resistance, self-care, liberty, and caring for others. He states that freedom is the ontological condition and the basis of ethics.[51] He defines ethics as a practice, a way of life, an "ethos," rather than as a theory or a codified set of rules.[52] He makes clear that self-care "implies complex relations with others" and that "this ethos of freedom is also a way of caring for others."[53] He states that power means "relationships of power," that resistance and freedom are implicit in power relations, and that "domination" is different from power. It is a situation in which "the relations of power are fixed in such a way that they are perpetually asymmetrical and the margin of liberty is extremely limited."[54] Foucault further concludes that the relationship between philosophy and politics is fundamental and that philosophy is charged with the duty of "challenging all phenomena of domination at whatever level or under whatever form they present themselves."[55]

This leads me to conclude that Foucault's idea of freedom as ethical agency involves choosing a life "style" and then integrating specific techniques of self-formation within an environment of power formations. The power context of life stylization further requires the cultivation of self-discipline and agonistic struggle to both resist disciplinary power matrices and carve out a space for self-empowerment and creative choice.

In other words, freedom entails a movement from resistance to ethics to political action. Resistance, the most primal expression of freedom, involves the revolt of the body against the normalizing effects of disciplinary biopower. This critical resistance, largely reactive and defensive, is channeled into an affirmative ethical project concerned with self-care.

The rejection of an imposed identity and a set of norms becomes the impetus for fashioning one's own ethical code and conduct. The ethical agent becomes a political actor in joining struggles that seek to alter power relations so that one can more freely live one's life. The battle is joined at the local and microlevels by countering norms with norms and techniques with techniques.

I further conclude that if, as I have argued, ours is a time of cultural postmodernization, of global-local flows of postmodern goods, services, and identities, of greater aesthetic-reflexive individuation, and of the pervasive effects of information and mass media in our lives, then quality of life and lifestyle issues should take (and have taken) on a greater importance in our daily social interactions, economic decisions, ethical considerations, and political concerns. Understood in this way, Foucault's idea of freedom as an aesthetic-ethical-political practice of lifestyle determination takes on greater significance. It is both a product of our late modern/postmodern transition and a new mode of being and normative guide in negotiating this condition.

Foucault's Critics

This model of aesthetic-ethical freedom and its implications for social and political life remain highly controversial. Foucault's critics have raised, and continue to raise, concerns regarding his normative criteria (or lack thereof), the risks and dangers of adopting an aesthetic model of ethics and politics, and the viability of a politics of resistance.

For Jürgen Habermas, Foucault does not provide acceptable normative standards because he rejects humanism and therefore cannot generate norms that are universally applicable. Furthermore, Habermas believes that aesthetic-expressive values cannot provide a reliable model for social interaction and politics because they are too unstable and employed in radically subjective ways.[56] Thomas McCarthy reads Foucault's ethic of self-care as an ethos of private freedom with minimal connection to social or political life.[57] Richard Bernstein also concludes that Foucault fails to affirm valid norms of critique because his "rhetoric of disruption" endorses a radical postmodern relativism.[58]

For Marxists such as Terry Eagleton, Alex Callinicos, Richard Wolin, and David Harvey, it is the centrality of aesthetics in Foucault's political ethic that makes it unacceptable.[59] It translates for them into a libertarian hedonism, the reduction of truth and ethics to pleasure and style, another imaginary myth of autonomous subjectivity, and a weak, defensive response to postmodern capitalism. They contend that Foucault has been seduced by the myth of artistic freedom and autonomy. In reality, modern art exists as both a safety valve for the release of marginalized countercultural values and as the grease that makes the wheels of advanced capitalism turn. Thus Foucault's modernist aesthetic-based critique is both easily managed or "disciplined" by existing power formations and commodified by advanced capitalism.

Finally, Leslie Paul Thiele regards Foucault's model of postmodern freedom as endorsing two unacceptable alternatives — action without limits and aesthetic self-mastery. Like Nietzsche, Foucault advocates a libertarian ethos that combines modernist aesthetics with a postmodern active nihilism.[60] The result, concludes Thiele, is freedom without responsibility and postmodern "homelessness."[61] Foucault's ethic, "born and nourished by existential resentment," strikes out "against an ambiguous and overpowering world" and therefore "betrays a resentful unwillingness to acknowledge and affirm the limitations and contingencies that constitute Being-in-the-world."[62]

Of these charges brought against Foucault, the weakest is the claim that his critical ontology lacks valid normative criteria. Foucault did not generate universally applicable norms, ideal models of justice, an ethic with a determinate content, or a politics of emancipation. This is because he maintained that universal humanist norms require grounding in a general theory of human nature, which is not attainable. The modern anthropocentric-epistemological claim of the existence of transhistorical truths about the nature of Man was exposed by Foucault as an achievement of power/knowledge. Modern norms are the product of a humanist regime of rationality whose regulative principles and techniques validate modern Western cultural power.

Yet Foucault's rejection of the Western scientific humanist "regime of truth" does not mean that he abandoned critical value judgments. He justified norms governing critique and action with respect to the contextual circumstances of specific locales and power fields. As Michael Kelly reminds us, for Foucault, "the demands of critique arise from and are met by practice."[63]

Susan Hekman maintains that Foucault questioned the value of universal concepts as analytic tools. Rather, he argued "that the specific instance of oppression will generate a specific resistance to that oppression. The oppression produces the resistance, no other grounding is required."[64]

For Hekman, the lesson of Foucault's work for contemporary feminism suggests

> that instead of appealing to an essential female nature we should attempt to understand how femininity is socially constructed in particular societies; instead of deploring the universality of patriarchy we should analyze the historical evolution of patriarchal structures; instead of proclaiming universal male dominance we should examine the specific instances of that phenomenon.[65]

Jane Bennett points out that what causes the most concern about Foucault's normative posture "is his refusal to place the moral 'code' — a 'prescriptive ensemble' of values, rules of action, and criteria of judgment — at the center of his ethics."[66] Code-based moralities require duty to established norms of moral conduct and the domestication of transgressive impulses. Yet Foucault embraced art precisely because of its transgressive qualities. Modernist literature and art always figured prominently in his work as models of freedom that fused resistance and creation. Art is both disruptive and radically reflexive.

Foucault did, however, consciously intertwine aesthetics, ethics, and politics with a postmodern emphasis on the "plebian aspect" of everyday life, rather than with a modernist emphasis on artistic autonomy.[67] He sought to radically democratize aesthetics and infuse it into everyday social and political life. Thus it is true that Foucault's aesthetic ethics and politics were created to disrupt rather than to stabilize social and political life. Furthermore, he provided us with no guarantees that this strategy would not be marginalized, commodified, or appropriated in the pursuit of domination. The idea of an "aesthetics of existence" offers us a more potent formula for freedom and self-empowerment. It is also a potentially risky course of action.

Yet Foucault's earlier endorsement of the modernist artist and radical protest was tempered by his later model of the disciplined, ethical agent. I would describe the ethical sensibility of the final Foucault as one that endorsed a kind of critical postmodern modesty more akin to the Renaissance skepticism of Michel de Montaigne. Foucault reached the conclusion that there can be no self without self-discipline, there can be no self-discipline without ethical practices, there can be no ethical life without aesthetics, there can be no ethics without a politics, and there can be no politics without an ethic of freedom.

What he left unexamined was the kind of social and political conditions that would need to be in place for his "ethic of care for the self as a practice of freedom" to become a "plebian" reality. That is, the conditions of both "leisure" and "democracy" required to pursue the "aesthetics of existence" remained to be addressed. He decided rather to undertake a research project on that complex technological apparatus that was responsible for the overall maintenance of these conditions. This involved analyzing government, or what Foucault called "governmentality."

Technologies of Government

The most neglected aspect of Foucault's work has been his research on modern government. In the late 1970s, his lectures and courses at the College de France were on the interrelated topics of modern government, liberalism, and "biopolitics."[68] In the 1979 Stanford University Tanner Lectures, Foucault presented his research on the origins of Western governmental rationality with reference to (1) "the pastoral modality of power"; (2) "the doctrine of reason of state"; and (3) "the police."[69] Connecting all these themes was the concept of "governmentality."[70] His work did not yield a detailed genealogical history. It has, however, resulted in the development of a new approach to political analysis.

Foucault defined governmentality "in the broad sense of techniques and procedures for directing human behavior."[71] He employed the term *government* "meaning not the institution of 'government,' of course, but the activity that consists in governing human behavior in the framework of, and by means of, state institutions."[72] Governmentality was used by Foucault to refer to the complex array of techniques — programs, procedures, practices, strategies and tactics — employed by both non-state administrative agencies and state institutions to shape the conduct of individuals and populations.

Governmental analysis focused on the who and what of governing rather than the why. It was concerned with how things got done and with how the exercise of government is rationalized. Examining government in this way, as a complex technological apparatus of behavior modification and control, shifted political analysis away from the question of legitimation (of how a political system is justified as right or just) and toward the question of operation (of how governance works and how its operating manuals can be deciphered).

Foucault's research, guided by this definition of modern government, located in the middle of the eighteenth century a noticeable proliferation of nonstate administrative agencies and techniques designed to guide and shape human conduct. Experts and social administrative agencies examined living conditions among various human populations, generating a host of "social problems" that required attention. Among these "problems" were issues of health, birthrates, sanitation, deviance, workplace conditions, and prisoner rehabilitation. Various social regulatory agencies came to "govern" specific populations.

These social governments were in turn legitimized by the nation-state's legal and bureaucratic framework. The entanglement between disciplines and their norms (standards, mechanisms, and goals of proper and improper conduct) and the state and its laws (of prohibition and punishment) resulted in what Foucault called the "governmentalization of the State."[73] Political scientists refer to this as "public policy." It involves direct government control of conduct through techniques ranging from the police to administrative regulation.

Yet Foucault broadened the historical scope of his investigation into government and governmental rationality to range across the terrain of Western history, making connections between what he described as ancient "pastoral power," the doctrine of "reason of state," the rise of disciplinary power, and the "welfare state problem." In the 1979 Stanford University Tanner Lectures, he identified two ancient models that shaped the Western political experience. The Judeo-Christian, shepherd-flock model exhibited a "pastoral rule," in which the shepherd watched over his flock through the constant, individualized care (paternalistic surveillance) of all its members.[74] The Greco-Roman, city-citizen model concerned itself with the unity of the city as a community of laws and citizens.[75] The early Christian model of pastoral power mixed Hebrew and Hellenistic elements into a governing formula of total obedience to God, self-knowledge, confession, and self-mortification.[76]

Christian pastoral power underwent a further mutation with the formation of modern government. It became an "individualizing power," legitimized under "reason of state" and implemented through the techniques of early modern policing. It realized its fullest modern deployment in the social welfare state. Once employed to ensure the salvation of the individual soul in the next world, modern pastoral power sought to ensure the secular salvation of individuals through a panoply of public, private, and nonprofit-sector agencies. A secular expert "pastorate" of social workers, psychologists, and health-care professionals came to guide the modern "flock."

The rationale of early modern government was formulated in two doctrines. "Reason of state" defined "how the principles and methods of state government differed, say, from the way God governed the world, the father his family, or a superior his community."[77] The "theory of police" defined "the nature of the objects of the state's rational activity . . . the nature of the aims it pursues, the general form of the instruments involved."[78]

Evident in sixteenth- and seventeenth-century Italian and German political literatures, "reason of state" was a form of knowledge specific to the art of governing states.[79] It drew its rationale from the state itself, thereby shifting the seat of political reason and legitimacy away from natural law and "the prince." It moved beyond Aquinas and Machiavelli to locate its principles of governance in the new "science of police," which translates as the "science of policy" in English. Reason of state was government in accordance with the reinforcement of state power, which required the accumulation of knowledge — the knowledge of the state's capacity in relation to a competing field of other nation-states.

Police technology was deployed to increase individual citizen happiness in order to enhance state power. The earliest form of modern public administration, policing was designed to forge a productive, healthy, secure populace by regulating social relations and maintaining an efficient infrastructure.[80] Such interventions, in Foucault's opinion, were both "totalizing" and "individualizing."[81] The purpose of government became not just territorial rule and conquest, but population health and growth, as well as wealth creation. Early modern police government thus focused on population development within a mercantile model.

Eighteenth-century liberal "economic government" emerged as a critique of police government.[82] It redirected the mechanisms of state control to ensure the security of "natural" economic processes. Liberal political economy became the new governmentality of the modernizing nation-state. The locus of governance shifted away from the state and police and toward "civil society" and the market. Liberal governance delimited state power, but it did not limit government. It rather deployed a new host of mechanisms, strategies, and tactics to allow a new economic power/knowledge network to regulate social and political activity. The resulting governmentality featured more impersonal economic and legal technologies. Foucault also discerned a shift from police regulation to the employment of new social disciplines. What we call "liberalism" was therefore neither a theory nor an ideology, but a way of rationalizing the exercise of government that pieced together the rationales and mechanisms of market regulation, the juridical power strategies of the new bourgeois political culture, and new social disciplines, resulting in a social contract mythology of the rights-bearing, productive, and "autonomous" individual subject.

The mutation of liberal "civil society" into "the social" as a new field of governmentality came with the formation of a mass working population.[83] The liberal governmental strategy of controlling the rapidly growing working classes combined the techniques of philanthropy and discipline. Yet it was overwhelmed by a host of urban social problems, including harsh factory conditions, unemployment, crime, suicide, and prostitution. The expansion of the state's scope in relation to this demographic development produced "social government." A strong interdependence between political and social security was forged as a new panoply of insurance programs and technologies, both public and private, settled into place. Social government would culminate in the Keynesian social-welfare state power structure.

The most recent neoliberal mutation in advanced Western governance has replaced the governmentality of a "welfare society" with that of an "enterprise culture."[84] Social welfare technologies have been scaled back in favor of more selective, privatized risk-management strategies of social and economic governance. Neoliberal governance has refashioned the governmentality of nineteenth-century liberalism by shifting from the state back to the market and from socialization to privatization. At the same time, the individual is less of a productive and responsible individual (the liberal bourgeois model) or a socialized citizen-client (the social welfare model) than a subject positioned within more complex intersecting and overlapping networks of consumer seduction and disciplinary moral codes.

Foucault concluded that three configurations of power have been in place in the modern West: the sovereignty-law-repression paradigm of juridical power, the disciplinary paradigm, and the governmental paradigm. Modern power first emerged as sovereign power during the late sixteenth and early seventeenth centuries with the emergence of the nation-state. Disciplinary power emerged in the eighteenth century. Governmentality achieved preeminence in the nineteenth and twentieth centuries, securing alliances of different power/knowledge circuits under the larger strategic umbrellas of "pastoral power" (individualized self-management) and "biopolitics" (population management).

Modern government's task has been to stitch up sovereign power, disciplinary power, and biopower into an even more totalizing, as well as individualizing, apparatus. However, Foucault made it clear that in the evolution from a sovereign to a disciplinary to a governmental society, one mode of power did not disappear to be replaced by another. Rather, a new layer of power appeared. Thus his mature model of power was a tripartite formulation of sovereignty-discipline-governmentality.[85]

Foucault's work on governmentality is suggestive not only for future research, but for responding to two major criticisms leveled against Foucault: (1) that his concept of power neglected the importance of macrostructures like the state; and (2) that his later work was on aesthetics and ethics, not politics.

Yet what is the nature of our present governmentality? Foucault did hint at a "new economy of power relations" emerging in our present time, yet he never ventured beyond that. Baudrillard and Bauman, among others, have asserted that "seduction" has replaced discipline and government as the main circuitry of contemporary power/knowledge networks.[86] If this is the case, we would need to direct our analysis toward examining how technologies of seduction, present in the market, the state, the media, and at the microlevel of self-identity and locality, operate today and how as desiring selves we can experience freedom within the confines of late modern/postmodern seductive power networks.

Foucault and Critical Postmodernism

Translating the work of Michel Foucault into a new theory, method, or type of knowledge (a set of posthumanist truths) is a risky undertaking. He was postmodern in his commitment to relentless critique, to the contingency of our thought constructs, to revealing the complexity of reality, and to a strategic ambiguity. His research exposed the contingent historical basis of the modern Enlightenment project and urged us to move beyond its conceptual system. Yet at the same time, he contributed to the revaluation of critique, emancipation, and reflexive self-determination, all integral features of the modern cultural ethos.

Foucault therefore situated his life and work in the tensional-transitional relationship between modernity and postmodernity. What he left us is a cluster of critical, analytical, and interpretive concepts, methods, and criteria that constitute an intellectual constellation that is both a critique of modernity and a complex mixture of ancient, modern, and postmodern cultural forms and practices. I believe one can further discern in this work a new interpretive-analytic perspective that incorporates the role of the body, cultural codes and practices, social power networks, and reflexive agency.

My idea of critical postmodernism adopts this approach to make sense of our late modern/postmodern transition. Like Foucault's outlook, critical postmodernism is "perspectivist" in that it asserts that our knowledge and understanding of the world is a function of the interpretive frameworks and contextual environments of particular knowers.[87] It equally draws a distinction between perspectivism and the extreme relativism that is commonly associated with postmodernism. As C. G. Prado explains:

> Contrary to the common assimilation of perspectivism to this sort of relativism, perspectivism is different in conception and not a simple, egalitarian leveling of all truth-claims to the same status consequent on the abandonment of objectivity. Instead, perspectivism is the denial of the possibility of descriptive completeness. Rather than denying that any truth-claim can be proven, and so making them all equal, perspectivism denies the possibility of a global and correct understanding or description of the world within which diverse individual interpretations could be integrated as so many true but incomplete points of view on 'the same thing.'[88]

Perspectivism does reject the modern Enlightenment belief that there are universally neutral, ahistorical standards of rationality that can effectively translate and integrate all languages and conceptual schemes. However, this does not force us into a radical relativist and multicultural separatist position in which only radically incommensurable and self-referential discourses exist. Different conceptual schemes and interpretive accounts of the facticity of the world frequently overlap. Therefore, many perspectives are intertranslatable. While they are not completely translatable, neither are they completely incommensurable. Brian Fay sums this up rather well when he points out that "people recognizably living in different cultures cannot be living in a different world; but they may well be living differently in the same world."[89]

Steven Best and Douglas Kellner contend that our present social condition requires a "multidimensional and multiperspectival critical theory" that draws on the strengths of both critical theory and postmodern theory and that merges micro- and macroperspectives. They write:

The term perspective suggests that one's optic or analytic frame never mirrors reality exactly as it is, that it is always selective and unavoidably mediated by one's pregiven assumptions, theories, values, and interests. The notion of perspective also implies that no one optic can ever fully illuminate the richness and complexity of any single phenomenon, let alone the infinite connections and aspects of all social reality.[90]

Critical postmodernism explains social and cultural reality in terms of four interrelated sets of variables: (1) biological evolution and the body field; (2) the reproduction of cultural practices; (3) organized social power networks; and (4) the interpretive self or reflexive agency. All of these four determinants of human identity, rationality, and action are influenced by Foucault's thinking on the body, the production of cultural artifacts, the nature of social power, and the self.

Foucault regarded the body and the question of "embodiment" as a core concern of social and political analysis. While not denying its biological makeup, he maintained that the body could not be understood outside of cultural codes and social power networks. In his early work, Foucault was concerned with demonstrating the cultural encoding and social production of bodies. The body was "the inscribed surface of events," "the locus of a dissociated self," and "in perpetual disintegration."[91] It was the site upon which different power configurations left their marks. In his final work, Foucault shifted to a concern with the embodied self as a reflexive agent with the capacity for freedom.

I contend that we should comprehend the body as consisting of biological drives and reflexive-interpretive capacities, both culturally encoded and socially structured. The body becomes a constructed "self" or "agent" through the forces of cultural reproduction, social structuration, and reflexivity. The body is the nexus or site in which all three determinants intersect. The organizational achievements of this intersection, namely social power networks, institutional orders, and disciplined individuals, are the products of the mobilization of power practices. The body is shaped and reshaped by these practices as they "inscribe" their effects on its bioreflexive makeup. The resulting "self," "subject," or "agent" is the assemblage of both constitutive capacities and historically structured effects.

Therefore, the real question is not whether the self is constitutive or constituted, but rather what the constitutive field is that organizes embodied experiences into a self, one neither sovereign nor radically decentered, but more accurately the achievement of a struggle that involves constitutive capacities and the effects of historically shaped power relations. Further, the self is the product of subjective, intersubjective, and object relations that are intertwined, but not reducible to each other. In other words, we are the product of an ongoing tensional interplay between self-other, self-world, and self-self relationships.

Human beings are bodies capable of generating cultural practices in reaction to environmental conditions. Cultural practices are produced to negotiate an organism-environment territory, or "body field," as humans learn to interpret, interrogate, adapt to, and modify the multiple environments of action in which they exist. A repertory of learned practices or a "culture" is developed to satisfy both a relatively fixed and constant set of biopsychological needs through the production of more plastic and modifiable sets of social norms and technologies.

I define culture as the historical transmission of a learned repertory of embodied human practices expressed in symbolic codes through which individuals and social groups develop and perpetuate a way of life. It is a set of signifying activities shaped by and infused with relations of power. Culture implies not only language, values, beliefs, and mores, but material objects and processes organized in space-time locations. Culture is therefore a complex social ecology of object, subject, and intersubjective relations.

I further distinguish cultural practices from their reproduction as a code and process of socialization. Embodied cultural practices, once organized into "a culture," become an infrastructure for generating requisite levels of social reflexivity into authoritative social structures in response to the individual and group needs of specific populations. Cultural learning evolves through the intertwined processes of material production and socialization, which are institutionally organized and legitimized through sanctioned cultural traditions. Here cultural practices take on the status of authoritative traditions.

Cultural reproduction involves a mode of transmission driven by an instructional or learning mechanism. Yet the human species also employs a mode of genetic transmission driven by a biological selection mechanism. Culture can be understood as the transmission of all nongenetic information generated by social learning. Different rules govern these transmittal processes. While biological evolution is Darwinian and slow, cultural evolution occurs at a faster pace. While genes are the primary units of biological evolution, social conventions or "mores" are the primary units of cultural reproduction. Zoologist Richard Dawkins describes these cultural agents as "memes." He further contends that in recent human evolution, memes have taken over genes as the primary agents shaping human behavior because cultural change occurs at a much faster pace than biological change.[92]

Leslie Paul Thiele explains this relationship as one in which "the leash on which genes hold culture is so long and flexible that culture has become the greatest force structuring most human relationships and activities."[93] Human memes are transmitted by way of "symbol pools" and are reproduced through human interaction as cultural practices are imitated, hybridized, and mutate. Under conditions of rapid cultural change, meme reproduction accelerates. Thus in today's postmodern environment, meme reproduction and hybridization are occurring at an unprecedented rate. Modern mores are under assault by postmodern mores that challenge the established limits of social and cultural norms.

Yet being human is more than following genetic and cultural codes. It is also the individual capacity to attribute meaning to experiences, to make choices, and to modify behavior. This human capacity for reflexive individuation and subjective interpretation involves both cognitive information processing and the narrative construction of reality bound up with the assembly of an identity. This activity is not determined by genetic codes, nor is it completely derivative of transmitted cultural information. However, the interpretive self or reflexive agent must be situated within the context of its genetic endowment, as well as its historically produced cultural codes and social power formations.

The historical production and reproduction of social power formations involves organizing cultural practices and social relations into circuits of power, which are further stabilized into power networks. These stabilized power networks facilitate the greater routinization, institutionalization, and legitimation of social power formations into structures and processes of social and systemic integration. The result of all this is the organizational translation of micro social power relations into dominant "social structures."

Critical postmodernism involves the application of this four-field framework of analysis to late modern/postmodern environments of social, cultural, and political change. It is concerned with understanding our present transition in terms of cultural and institutional analyses at both the micro and macro levels. Critical postmodernism grasps our present reality in terms of the complexity and plurality of social spaces and environments. Therefore, analysis and interpretation is required from a multiplicity of vantage points within the four interrelated fields of the body, cultural reproduction, organized social power networks, and individual agency.

Critical postmodernism is the optic or analytic frame that provides us with what I believe to be a significant picture of our current social, cultural, and political condition. It is, in my opinion, the theoretical perspective best able to make sense of the complex phenomenon of our late modern/postmodern transition. The case I have made here for critical postmodernism is indebted to the final and unfinished work of Michel Foucault. Armed with this interpretive-analytic perspective, I now proceed to come to terms with the condition of democracy in our present time.

Part III

5 — Complexity, Governmentality, and the Fate of Democracy

> [I]t is the idea of complexity — along with the closely
> related notion of social complexity — which opens the way
> to a realistic analysis of the condition and fate of
> democracy in post-industrial societies.
> — Danilo Zolo, *Democracy and Complexity:*
>   *A Realist Approach*

The Relocation of the Political

Today when political theorists talk and write about politics, they often refer to the idea of "the political." Thus we encounter phrases such as "the return of the political," "rethinking the political," "the fate of the political," and "contesting the boundaries of the political."[1] Yet what do they mean? French philosopher and political theorist Claude Lefort contends that the distinction between "politics" (*la politique*) and "the political" (*le politique*) is crucial to understanding both the nature of political inquiry and democracy.[2] For while politics is about the specific behaviors, strategies, and policies of political actors and institutions, the political is the constitutive framework and sociopolitical space within which politics happens and through which meaning is assigned to events.

Lefort maintains that political science concentrates its analysis on politics and ignores the political.[3] This impoverishes political analysis because phenomena are described and explained with respect to analytic frameworks that remain disconnected from, and thus do not take into consideration, the "form of society" that frames human action and meaning.

Politics takes place within the bounded space of a "society," a forma-tion of social relations that is the product of a historically constituted symbolic order, set of social practices, institutions, and norms.[4] Society gives politics its structure and meaning through the medium of "the political." The recognition of new types of politics is the result of the re-configuration of the political, which can be further traced to a mutation in society. Therefore, political analysis requires an investigation into the political, which necessitates an inquiry into "the social."

It is Lefort's contention that modern society is a formation whose space-time constitution and identity are attributable to the democrati-zation of social, cultural, and political life. The democratic shaping of society and politics is the distinctive feature of modernity. He further claims that this

> is instituted and sustained by the dissolution of markers of certainty. It inaugurates a history in which people experience a fundamental indeter-minacy as to the basis of power, law, and knowledge, and as to the basis of relations between self and other, at every level of social life.[5]

Lefort defines modern democracy as an "empty place."[6] By this he means that the modern democratization of society reconfigured political space from a visible and organic sovereign power structure, a Leviathan-like relation between a sovereign (monarch) and subjects (a people), to a new model of sovereign power as an impersonal (i.e., legally circum-scribed) space of action whereby a plurality of political actors compete for the opportunity to temporarily rule. Modern democracy rests on the legitimizing principle of popular sovereignty. However, "the people" is not an organic totality. It is an aggregate majority of diverse individu-als and groups whose "will" is a temporary identity. The structure of democracy ensures a rule-governed struggle for power that reflects the dynamic nature of a modern pluralistic society.

However, modern democracy has never been as "empty" a public space as Lefort maintains it should be. The history of modern democracy re-veals constant attempts to attribute a unified identity to "the people." This has been most evident in the ideologies of nationalism, socialism, and populism. To claim to represent what Lefort calls "the People-as-One" is to distort the meaning of democracy.[7] It is to reconfigure the social into "a homogeneous and self-transparent society" and thus revert the political back to its traditional symbolic and spatial form. Thus Lefort warns us that democracy faces a threat from totalitarianisms of the Right and the Left, as well as from behaviorism and functionalism, political movements and scientific methods that deny the political.[8]

Postmodern thinkers have used Lefort's ideas to deconstruct modern democracy.[9] For if democracy is defined as a structure of power that belongs to no one, where those who exercise power do not possess it, and where the political community is continually reinvented, then the apparent solidity of modern democratic politics is open to question. The essential feature of democracy is its indeterminacy. A truly democratic society allows for no permanent representation of authority, no final legitimation, no determinate identity. The space of democracy is one of incessant conflict, contradiction, heterogeneity, and ambiguity.

This in turn raises the question of whether a modern democratic society really exists. For if, as postmoderns contend, modern society no longer exists, then the political needs to be relocated and politics redefined. The distinctive feature of democracy lies not in its modernity, but in its postmodernity. Understood this way, democracy is best summed up by Sheldon Wolin as "the continuing self-fashioning of the demos."[10]

While the spirit of the *demos* may be postmodern, much of contemporary democratic politics is still bound up with a condition that is largely modern. A Euro-American creation, the modern political condition has developed over the past two hundred years into a global force. Western political modernity has been shaped by: (1) a representative order through which flows mass public opinion as mediated by electoral systems, political parties, trade unions, interest groups, and newspaper, radio, and television communications media; (2) the principle of individual autonomy enshrined in a legal-constitutional framework that provides for a system of rights or liberties; (3) the separation of human activities into public and private domains; (4) the organization of political communities of interest around discernible social classes and class differences; (5) a politics organized within a bounded sovereign national arena and focused on the control of state power; and (6) the translation of Enlightenment humanist ideologies of emancipation into the democratic power of the people.

Yet today this political condition finds itself significantly disconnected from the kernel of social and political life in advanced Western societies. While its institutions plod along like creaking megamachines, new technologies propel us forward in a juggernaut fashion. The disjuncture between these new technologies of politics and old institutions of governance is noticeable. We invoke early modern constitutional principles, interpretations, and values in dealing with a late modern/post-modern world driven by high-tech media and marketing strategies. To this we must add the exhaustion of the modern social paradigm of a class-structured, industrial-manufacturing society bounded by the nation-state. Our world is shaped more by consumption than by production in the economy and culture, by global-local (glocal) flows, by more flexible decentralized organizational forms, by hyperreal media technologies, and by issues related to subjective well-being, to identity, lifestyle, and recreation.

Today "the political" is located in a transitional late modern/postmodern social and cultural space. We find ourselves in the midst of a shift from a modern to a "postmodern political condition." Our mode of governance and our political styles and strategies partake of both modern and postmodern features. That is in part why it is difficult to plot politics along a modern Left-Right ideological continuum. Socialism and welfare-state liberalism, like economic neoliberalism and moral neoconservatism, struggle to remap a political landscape that no longer corresponds to a modern condition that was once taken for granted.

If the defining features of the modern political condition were Enlightenment rationalism, secular humanism, universal emancipation, individual autonomy, the sovereign nation-state, liberal representative democracy, industrial capitalism, social class, the mass political party, binary governance, and mass media, then the defining features of the postmodern political condition are postmodern perspectivism, global-local flows, information, hyperreality, identity, resistance, leisure, self-care, performative action, pluralization, and the democratic questioning of all areas of human existence.

Modern politics is being bypassed for a postmodern politics that exists more as an ethos than as a set of institutions and a programmatic agenda. The frameworks and models of modern governance — constitutions, mass elections, political parties, parliaments, professional politicians, and bureaucracies — continue to operate largely due to the sheer weight of tradition and organizational infrastructure. Modern politics, observes Geoff Mulgan, is a predictable binary game of government and opposition "institutionalized not only in the forms of parliamentary life but also in the media which structure reporting and argument into binary forms."[11] This formal binary governmentality legitimizes and reproduces a techno-oligarchic social structure in the process of adapting to a new power environment. It is an environment shaped by a host of new issues that are largely global and personal, concerns solved more by cultural changes than by new laws.

What, then, has become of democracy as an actually existing public space and organizational order? I submit that the regime occupying this space in the name of democracy is what I would call, thinking with Foucault, a "postmodern, neoliberal, techno-oligarchic governmentality." Yet if this is the case, where do we find the *demos* today? Where is the political space of democratic life to be found? I contend that the locus of democracy has shifted from modern governance to postmodern resistance and the radical democratic questioning of all areas of human existence. This has resulted in a revaluation of democracy as an idea and its relocation away from being a form of governance to that of an ethos or way of life.

Our Postmodern, Neoliberal, Techno-Oligarchic Governmentality

The dominant mode of governance in advanced Western polities is best characterized as a postmodern, neoliberal, techno-oligarchy. That is, government today consists of a complex array of techniques for directing human behavior that are postmodern, neoliberal, and techno-oligarchic. The real world of democracy is shaped by the forces of techno-oligarchic globalization, hyperreal technologies of media governance, and new advanced liberal strategies of individual-society-market-state relations.

In employing Foucault's concept of "governmentality," I define governance in the broad sense of techniques that shape human conduct employed by state and nonstate institutions. Foucault defined government in two interrelated senses. It referred to those techniques, strategies, and procedures of behavior modification that shape human conduct. It also referred to a political rationality of rule, a formula that gives coherence to this complex array of techniques. Governmentality is the principle or method that rationalizes the exercise of government and makes reality amenable to public policies. Thus as a technology of government, democracy today is a postmodern, neoliberal, techno-oligarchy. Its rationalization is "neoliberalism."

How is governance postmodern? This is most evident in our techno-oligarchic, hyperreal public sphere. The axis of governance today is a media-information complex or "mediocracy" (rule by means of images). This is because of the hegemonic and ubiquitous impact of microelectronic information, communication, and entertainment media (television, radio, newspapers, magazines, film, music, computers, E-mail, fax machines, CD-ROMs, and the Internet) upon individuals, social segments, politics, and mass publics. This mediocracy is corporate-controlled, globalized, and hyperreal.

Media globalization and corporate consolidation took off in the mid-1980s.[12] It is a function of technological innovations such as fiber optics, digital transmission, cable television, videocassettes, satellite dishes, new computer software, and the Internet, combined with neoliberal strategies of deregulation and privatization. This restructuring of media industries on a global scale has produced a new media-information order dominated by ten transnational conglomerates — Time Warner, Disney, Bertelsmann, Viacom, Rupert Murdoch's News Corporation, Universal (Seagram), Sony, PolyGram (Philips), and NBC (General Electric).[13] The strategy of these megacorporations is not just global expansion, but also the vertical integration of multiple media in order to control all phases of the image production and distribution process.[14]

This media-information complex is corporate-controlled, homogenized, and mainstream. News media networks such as NBC, ABC, CBS, CNN, FOX, and PBS are neither liberal nor conservative, but corporate. Their content largely consists of mass entertainment, consumer information, and elite propaganda. News and infotainment are produced and disseminated through several narrowing filters, which include transnational corporate owners, managers, editors, advertisers, corporate and government agency news sources, and journalists who are trained, disciplined, and rewarded to become elite stenographers, public relations mouthpieces, and personalities rather than critical democratic investigators. The finished product of national and international news and information is stylistically and substantively corporate and "Roman" right down to its theme music.

More than this, our globalized and corporate-controlled media-information complex has produced such a surplus of symbols, signs, simulations, and images moving at a rapid pace that they have taken on a life of their own, creating a postmodern mediascape or hyperspace. This condition of mediated experience is known as "hyperreality." It is one in which words, symbols, and images are disconnected from their empirical referents and effectively displace the experiential reality of everyday life with a simulated reality. The decoupling of signs from referents, of visual images from real contexts, and their promiscuous and manipulated recombination by way of microelectronic communications and information media, creates a "collage effect."[15]

Hyperreality therefore describes the surplus production of symbols and images, their detachment from the reality of everyday life, the construction of a parallel simulated reality more real than the real world, and the resulting collapse of clear boundaries between hyperspace and real-world experience and between knowledge, entertainment, fantasy, advertising, politics, and real life. The result is a melange of "infotainment" speeding across television and computer screens. These hyperreal images and epiphenomenal symbols, with a tenuous rootedness in empirical reality, come to increasingly govern our cultural, social, economic, and political worlds. It is a world of "hypertexts" without sufficient context.

The political effects of this condition, concludes Italian political philosopher Danilo Zolo, are devastating for democracy. This is largely due to the actual structure of the medium of most electronic communication, which is asymmetric, selective, and noninteractive.[16] For while media producers are "highly cohesive professional groups formally organized as capitalist business concerns or as bureaucractic structures," media consumers "have no specific form of social cohesion, possess no collective perception of themselves as a group with a role to play, and make use of a symbolic universe already severely reduced in scale through the selections of the information-producing class."[17]

This mass-media producing class does not reveal the means by which their product is obtained or the ingredients that go into it; nor does it give the public sufficient critical context. Television news involves "a systematic decontextualization and fragmentation of events" in which items are "constructed in the form of a narrative flash which is self-standing and conclusive in itself."[18] The focus of narration is on the "what" and not the "why" of the happening. More importantly, this process transmits "the mental framework through which the selection and distortion takes place."[19] Over time, it establishes itself in the public psyche, determining the nature and scope of relevant reality. This is achieved by way of two key properties of electronic mass media: "cumulativity" (its ability to impose a topic on the public through constant repetition) and "consonance" (the consolidation of similarities, the ironing out of dissonances, and the production of consensus).[20]

The construction of a hyperreal image of social and political reality becomes the only relevant reality over the long term. The mass-media self-referentially impose this reality on the public. The overall effect of media hyperreality, cumulativity, and consonance leads to a heightened dependency on the gratification one obtains from mediated experience. Zolo describes this as a "narcotizing dysfunction" that comes with consuming "the continual repetition of stereotyped representations." He further notes "a tendency to take refuge in the inner sphere of private experience and personal relationships."[21]

What has become a "telecharismatic" public sphere is dominated by consumer-spectators rather than citizens, by telegenic politicians and pundits, and by "demoscopic agencies" (public opinion assessors). A key feature of this televisual democracy is "the growing transformation of political campaigns into 'meta-campaigns' and of electorates into 'meta-electorates.' "[22] Publicity specialists, pollsters, and media pundits select the appropriate candidates and issues, and frame the boundaries of electoral competition. Public opinion assessors create a surrogate electorate more important than the real one. The real voters "see themselves replaced by their own demoscopic and televisual projection, which anticipates them and leaves them the passive observers of themselves."[23] Zolo concludes that democracies today are self-legitimizing liberal oligarchies whose central organizing dynamic is the mass media.

Techno-oligarchic globalization refers to the unprecedented power and scope of the "new" capitalism described and explained in chapter 2. Its main features include global telecommunication technologies and structures, deregulated global capital markets, microelectronic information superhighways, reorganized transnational corporations, new global cities, and postmodern goods and services (which are composed of a significant aesthetic content and image value) circulating through these globalized networks and transnational flows. Modern corporations, vertically integrated and spatially concentrated, have been transformed into entities more vertically dis-integrated and spatially dispersed. This has accelerated the decentering of the boundaries associated with the modern nation-state and has increasingly recentered them around new global-local power points and conduits.

We therefore find ourselves in a new phase of capitalism organized around recreational consumption and postmodern goods and services, and fueled by postindustrial technologies and strategies of globalization. Advanced societies have in turn been restratified around five main socioeconomic status groups: (1) a finance-knowledge-media elite; (2) a new postmodern middle class of information, telecommunication, and symbolic workers and consumers; (3) a smaller industrial working class reorganized by high-tech; (4) a postindustrial service class; and (5) an impoverished and largely marginalized underclass.

These techno-oligarchic and hyperreal-media features go hand in hand with the neoliberal marketing strategies that equally shape contemporary governance. Neoliberalism confidently heralds the triumph of economic and political liberalism over the social and political paradigms of socialism and the Keynesian social-welfare state. Its formula of governance advances the imperatives of global capitalist enterprise, individual autonomy, federal devolution, the dismantling of the regulative and redistributive welfare state, privatization, and community self-reliance.[24]

Adopting Foucault's concept of governmentality, Nikolas Rose describes neoliberalism as techniques of government that "create a distance between the decisions of formal political institutions and other social actors, conceive of these actors in new ways as subjects of responsibility, autonomy and choice, and seek to act upon them through shaping and utilizing their freedom."[25] This amounts to "a new formula for the relation between government, expertise and subjectivity."[26]

Rose discerns a new relationship between expertise and politics in the deployment of welfare services. The shaping of conduct is now more a function of market expertise than of welfare bureaucracies. Power once accorded to social scientific experts and social welfare governmental networks is being "transferred to the calculative regimes of accounting and financial management" and the techniques of "budget disciplines, accountancy and audit."[27] This shift to marketization has turned welfare agencies "into 'purchasers' who can choose to 'buy' services from the range of options available."[28] Clients are now consumers, and experts are now providers. Professional experts are less autonomous and authoritative, are under greater budgetary discipline, and are subject to more frequent audits and performance review. The discourse of "welfare" has been altered from one bound up with the socialization of risk to that of "governing at a distance."[29]

This "de-statization of government" that is under way has allowed for "a new pluralization of 'social' technologies."[30] That is, neoliberal governance has been decoupling social regulatory programs and techniques from their central mooring in "the State" through the strategies of deregulation and privatization. The result is a proliferation of nongovernmental (nonstate-centered) regulatory organizations that are doing more of the governing. Rose attributes this to "a mutation in the notion of 'the social'" where the relationship "between the responsible individual and their self-governing community comes to substitute for that between the social citizen and their common society."[31]

The result of this change in the social welfare model of society is a new subject of government. This new regime of the self is based on the model of the enterprising individual or "the actively responsible self."[32] Neoliberal programs, techniques, and networks of social governance urge individuals to "fulfil themselves within a variety of micro-moral domains or 'communities.'"[33] Thus the new individualism is intimately bound up with the new communitarianism. The formula is that of the individual within a moral community. Rose observes that this new notion of the self is in place "because of the development of new apparatuses that integrate subjects into a moral nexus of identifications and allegiances in the very processes in which they appear to act out their most personal choices."[34]

Social security has become more of a private obligation. The individual is required "to adopt a calculative prudent personal relation to fate."[35] Social work has shifted from the "civilization under tutelage" model to that of "the private counselor, the self-help manual and the telephone helpline."[36] The regulation of lifestyles, more outside the control of the social-welfare state, is increasingly influenced by mass media communication networks. It "becomes a matter of each individual's desire to govern their own conduct freely in the service of the maximization of a version of their happiness and fulfilment that they take to be their own, but such lifestyle maximization entails a relation to authority in the very moment as it pronounces itself the outcome of free choice."[37]

Rose concludes that while the social welfare state model "sought to govern through society," neoliberal governance strives "to govern without governing society."[38] This takes place through "the regulative and accountable choices of autonomous agents — citizens, consumers, parents, employees, managers, investors — and governs through intensifying and acting upon their allegiance to particular 'communities.'"[39]

The convergence of new media technologies, neoliberal market strategies, and a globalized techno-oligarchic capitalism into a new electoral governmentality has further mutated our system of representative government. The result is a sophisticated electoral technopolitics geared as much toward demobilization as toward mobilization. It is driven by a panoply of new technologies and formats, including "push polling" (which involves asking respondents loaded questions to elicit answers desired by the pollster), the computerized identification of "bellwether districts" (that predict the attitudes of larger population segments), "infomercials," talk show interviews, electronic town hall meetings, targeted direct mail, phone banks, focus groups, and television and radio advertising. This trend has also recast political parties into large fund-raising machines or PACs (political action committees). It has also made campaign finance reform nearly impossible to achieve.

Professional public relations consultants and strategies dominate the "business" of electoral politics. They employ the techniques mentioned above to test out issues that will connect with pivotal voting groups. These groups are usually composed of highly ideological, single-issue voters who can be easily mobilized. Combine this with tactics that turn off moderate voters, like negative advertising, and you have the strategy of our current electoral governmentality. It is dedicated to mass demobilization combined with niche mobilization in a time of high-tech, capital-intensive, media politics.

Contemporary Models of Democracy

In examining the fate of democracy in advanced Western societies, one must not only elucidate the reality of neoliberal democracy, but also assess the viability of alternative models that challenge the current governmental order of things. In doing so, I would identify four normative models of democracy that have emerged to occupy center stage in recent debates in democratic theory. They are the communitarian, deliberative, agonistic, and associative models of democracy. These new models have been conceptualized in opposition to neoliberalism and have focused on the respective tasks of rethinking community, public deliberation, identity/difference, and civic association.[40]

Communitarian Democracy

Communitarianism has become an influential public philosophy thanks to the work of its leading proponents Benjamin Barber, Daniel Bell, Robert Bellah, Jean Bethke Elshtain, Amitai Etzioni, William Galston, Michael Sandel, Thomas Spragens, and Charles Taylor, among others.[41] Forged in response to John Rawls's reconstruction of liberalism in the 1970s and the new libertarianism of the 1980s,[42] communitarianism has established itself at the end of the 1990s as a major American social and political movement of moral and civic regeneration.[43] It became part of President Clinton's domestic policy agenda.[44] It is therefore an intellectual and political force to be reckoned with.

The communitarian model asserts that our sense of justice is the product of our participation in a bounded community that defines the good life. The liberal prioritization of individual rights, instrumental rationality, self-interest, and procedural justice over that of the common good is derived from its model of the autonomous, rational, unencumbered self.[45] Communitarians contend that liberals and libertarians fail to realize that social communities are a deep-seated part of both human nature and the human condition. The human capacity for individuality is the product of a social nexus of affective bonds and established norms. Etzioni defines the self as "congenitally contextuated within a community."[46] He argues that human nature consists of "a universal set of basic human needs" that are "independent of the social structure, cultural patterns, or socialization processes."[47] Chief among these essential human needs are those of "social bonds (or attachments)" and "normative (or moral) guidance."[48]

Communitarian morality is therefore based on the idea of an identifiable, common, moral good bound up with the immutable features of human nature. A common human nature is the basis for shared moral values. Etzioni is confident that we can develop "an evolving framework of shared values, which all subcultures will be expected to endorse and support without losing their distinct identities and subcultures."[49] He believes we can attain a common moral voice. This community ethos requires "a synthesis of some elements of traditionalism with some elements of modernity, recasting both in the process."[50] A good society must strike a balance between a "thick" social order based on core values and "bounded autonomy."[51]

Yet this morality must be nurtured by strong civic institutions. Therefore, we must strengthen the institutions of civil society — the family, schools, churches, and neighborhoods. The preferred means for achieving this include education, moral dialogue, faith, civic voluntarism, and moral leadership. By recementing the social glue that holds the moral order together, civil society will be bolstered. Therefore, we can repair civic life and reactivate self-government, tasks of social integration that cannot be secured by the liberal law state, bureaucracies, or globalized markets.

Where, then, does political democracy fit into this model? Communitarians "favor strong democracy" and "seek to make government more representative, more participatory, and more responsive to all members of the community."[52] More precisely, democracy is the means by which we can realize a common good based on the mobilization of shared moral values, thus achieving a strong consensus that carries more relative weight than the majoritarian aggregation of diverse interests and individual rights. The primary site of the democratic experience is not government or the market, but communities, beginning with families and neighborhoods and extending to towns, cities, and nations, which fit together like Russian nesting dolls.

The appropriate model of governance, therefore, is a civil society of strong communities and a lean, constitutional republic. The common good is best realized in the voluntary realm of civil society. Strong communities obviate the need for a strong centralized state. It would also facilitate the downsizing of the federal government's social engineering and welfare functions and the redirecting of its juridical apparatus toward rebalancing the relationship between individual rights and social obligations. It would foster a political culture whose central value is less individual liberty, than individuality within community.

Deliberative Democracy

The deliberative model of democracy claims that collective public deliberation is the definitive democratic experience. Deliberative theorists include Seyla Benhabib, James Bohman, John Dryzek, James Fishkin, Jürgen Habermas, and Mark Warren.[53] Benhabib states that "it is a necessary condition for attaining legitimacy and rationality with regard to collective decision making processes in a polity, that the institutions of this polity are so arranged that what is considered in the common interest of all results from processes of collective deliberation conducted rationally and fairly among free and equal individuals."[54] Deliberative democrats locate the political in the "public sphere," that mediating realm between civil society and the state connected to both spheres, yet distinct from them and from the economy. It consists of civic associations, social movements, interest groups, the media, and arenas of public opinion formation. It is the space where citizens talk about their common affairs, the site where public discourses circulate.[55]

Deliberative democracy consists of four key features: (1) a free public sphere in which citizen discussion and debate can take place; (2) a set of procedures to ensure that this collective deliberation is fair, equal, and impartial for all participants; (3) that deliberation be conducted discursively and rationally, and that citizens engage in public reasoning on the greater public interest; and (4) that governmental bodies effectively translate this consensus into laws and policies.

Jürgen Habermas's "Three Normative Models of Democracy" (1994) captures the essential features of this model. He situates deliberative democracy between liberal and communitarian models of democracy. In the liberal model, the state is the guardian of a market society and its values of instrumental rationality. It draws its legitimacy from a constitutional framework of basic rights, majority rule, representation, and procedural fairness. In the communitarian model, the state is the product of a public sphere anchored in the collective identity of an ethical community. Citizens come to decisions within the boundaries of a shared concept of the common good. Habermas takes the proceduralism from liberalism and the civic-deliberative dimension from communitarian republicanism, while jettisoning the former's grounding in the strategic, market model and the latter's reliance on a substantive ethical community.[56]

Habermas thus arrives at a procedural-deliberative model of democracy. Practical reason, he claims, resides neither in the individual, nor in a community, but in the rules inherent in "the very structure of communicative actions."[57] This in turn presupposes a "postconventional" moral consciousness among citizens and a principled ethical orientation that requires critical reflexivity, logical consistency, and universality.[58] The normative content of deliberative democracy is stronger than liberalism, yet weaker than communitarian republicanism.[59] Thus while Habermas believes that a common good is attainable, he rejects the communitarian desire to base this good on a community ethos. Furthermore, popular sovereignty resides neither in a majority, nor in a collective citizenry, but in "the subjectless forms of communication that regulate the flow of deliberations."[60]

This model can be spatially represented as a three-tiered configuration. At its base is a pluralistic civil society. Its second tier is the public sphere, which Habermas describes as a linguistically constituted public space of informal opinion formation. The reality of the public sphere is that it is dominated by a corporate-controlled media-information complex. The third tier is that of formal, governmental, decision-making institutions.

Habermas's strategy is to elevate the level of dialogue in both the informal public sphere and formal state institutions to a "higher-level intersubjectivity."[61] Once elevated to a significant level of political-cultural force, the norms of democratic discourse must be encoded through legal and constitutional reforms into new principles of democratic legitimacy. Thus deliberative democracy's goal is to channel public opinion into a higher and more thematic level of discursive consensus ("communicative power") that can influence government ("administrative power").[62]

Deliberative democracy, therefore, forges a strong connection between a well-functioning public sphere of free, equal, and rational discourse and more deliberatively organized political institutions. It rests on the premise that ordinary citizens can engage in deliberative reasoning if genuine democratic public spaces are maintained. It also holds governmental institutions to a much higher standard of legitimacy. They satisfy deliberative criteria if their laws and policies are the result of a process of collective deliberation in which both citizens and representatives engage in rational debate and justify their positions by appealing to the norms of moral-practical reason and the greater public interest.

Agonistic Democracy

Like deliberative democracy, agonistic democracy is an activist model of participatory democracy. Yet unlike deliberative democrats, agonistic democrats view politics in terms of conflict rather than consensus, are dedicated to difference rather than the general interest, and are radically oppositional rather than reformist. They locate the political in the existential struggle to form identities and advance different ways of life in an environment of contingency, plurality, and power. If Habermas is the philosopher of deliberative democracy, Foucault is the philosopher of agonistic democracy.[63]

This model of the political as radical democracy reflects the postmodern model of society as a world of multiple, intersecting social fields and networks. Postmodern subcultures are spaces of hybrid identities, experimentation, and deconstructive discourses. This translates into a political ethos of multicultural difference employed to challenge hegemonic liberal and communitarian identities. Agonistic democracy calls for a radical pluralistic public sphere of contestive identities, moralities, and discourses. It endorses a politics of diverse social, cultural, and political movements organized around the values of cultural recognition, direct democracy, and performative resistance.

William Connolly has described postmodern democracy as an "ethos of pluralization"[64] that "affirms the indispensability of identity to life, disturbs the dogmatization of identity, and folds care for the protean diversity of human life into the strife and interdependence of identity\difference."[65] It promotes genealogical critique, respect for difference, the contesting of fundamentalist moral and political codes, and a more equitable distribution of social goods. It is focused less on organized interests and governance than on the reconstitution of cultural life.

The idea of a postmodern civic republicanism advanced by French political philosopher Chantal Mouffe exemplifies the model of agonistic democracy. In contrast to the prevailing discourses of Rawlsian liberalism, communitarianism, and Habermasian deliberative democracy, Mouffe contends that democracy today should be dedicated to maximizing liberty and equality through a set of public values (a civic identity) that defines politics as the struggle to establish the hegemony of radical pluralism.

The modern democratic ideals of liberty and equality should be understood as contingent and intertwined historical projects. They are ensembles of social and political practices, not essential foundations of the human condition. The constitution of democracy as a social and political space occurs "precisely in the tension between the democratic logic of equality and the liberal logic of liberty."[66] We therefore should not reconcile equality and liberty, but rather affirm their "unresolvable tension" and extend these "principles to the widest possible set of social relations."[67]

Mouffe contends that while we should retain the modern Enlightenment political project of liberty and equality for all, we should jettison the Enlightenment's rationalist epistemological project.[68] Why? Because rationality, universality, and individual subjectivity are in reality pluralistic, culturally constructed, and entangled with power relations. We need "a theory of the subject as a decentered, detotalized agent, a subject constructed at the point of intersection of a multiplicity of subject positions between which there exists no *a priori* or necessary relation and whose articulation is the result of hegemonic practices."[69]

Mouffe redefines modern equality and liberty to arrive at a new formulation of the political. Equality is rearticulated as the maximization of egalitarian spaces of difference, while liberty is construed as public liberty and the maximization of democratic rights. The result is a new radical democratic logic of pluralist difference and "democratic equivalence."[70] The glue that holds this democratic model together is a shared language and norms of civic intercourse that Mouffe calls "agonistic pluralism."[71] She believes that diverse subjects can coalesce around the common political identity of radical democratic citizenship. This civic identity seeks to construct a new "we" through a "chain of democratic equivalence" that goes beyond "a mere alliance between given interests" to "actually modifying the very identity of these forces."[72]

Like communitarian and deliberative models of democracy, agonistic democracy relies on the active citizen model. Yet the agonistic citizen is not motivated to achieve the common moral good or a deliberative consensus. She is rather dedicated to a civic ethos that grasps the nature of the political as a pluralistic field of constructed identities and values shaped by power, struggle, and a commitment to radical democracy.

Associative Democracy

Associative democracy is the most recent product of the tradition of "associationalism," which originated in the shadow of nineteenth-century Marxist socialism. Its sources can be found in Robert Owen, Pierre-Joseph Proudhon, G. D. H. Cole, Harold J. Laski, French labor syndicalism, and German corporatism. Paul Hirst has defined its two central principles as: (1) "the advocacy of a decentralized economy based on the non-capitalistic principles of cooperation and mutuality"; and (2) "the criticism of the centralized and sovereign state, with radical federalist and political pluralist ideas advanced as a substitute."[73] Today, associationalism has been resurrected as associative democracy not only by Hirst, but by Joshua Cohen and Joel Rogers.

Cohen and Rogers want to structurally transform American liberal pluralism into a European model of social democratic corporatism. They advocate a greater role for "secondary associations" in the policy process.[74] This amounts to changing America's "iron triangle" mode of governance, a special-interest-group bazaar of "pork"-saturated bargaining dominated by business groups. In its place would be a mode of governance in which the state formally integrates special interest groups into the policy process. It would match them up with administrative agencies and democratize this policy process by making its operation amenable to egalitarian and deliberative norms enacted into law by the legislative branch and enforced by the executive branch.

This statist colonization and democratic transformation of interest groups would shift the group basis of American politics toward a deliberative egalitarianism. It would further require politicians and bureaucrats to free themselves from being in the thrall of special interest groups, to reconnect with a mass majoritarian democratic politics, and to use the state to radically reorganize neoliberal pluralism into a more equal group system, enabling state agencies to empower weak and excluded interests and to tame and disempower oligarchic interests.

Cohen and Rogers call for the reinvention of the social welfare state based on six fundamental norms: popular sovereignty, political equality, distributive equity, civic consciousness, good economic performance, and state competence.[75] This translates as "the organization and representation of underrepresented interests," "active labor policies aimed at ensuring full employment," "mandatory programs of public service," "more ambitious schemes to finance party competition largely out of public funds," "productivity improvement in enhancing the general welfare," and "the construction of new arenas for public deliberation."[76]

Paul Hirst's model identifies voluntary associations, rather than interest groups, as the key actors in governance. These civic associations range from nonprofit organizations helping the elderly, the poor, victims of sexual abuse, people with disabilities, and immigrants, to neighborhood associations, church groups, tenant organizations, animal welfare societies, and toxics-free environmental groups. His strategy is local and designed to work from the bottom up. He advocates building strong social networks and associational cultures that promote voluntary action, pluralistic mutual aid, and self-governance. Civic associations should form mutual-aid alliances, creating a strong local civic infrastructure. Building on this base, local civic alliances and governments can pressure state governments and business firms to build more collaborative and democratic relations between government, workers, and business, and to sustain local and regional economies.

Hirst's more ambitious goal is to dismantle the bureaucratic welfare state and replace it with an "associationalist welfare system" in which "voluntary self-governing associations gradually and progressively become the primary means of democratic governance of economic and social affairs."[77] This shift would require radical reformist legislation and structural changes. The key component parts of Hirst's ideal model of democracy are a decentralized federal state, public welfare services provided by voluntary self-governing associations, public money with which to fund and oversee these organizations, democratized capitalist firms, regional economic regulation, and a guaranteed minimum income plan.[78]

Although the models advanced by Cohen and Rogers and Hirst are quite different, they both adhere to an underlying associationalist political ethic:

Associative democracy draws on an egalitarian ideal of social association. The core of that ideal is that the members of a society ought to be treated as equals in fixing the basic terms of social cooperation — including the ways that authoritative collective decisions are made, the ways that resources are produced and distributed, and the ways that social life more broadly is organized. The substantive commitments of the ideal include concerns about fair conditions for citizen participation in politics and robust public debate, an equitable distribution of resources, and the protection of individual choice.[79]

The Prospects for an Alternative Model of Democracy

The heart of the democratic experience for communitarians is "the community" understood as a group of people who share the same values. For deliberative democrats, it is "the public sphere" understood as a public space of rational collective deliberation. For agonistic democrats, it is "identity/difference" understood as the egalitarian reconstitution of cultural life within a radically pluralized, postmodern polity. For associative democrats, it is "social association" understood as the cooperative interaction of diverse groups in civil society.

Yet how do these alternative normative models of democracy fare against the powerful complex of postmodern, neoliberal, techno-oligarchic governance? In my view, these models lack sufficient sociological and political realism. With their radical reformist and antisystemic features, they have little hope of replacing our current governmentality. Indeed, some of these models fit rather nicely as supplemental adjuncts to existing neoliberal democracy. Other models, however, could be reinvented as local and microlevel strategies of democratic resistance and self-governance.

Communitarianism is largely a reincarnation of the turn-of-the-century Progressive movement. It articulates a general set of moral and humanitarian goals tied to a policy agenda of "good government" reforms and local community moral revitalization. Yet several problems plague the communitarian model of democracy. First, the current disintegration and denigration of civil society, public morality, and community life is not primarily due to the perceived rampant spread of libertarianism and the proliferation, trivialization, and privatization of individual rights. The principal threat to communities, from families to nation-states, comes from the powerful disruptive effects of advanced capitalist markets and their high-tech, deregulated globalization. Yet communitarians do not offer us an analysis of how high-tech economic globalization is changing social life in advanced Western societies. Nor do they challenge the power of advanced capitalism.

Second, the notion of a strong community with shared values is only workable in small, homogeneous locales, in neighborhoods, small towns, and suburbs, where sameness is dominant. And strong, cohesive communities based on a clear set of values are usually authoritarian rather than democratic, monocultural rather than multicultural, and rest upon subtle and not-so-subtle norms of inclusion and exclusion. Thus the wider application of the idea of the moral community is undermined by the realities of social complexity, cultural pluralism, and economic inequality.

The problem with communitarianism is that its conflation of the common moral good with the common political good infects its agenda of empowering civil society with an overbearing code of moral discipline. Its policy agenda includes a mandatory waiting period and counseling before couples get married, laws restricting divorce, providing moral education in schools by teaching a set of substantive values common to all Americans, having students wear school uniforms, mandating public service, promoting more personal responsibility and self-help, expanding what constitutes reasonable search and seizure, and instituting curfews.[80]

Finally, communitarianism is a supplemental adjunct to existing neoliberal democracy. Its goal of balancing individual rights with social responsibilities helps stabilize and legitimize neoliberal governance. It fits in nicely with the current political formula of "devolution federalism," whereby responsibilites once assumed by the federal government are being placed on state and local governments and communities. This strategy stresses entrepreneurial governance, public-private partnerships, decentralization, and local community self-reliance. With the high-tech globalization of capitalism and the downsizing of the social welfare state, local communities are increasingly taking on tasks that the economy and government are unwilling to deal with.

Yet civic voluntarism, calls for greater moral and civic virtue, and recovering the spirit of community will not be enough to fill the void created by federal governmental devolution (which is as much fiscal as it is bureaucratic) and high-tech, corporate globalization. What we are seeing is the creation of a neofeudal landscape, a patchwork of local, state, and regional social contracts between techno-oligarchs and communities brokered by governmental institutions. This fusion of liberal, techno-oligarchic power structures with a disciplinary communitarianism is the ideal formula for neofeudal governance.

Turn, then, to deliberative democrats, who encourage all citizens to participate in democratic discussion. Democracy should rest on a well-informed citizenry with access to public spaces of open communication and reasoned debate. Reasoned public opinion, not interest group competition, should be the basis of democratic governance. This in turn requires that citizens follow a set of rules shaped by the norms of secular rational dialogue. This public discourse, whose form and content are shaped by Enlightenment rationality, also requires that we justify our positions through a practical reasoning process that others accept. The "force of the better argument" within the framework of fair deliberative procedures and a "postconventional moral reflexivity" is the criterion of democratic legitimacy.

Yet these norms privilege a type of speech that is formal and argumentative, articulate and dispassionate; that abstracts from ascriptive characteristics of race, class, gender, lifestyle, and religion; and that is oriented toward the greater public good. Other types of speech are relegated to second-class status, including speech that is dramatic, expressive, rhetorical, and testimonial; that involves storytelling, humor, irony, and figures of speech; and that takes place in discussion settings that focus on cultural difference, listening, and protest and performative resistance.[81]

More than this, the demands put on citizens to embrace a postconventional morality, to bracket and test normative validity claims, to argue from the position of universalizable principles, and to achieve a rational consensus are unreasonable. This rational discourse model is more at home in formal, procedural, and methodologically structured parliamentary, judicial, and academic institutional settings than in populist civic forums. In open civic forums, the cognitive use of language cannot be separated from noncognitive speech. Indeed, the discourses and judgments that occur in both the specialized world of experts and the everyday world of citizens involve a complex mix of context-dependent cognitive, normative, aesthetic, hermeneutic, and strategic types of speech that cannot be disentangled and logically analyzed.

Then there is the public sphere itself. Where does democratic discourse fit into this high-tech, corporate-controlled, postmodern environment?

If a deliberative public sphere is necessary for democracy, then our mass media–information order must undergo structural and cultural changes. Yet most deliberative theorists focus on constructing elaborate discourses of justification and not on critical media studies. Furthermore, new models of citizen deliberation ranging from televised town meetings to "deliberative opinion polls" to interactive cable systems are supplemental adjuncts to existing neoliberal democracy. High-tech citizen discussions of policy issues are carefully orchestrated to ensure deliberation within narrow boundaries.

Agonistic democracy provides us with a needed counterweight to the more conformist communitarian and deliberative moral-political logics. Its conception of democracy and citizenship is informed by an ethos of opposition and dissidence. The communitarian emphasis on restoring the moral community and the deliberative emphasis on restoring democratic legitimacy converge in the regulatory ideal of republican self-governance. Opposition to government is downplayed. Indeed, communitarian conformity and deliberative consensus inhibit dissent.

Agonistic democrats also have a more sophisticated and realistic view of our postmodern political condition. They locate the political in the triangular relationship between technologies of governance, individuals and social groups operating in a more pluralized and identity-conscious civil society, and our mass-mediated, hyperreal public sphere. Given the nature of our current governmentality, the challenge of opening up democratic public spaces in a corporate-controlled mediocracy demands much more than deliberative forums. It requires a more expressive, disclosive, and agonistic strategy. In a late modern/postmodern world, the democratic illumination of public space requires a political dramatics that channels critical publicity into powerful catalytic and cathartic acts of revelation and resistance.

Yet at the same time, radical postmodern democrats tend to minimize several crucial variables. These include: (1) the relative scarcity of resources available to accommodate the demands of radically democratized groups without major systemic reforms; (2) the importance of economic issues and the linkage between cultural struggle and economic inequality; (3) the dangers of tribalism and violence generated in the wake of an agonistic politics; (4) the problem of communication and coordination in sustaining social movements and coalitions mobilized by the politics of difference rather than solidarity; and (5) the decline of social movements organized around identity and the emergence of new grass-roots, social justice movements organized around locally intertwined economic, environmental, and cultural issues.[82]

Finally, in turning to associative democracy, I value Hirst's model over that of Cohen and Rogers. They themselves admit to the limited relevance of their model. America, they conclude, "has a strongly anti-collectivist political culture, a weak state, and a civil society dominated by business interests."[83] Furthermore, in a society of numerous civic, social, and cultural groups, as well as economic and occupational interest groups, wouldn't associative governance institute a two-tiered democracy? Wouldn't associations not functionally matched with existing bureaucratic agencies or those regarded as representing nonvital interests be marginalized? And isn't the main purpose of the Cohen and Rogers model to empower a weak labor movement through active state intervention?

Hirst's idea of rebuilding civic associations from below by revitalizing voluntarist and libertarian currents in civil society is a much more plausible strategy.[84] The revitalization of civil society, that space of collective life distinct from the state and business sectors, is an integral component of the communitarian, deliberative, and agonistic models of democracy. Yet the civic associational model differs from them in significant ways. Its conception of civil society is sustained by a plurality of civic associations, rather than by moral communities. Its civic pluralist ethos eschews communitarianism's paternalistic "moral voice." Its spirit of social association and cooperation is also at odds with the postmodern ethos of radical agonistic pluralism. It is dedicated to pluralistic mutual aid in the midst of cultural difference. Finally, it contends that the public sphere is sustained more by the "social capital" and pragmatic experimentalism of civic associations than by the discourses of deliberative citizens.[85]

As for the fate of democracy in our late modern/postmodern times, I believe that its trajectory will unfold as a two-track dynamic. We will continue to see the deployment of a postmodern, neoliberal, techno-oligarchic mode of governance as the dominant power framework. Yet we will also see the growth of a local civic associationalism and postmodern strategies of resistance. These local and microlevel adaptations open up possibilities for new strategies of democracy. Furthermore, these trends toward greater techno-oligarchic governance, local civic associationalism, and postmodern resistance will continue to come at the expense of the now outmoded, modern, liberal-representative model of democracy.

Complexity and the Fate of Democracy

It is my view that the concept of "complexity" defines our current political condition more accurately than do the models of the moral community, public deliberation, identity/difference, or social association. Calls for the recovery of community, for democracy as critical reflective dialogue, for radical pluralization, and for a more robust civic associational life are all effects of the greater forces of technological and social complexity. This condition of complexity is the product of high-tech capitalist globalization, time-space compression, the information revolution, increased social and self-reflexivity, the pervasive influence of mass-media communication, and postmodern cultural change.

That is why I believe the work of Danilo Zolo in *Democracy and Complexity: A Realist Approach* (1992) is the most powerful and disturbing contribution to the analysis of contemporary democracy and democratic theory. Zolo asserts that "it is the idea of complexity—along with the closely related notion of social complexity—which opens the way to a realistic analysis of the condition and fate of democracy in post-industrial societies."[86] He defines complexity in terms of "the wider scope of possible choices and the higher number of variables which agents have to take account of in their attempts to resolve problems of knowledge, adaptation, and organization."[87] As environments of action become more complex, he says, "the more interdependent the variables become" and "a larger amount of information is then needed to arrange and control the environment."[88] Environments become more turbulent and unpredictable as the number of variable correlations increases. This situation of increased contingency or aperiodic behavior within complex environments in turn fuels the imperative for increased technological innovation and control.

The central function of the state in complex technological societies is "that of regulating selectively the distribution of social risks, and so of reducing fear, through the competitive allocation of 'security values.' "[89] State legitimacy is a function of complexity reduction, rather than representation, participation, or consensus. Diverse groups compete for the distribution of security values in an environment of heightened risk. The state engages in an ongoing reconfiguration of political space in terms of security and risk zones. It shapes these spaces of inclusion and exclusion through various means, including administrative agencies with rule-making discretion and extensive regulatory powers, elite interest groups, networks of marketized governance, a self-referential party system that promotes programmatic homogeneity and marginalizes real alternatives, and a corporate mass media that manufactures "public opinion" and "consensus."[90]

Zolo's analysis reveals an abyss between the ideal principles of liberal democracy as formulated by Robert Dahl and Norberto Bobbio and the performance of Western polities. He asserts that: (1) popular sovereignty "has been completely drained of effect by the growth of public bureaucracies"; (2) pluralist society "has resulted in the suffocation of the postulate of individualism"; (3) in a high-tech society, democracy has become expertocracy; (4) the promise of an educated and responsive citizenry confronts "the widespread diffusion of mass conformity and political apathy among voters"; (5) democracy "has never succeeded in dispensing with oligarchic power"; (6) democracy has not established itself in the larger social realm or in "everyday institutions such as the family, schools or hospitals"; and (7) democracy has failed to eliminate "invisible power," the extensive covert power networks that make up a parallel "invisible State."[91]

What, then, is the impact of this condition on democratic theory? Most models of democracy, modern and contemporary, are obsolete. Their conceptual infrastructures are outmoded. The "classical" model of democracy, which translated the ancient democratic *polis* ideal into modern times through the Enlightenment conceptions of individual autonomy, popular sovereignty, and emancipation, has been negated by a modernization process that has produced complex, differentiated societies.[92] The model of "pluralistic democracy" or "democratic elitism," crafted by Joseph Schumpeter, Robert Dahl, and Giovanni Sartori jettisoned much of this Enlightenment fantasy. It was replaced with a more realistic formulation that rested on the axioms of formal political equality, electoral proceduralism, interest group pluralism, elite selection, and citizens as rational consumer-voters.[93]

Yet this pluralistic model is also outmoded.[94] It rests on the "polyarchic" assumption that there exists a relative equal distribution of resources and opportunities between competing interest groups. This is not the case. The public realm is largely determined by oligopolistic power structures, just as the economic market is shaped by transnational corporations. Furthermore, citizen-voters do not possess the requisite information and autonomy of choice to qualify as free and rational actors. The sovereignty of the political consumer has been effectively undermined by a corporate mass media whose medium of hyperreality and whose message of consumer dependency dwarfs its informational and civic functions. In short, Zolo maintains that neither pluralistic competition nor citizens exist in contemporary mass democratic societies.

As for contemporary models of democracy, Zolo argues that theorizing democracy in terms of a community moral good, rational deliberation, and a reinvention of the Greek *agora* (as Arendt and postmoderns do) is not feasible in today's highly differentiated, complex societies. Normative theories that rest on the assumption of ethical cognitivism (the knowability of universal moral intuitions) and communitarian notions of an identifiable substantive common good are unrealistic because in complex societies, standards of both right and good have been radically pluralized. According to Zolo, Habermas, Rawls, and communitarians (like Rousseau and Marx) lack "a perception of the variety, particularism, and mutual incompatibility of social expectations in non-elementary societies."[95]

Zolo is forced to conclude that Western liberal democracies are in reality "differentiated and limited autocratic systems."[96] Contrary to the proclamation of Francis Fukuyama, we are not witnessing the triumph of liberal democracy over all other contenders.[97] Rather, both socialism and liberal representative democracy are dead. Our post–Cold War world is as postdemocratic as it is postsocialist. We have reached the end point of political modernity. What has triumphed is a techno-oligarchic mode of governance. Zolo speculates that if there is any discernible trend in the evolution of democracy, it is toward a "Singapore model":

> In today's world, no more perfect example could be found of the modern antipolis, characterized as it is by the highest technological efficiency, extensive use of information instruments, widespread prosperity, excellent public services (especially schools and hospitals), high levels of employment, efficient and enlightened bureaucracy, social relations aseptically mediated by exclusive functional requirements and a total lack of political ideologies or public discussion.[98]

In many respects, Zolo's model of contemporary democracy comes close to my notion of a reigning postmodern, neoliberal techno-oligarchy. And like Zolo, I believe we have entered a period of "post-representative democracy."[99] Western societies are moving in the neofeudal direction of being determined by transnational corporate fiefdoms, a new middle class/senior citizen social-welfare contract, an upgraded surveillance state, and more privatized forms of risk management.

There is a significant weakness, however, in Zolo's analysis. He adopts a functionalist approach that portrays Western societies as differentiated subsystems operating on the basis of distinct and autonomous functional codes.[100] Government is a cybernetic system steered by its state-centric political code. This code is defined in terms of the systemic viability of the state as an organized set of "functions and behavior patterns of an adaptive type which tend towards the collective alleviation of insecurity and which are based on a logic of the avoidance of risk."[101]

This Hobbesian approach, which marginalizes human agency, allows no space for democratic action to take place. Zolo's harsh indictment of alternative models of democracy is justified to the extent that their radical reformist features are shown to lack sufficient sociological and political realism. Yet he is incapable of theorizing democratic action oriented toward local and microlevel adaptations to complexity and techno-oligarchy.

What is particularly striking is that Zolo's analysis of governance is similar to Foucault's. Government exists as a vast array of technologies, strategies, and tactics that discipline and seduce both the body politic and individual subjects. While novel microlevel forms of resistance do manifest themselves, they are most often channeled into new modes of conformist assimilation.

Yet Foucault had more faith in the possibilities for freedom at the local and microlevels. He developed a realist approach that combined the analysis of both governance and resistance. Government disciplines and seduces; yet it also sends into motion diverse points of resistance. These points of resistance are channeled back toward the reigning mode of governance and are most often assimilated effectively. Yet they also open up spaces for advancing freedom and democratic action. Therefore, the prospect for new types of democratic politics at the local and microlevels needs to be addressed. In doing this, I again return to Foucault. For in Foucualt one can find a political ethic of freedom and strategies of democracy with which to negotiate our current mode of democratic governance. Furthermore, they can be fashioned into an alternative "critical postmodern democratic politics."

6 — Postmodern Strategies and Democratic Politics

Democracy needs to be reconceived as something other than a form of government: as a mode of being that is conditioned by bitter experience, doomed to succeed only temporarily, but is a recurrent possibility as long as the memory of the political survives.
— Sheldon Wolin, "Fugitive Democracy"

The Revaluation of Democratic Self-Governance

Democracy is most often defined as a specific mode of governance in which political power is exercised by citizens through direct and mediated means of participation in collective decision-making and policy implementation processes. Democracy is based on the principle of political equality and designates that all citizens have the right to exercise political power. Oligarchy is a mode of governance in which an elite minority controls most of the governing decisions. Authoritarian and autocratic modes of governance recognize few or no formal limits on government.

Modern governments have always been a mixture of oligarchic, democratic, and bureaucratic features. Today, while these features remain integral to their functioning, governments operate through the workings of complex policy networks that coordinate a multiplicity of power techniques, strategies, and tactics. That is why I conclude that the dominant mode of governance in advanced Western societies today is neither democracy, nor oligarchy, nor bureaucracy, but governmentality.

Our current mode of government is not the rule of the people. First, "the people" do not exist as an entity with a common identity, a determinate will, or a majoritarian voice. These populist identities are largely manufactured by media and public opinion governmentalities in the production of "news," "polls," and electoral "majorities." Second, people do not exercise sovereign power over a political state. Governmental power is exercised by complex power and policy networks. We are connected to government through varied representations and simulations of democracy. This is not government by the people. Nor is it government by elites. Rather, it is government by complex power networks as negotiated by the few in the name of the many.

I have described this mode of governance as a postmodern, neoliberal, techno-oligarchy. When the word *democracy* is used, it is most often invoked as the legitimizing label for this type of government. Yet I would argue that democracy is not principally about government; rather, it describes a mode of existence bound up with the political condition of the *demos*. And in its contemporary manifestation, democracy is an ethos of resistance to our existing mode of governance. Understood this way, democracy is a way of life in which ordinary people engage in the practice of self-governance through the discovery of freedom among others. This activity is principally experienced in opposition to government.

Sheldon Wolin has characterized democracy as an event that occurs when ordinary people become "political beings through the self-discovery of common concerns and modes of action for realizing them."[1] The moment when the political manifests itself as democracy is further defined by Wolin as one that is episodic, transgressive, and "fugitive." The *demos* is activated and takes shape in the midst of revolt, resistance, and revolution, releases of human energies that contest established boundaries, institutions, and practices.

This concept of democracy is postmodern in its description of the *demos* as a "mode of being" that challenges boundaries. The notion of boundaries, explains Wolin, defines not only the modern political condition, but also the Western tradition of political philosophy. From its inception in ancient Athens, political theory has been primarily concerned with the legitimation of political orders. This involves the demarcation of a circumscribed space designed to shape a population as belonging together. From the "myth of the metals" to the "state of nature" to the "general will" to the "original position" to the "ideal speech situation," Western political and social theory has been driven by a will to *domus*— a bounded political community where likeness and unity dwell.[2]

Wolin writes that "boundaries signify the will to contextualize."[3] Politically this "signifies the domestication of politics in a double sense."[4]

A political community is established and a domestic politics created to control and pacify the contents of this bounded space. Two key institutional devices ensure this process of domestication: the state and the constitution. Our modern political condition is the product of the constititutional nation-state as both the bearer of the political and the form of democracy. It is a political condition dedicated to "the containment of democracy."[5] This is implicit in the operational codes of the modern constitutional-representative state. They delimit the *demos* and relegate it to a subsidiary adjunct of sovereign power, governmental separation of powers and checks and balances, and electoral procedures and mechanisms.

Democracy as a form of government must therefore be replaced with democracy as a mode of being. Democracy conceived as a mode of governance tells us how the *demos* has been effectively colonized by the modern *domus*. It does not tell us where democracy, understood as a mode of existence concerned with "the political potentialites of ordinary citizens,"[6] is located and how it is experienced. It tells us, asserts Wolin, how "the labor, wealth, and psyches of the citizenry are simultaneously defended and exploited, protected and extracted, nurtured and fleeced, rewarded and commanded, flattered and threatened."[7]

Yet if this is the case, then where is the contemporary *demos* to be located and experienced? Wolin writes:

> The possibility of renewal draws on a simple fact: that ordinary individuals are capable of creating new cultural patterns of commonality at any moment. Individuals who concert their powers for low income housing, worker ownership of factories, better schools, better health care, safer water, control over toxic waste disposals, and a thousand other common concerns of ordinary lives are experiencing a democratic moment and contributing to the discovery, care, and tending of a commonality of shared concerns. Without necessarily intending it, they are renewing the political by contesting the forms of unequal power that democratic liberty and democratic equality have made possible and that democracy can eliminate only by betraying its own values.[8]

This revaluation of democracy from a bounded, state-centered *domus* to a transgressive demos illuminates my idea of a critical postmodern democratic politics. Returning to the ancient Greek meaning of democracy, the rule (*kratos*) of the people (*demos*) should be rephrased. Democracy is the struggle (*agon*) of ordinary people (*demos*) to create (*praxis*) a free (*eleutheria*) way of life (*ethos*) in opposition to the government (*politeia*) of complex power networks (*techne sustema*).

Democracy, defined as the struggle of ordinary individuals to experience a free way of life among others, occurs at the very edges of our postmodern, neoliberal, techno-oligarchic governmentality and in opposition to it. Its location is most evident at the local and microlevels of adaptation and resistance to complex, governmental power frameworks. It is here that Wolin's vision of the *demos* and Foucault's ethos of creative resistance intersect. Wolin's revaluation of democracy as a mode of being and vision of the *demos* as "the political moment when the political is remembered and re-created"[9] requires effective strategies. Foucault provides us with those strategies, yet he lacks a vision of the *demos*. This is provided by Wolin. Together, they illuminate the prospect of a critical postmodern democratic politics.

Strategies of Democracy

Democracy today is the struggle of ordinary people to create a free way of life in opposition to our dominant techno-oligarchic governmentality. I have defined governmentality as those techniques, procedures, strategies, and tactics of behavior modification employed by state and nonstate institutions to shape human conduct. Therefore, democracy stands in opposition to government and manifests itself as an activity in a tensional relationship to our dominant mode of governance. Given this characterization of democracy and government today, the task facing a critical postmodern democratic politics is to develop alternative "strategies" rather than alternative "models" of democracy.

The idea of "strategies of democracy" is in keeping with Michel Foucault's understanding of the role of the intellectual. A model of democracy is an ideal theoretical construct that embodies a normative alternative to our present system. It is the product of a "universal" intellectual disposition that aspires to be the bearer of a universal truth, rational knowledge, or ideal way of life applicable to all reasonable human beings. By contrast, what Foucault described as a "specific" or "local" intellectual exposes the concrete operations of specific power/knowledge networks and identifies strategies effective in opening up spaces of resistance, critique, and freedom. Foucault's concern was to create the conditions for struggle, not an ideal model that too often is the product of the very power system one wishes to radically reform.[10]

I regard the following practices endorsed by Foucault as strategies worthy of our consideration in advancing a critical postmodern democratic politics. These strategies are oriented to microlevel and local modes of resistance and adaptation to modern frameworks and technologies of power. They are transgressive negation, self-care, performative action, agonistic *praxis, parrhesia,* and local resistance.

Transgressive Negation

The transgression of limits was a major defining theme of Foucault's thought.[11] His message was that we need to analyze, test, and go beyond the limits imposed on us by modern discourse, knowledge, subjectivity, and government. Trangressive actions expose the boundaries of our culture, which are also the boundaries of our reality. They illuminate the limit lines that determine what is reasonable and what is unreasonable, what is normal and what is deviant or pathological, what is good and what is evil. In crossing these boundaries, we demonstrate that the bounded character of our reality is not the product of an absolute, essential, or natural condition. It is the result of the battle lines of historical power relations that have coalesced into spaces of containment. The act itself is risky, unstable, unpredictable, and in some cases life-threatening. Yet at the same time, it is a risk that is calculated. It involves skill, planning, and positioning onself in a specific set of circumstances. It is a strategy.

I would define Foucault's idea of transgression as the will to a negation of limits through the experiential cultivation of excess.[12] This excess is achieved by taking the existing artifacts and practices of one's culture and working them to exceed both their normal allowances and prohibitions. By deliberately opening what one's society regards as dangerous portals into the abyss of primal chaos or otherness, gateways under constant monitoring and security, the transgressor illuminates both our confinement and the territory beyond the divide. She or he bears the marks of the transgressive experience as evidence of the limits of our culture, the largely uncontested boundaries of our reality, and worlds beyond our sanctioned existence.

Foucault identified and valued several transgressive sites, ranging from the aesthetic to the theoretical to the personal to the political. Modernist art, avant-garde literature, the cultivation of states of "madness," the exploration of the unconscious, the deconstruction of categories of thought, drug use, sadomasochistic sexuality and other taboo bodily practices, radical protest, and revolutionary battle were all endorsed by Foucault at different times in his life and work.[13]

Foucault regarded transgression as specific acts or a series of cultural experiments that reveal the limits of our known existence. He did not believe that one could live a life without limits or create a culture or society based on transgression.[14] And while many of these practices are self-referential, it is their public character (their being done in public or made public) that makes them relevant as strategies of democracy. To the extent that these events disrupt one's culture, society, the lives of ordinary people, and governments, they are democratic. These acts force us to confront our limits. And in doing so, we must acknowledge, define, defend, redraw, and redeploy existing boundaries. Transgressive negation is the boldest strategy in testing the limits of reality. It is also very risky. It sets the context for a backlash, an equally excessive and violent reaction.

Self-Care

The idea of an ethic of self-care, developed toward the end of Foucault's life, was shaped by the idea of transfiguration rather than by transgression.[15] Both transgression and self-care challenge the boundaries of our culture and our selves. Yet they are different strategies. Transgression introduces excess into one's life in order to expose and go beyond limits. It is a strategy dedicated to bursting barriers. It is an ethic of negation that channels human energy into acts of creative destruction, disintegration, and existential confrontation.

Self-care is an ethical project of self-reformation. It is the ability to intentionally create a distinctive lifestyle. This entails adopting a more moderate aesthetic stance in examining, selecting, and weaving together various techniques of self-mastery. The goal is to fashion a mode of ethical conduct that exemplifies a free relationship to one's self. This implies a self-disciplined form of activity. Self-care is an affirmative ethic geared toward the experience of freedom associated with creativity. Conformity is challenged and the self is reflexively refashioned.

Yet what is the political relevance of an ethic that is primarily self-focused? Or is it? Is not developing an aesthetic relation to oneself more about recreating personal autonomy than about renewing the *demos*? Or is it about both? And is not the imperative to stylize one's conduct a private rather than a public concern? Or is it both?

I maintain that self-care is as political as it is personal. It occurs at the intersection of the public and the private domains and illuminates their more complex intertwinement. Self-care forces us to rethink what we mean by autonomy. It also demands the democratization of personal life. The ethical imperative to care for one's self is forged in response to interventions into and the micromanagement of the most intimate details of our everyday and private lives. As concerns regarding relationships, the body, sexuality, identity, health care, food, and personal habits and tastes become more politicized and regulated by bureaucracies, consumer markets, the workplace, civic groups, and moral communities, self-care becomes a high priority.

We respond to these disciplinary adjustments by both conforming to and resisting them. It is when we begin to openly challenge the existing mores and codes that structure the details of our lives that the search for a more original sense of self becomes critical. The existential question that always lurked in the background but was never fully confronted — how should one live one's life? — comes to the foreground. It puts the catalogs of available identities and self-presentations into question.

The pursuit of self-care therefore implies resistance to the governance of our daily lives and a critical reevaluation of those identities that are produced for us so that we can assume our proper social roles and fulfill societal norms. The disruption of this process of socialization creates a space of cultural criticism and relearning. The available practices that we find in our culture come under strict scrutiny. We critically survey our habitat and our perceived sense of self-identity.

Self-care is the product of a rupture in one's self-identity that sets into motion a dynamic of self-disassembly and reassembly. We discover that we are a composite of many drives, emotions, and habits that have been forged by circumstances significantly beyond our control. Our self-identity must either be restabilized or further destabilized to the point of embarking on a lifestyle change. If the latter course is undertaken, the path toward self-reformation may result in the kind of ethical and aesthetic journey that Foucault advocated. Again, there are no guarantees. We are, however, provided with the opportunity to change ourselves and our conduct and in so doing to transform our relationship to others.

Performative Action

Foucault believed that political action was possible in a world of disciplinary governance. Yet the kind of action that follows from his analysis is very different from the liberal humanist model of emancipatory action. Emancipatory action is conceived of as the achievement of intentional actors who believe themselves to be autonomous beings with self-evident interests. Their actions are shaped by a deliberate purpose or fixed desire. These actions are perceived as representative of stable identities, as the sovereign and instrumental exercise of power, and as designed to liberate individuals and groups from domination. Power is harnessed to reduce or eliminate the impediments to freedom. Agents thereby gain greater control over their environment. Their goal is a social and political order that facilitates greater autonomy of action among free and equal individuals.[16]

Performative action is not grounded in the logic of the modern liberal utilitarian model. It does not regard the individual as a substantial unity and self-determinant ego-identity. It does not hold to an instrumental view of action whereby human interests are efficiently advanced to attain self-chosen ends. It does not regard the goal of this action as that of creating or maintaining a protected space free from power or coercive interference. And it does not believe that we can achieve maximum control over the environments or contexts in which action takes place.

The performative model reverses this logic. Action is the product of the complex and subtle interaction of largely diffuse and anonymous power networks. The rules and norms of different social power environments shape our identities and interests. The individual is therefore one of the key effects of the social power environment. Our actions do not liberate us from oppressive power relations; instead they shift and recreate power relations.

Conscious of the way power operates, performative resistance, rather than emancipation, is regarded as the kind of action most effective in situations of contemporary disciplinary governance.[17] When we resist control as a public act, we engage in a series of expressions, utterances, and demonstrations that bring into being a public persona perceived by others as our self, our identity, our citizen character. The action itself constitutes the reality of our identity. It is a kind of action that refers to the context in which the action takes place, not to the individual person that existed prior to the action. Indeed, we experience a sense of distance between our own sense of self and the self (or selves) we portray as a public actor. In other words, our public identity is contingently created by our action, which is a reaction to the power environment we find ourselves in.

Performative action stems from a public act of resistance to a particular power situation. It is an act of revolt, rebellion, or disruption that creates a citizen in protest. It is an act of defiance that exposes power relations. It is also a public performance or demonstration. It can range from an accidental occurrence to a staged event. The key here is that the action is primarily expressive and aesthetic. It is judged with reference to how one's appearance and actions reveal the operation of power. The action is more disclosive and agonistic than intentional and emancipatory. It often involves taking ordinary, everyday activities and routines and turning them into vehicles for protest.

In a time shaped by mass media, performative action takes on a more significant role as a strategy. In a televisual democracy, it is the dramatized rather than the deliberative character of events that carries more weight in shaping perceptions and opinions. The deployment of language and images in a performative way governs much of our symbolic production and consumption. Therefore, our ability to redeploy this language and imagery in ways that illuminate relations of power and acts of resistance is a valuable resource. Spontaneous events and staged performances, both individual and collective, have become integral sites of political action and citizen participation. At the same time, the mass media, increasingly reliant on staged spectacles, has the capacity to trivialize and distort meaningful acts of resistance. The actor faces the very real prospect of having creative resistance effectively manipulated into a media circus performance. Performative action, therefore, is not without its risks and unanticipated consequences.

Agonistic Engagement

In the essay "Homer on Competition," Nietzsche examined the role that creative struggle or contest (*agon*) played in sustaining the cultural health of society in Homer's Greece.[18] The role of the *agon* in the arts, politics, athletics, and rhetoric allowed the Greeks to recognize the importance of man's violent, aggressive, and jealous passions and channel them in a direction that cultivated both individual excellence and overall cultural vitality. Nietzsche admired their Apollonian/Dionysian cultural ethos, rituals, and institutional designs because they affirmed life as an exhilarating tightrope walk between disciplined creative expression and destructive instinctual desires.

Nietzsche admired the Greek *agon* primarily as an aristocratic practice that helped to promote cultural excellence and combat egalitarian

leveling and cultural degeneration. He did not examine the role of agonistics in Greek democracy. It was Hannah Arendt who returned to the
Greek *polis* to illuminate the idea of political action as an agonistic, aesthetic, and virtuosic activity. The importance of agonistic *praxis* in Foucault's thought is traceable primarily to Nietzsche's idea of existential
struggle. Foucault, however, rejected Nietzsche's elitist vision of building a heroic culture and a great politics. He was concerned with the role
of agonistic engagement in furthering resistance, freedom, and everyday
plebian struggles. Leslie Paul Thiele captured both the role of agonistic
praxis in Foucault's thought and his relationship to Nietzsche when he
wrote:

> Nietzsche's struggle to order his soul led him to disdain and depreciate
> politics. Foucault opted for its proliferation. In short, Foucault politi-
> cized what Nietzsche had internalized: the will to struggle.[19]

The will to struggle has always been an integral feature of both politics and democracy. That is why democracy has so often been opposed,
contained, domesticated, checked and balanced, and redescribed throughout much of human history. The ancient Greeks are romanticized as the
founders of Western democracy, but their model is rejected. The tradition of Western political theory was founded in opposition to democracy, as was the American constitutional republic. Agonistic democracy
is therefore dismissed as an impractical model of government.

Agonistic practices and mechanisms have been a part of modern liberal democratic government. One can view political campaigns, elections, interest group competition, political debates, our adversarial legal
system, public protest, and civil disobedience as agonistic features of contemporary democratic governance. Yet while conflict is part of all of these
features of modern governance, it is regarded as a "necessary evil" that
must be overcome through greater and more positive appeals to order,
consensus, bargaining, and compromise. The emphasis is placed on the
resolution of conflict, the reconciliation of differences, and more comprehensive solutions. Political agonistics is something to be managed and
effectively overcome. The goal of a proper functioning politics, democracy, and government is not agonistic *praxis*.

For Foucault, agonistic engagement was the key to a healthy culture,
self, philosophy, and politics. The interconnection that Foucault said
existed between self-fashioning and agonistic engagement resulted in
his understanding of politics as creative struggle. To live a life without

struggle is to live a passive existence, to not experience freedom, and thus to not experience self-creation. It is to conform to existing power relations, or to re-form them in the interest of a greater consensus, stability, identity, community, or humanity. To make creative struggle the core of one's sense of self is to both experience moments of creative individuality and to contest the ongoing accumulation and disciplinary deployment of power and government.

If struggle creates the conditions for freedom, then the exercise of freedom illuminates the prospects for democracy. Democracy is the condition in which self-creation (freedom) is made possible for ordinary people. At the same time, democratic action occurs within the framework of modern power relations and technologies of governance. Government is the condition by which power relations discipline and control freedom. Democracy is thus the condition of freedom among others, in which power relations and existing governance are challenged.

As a strategy of creative struggle, agonistic *praxis* is also distinguished by the norm of democratic inclusiveness, even though the active contesting of normative standards is integral to agonistic democracy.[20] The agonistic contest is open to all participants who struggle to enhance the demos. No discourse, action, or identity is excluded if it seeks to test the limits of power and government, truth and subjectivity. If it seeks to deny the voice of different perspectives to destroy other contestants, or to achieve overall domination, then it reveals itself as a strategy of nondemocratic exclusion. In the face of this challenge, a *demos* would be forged to counter this threat. There are no guarantees that this particular demos would survive this threat. What would survive, however, is the ethos of the democratic questioning of all aspects of human existence.

Parrhesia

One of the last topics that Foucault lectured on at the University of California at Berkeley in 1983 and at the College de France in March of 1984 was the ancient Greek idea and practice of *parrhesia*, or "frank speech."[21] His research focused on *parrhesia* as a philosophical strategy of "truth-telling" developed by Socrates, the Cynics, and the Stoics. Foucault preferred the Cynic strategy, which radicalized the Socratic ethic to confront truth claims in a highly personal and political manner, rather than through the logic of the dialectic method. The Cynic "game of truth" involved contempt for theoretical knowledge, minimalist simplicity, the scandalous flouting of conventions, agonistic debate, critical preaching to large public audiences, and confronting tyrants and mobs.[22] In searching for a model of the philosophic life, Foucault found his exemplar not in Seneca or Socrates, but in Diogenes.[23]

Yet *parrhesia* was as much an integral feature of ancient Athenian culture and democracy as it was a philosophical strategy.[24] The idea of *parrhesia* emerged in ancient Athens during the fifth century B.C. after the democratic reforms of Cleisthenes. Frank speech, or speaking one's mind, was an important feature of daily life in the *agora,* in the Assembly, in friendships, in the theater (especially comedy), and in rhetoric. It combined confrontational criticism with a claim to be telling the truth. This was not necessarily an appeal to a transcendent, absolute Truth, but rather meant that the speaker held a strong and sincere view of reality that he believed needed to be spoken in public. There was also an element of risk in this kind of outspoken activity because *parrhesia* involved a direct confrontation with popular views, authority figures, and dominant regimes of truth. The speaker risked humiliation, fines, ostracism, and in some cases death.

Parrhesia was also associated with the common man. It was direct and unadorned speech, often contrasted with flattery and expert oratory. *Parrhesia* was synonomous with plain sentiments, straightforward honesty, and personal integrity. It was employed by ordinary citizens in Assembly debates to counter the sophisticated techniques, flowery discourse, and clever logistics of those citizens schooled in the arts of rhetoric. *Parrhesia* appeared in Euripides' plays. Of all the Greek playwrights, he had the most to say about the frank speech of common men and women. Euripides employed the language of the ordinary people, praised egalitarian democracy, and criticized aristocratic life.

Foucault was interested in reinventing *parrhesia* under present-day conditions and contrasted it with the modern liberal right of "free speech."[25] He defined the parrhesiatic act in terms of two key features: the opening up of a new space of freedom and the transformation of the individual speaker. For Foucault, *parrhesia* involved confronting someone of authority or elite social status with an unpleasant truth. This truth both erupted and disrupted public life. It opened up a space of freedom occupied by a stark revelation whose impact went far beyond its specific target. Thus one put oneself at risk not only by challenging a powerful individual or power structure, but also by potentially alienating larger groups of people. A direct moral confrontation with both elites and the mass public carried with it an unpredictable reaction.

Yet in putting oneself on the line, by entering the fray and risking a fight, one experienced a rare episode of freedom that had the potential to be a life-altering event. The act of *parrhesia* placed one on the public stage, a stage where the course of future events could not be determined. The unintended consequences of one's action could propel one in an unanticipated direction. One entered a turbulent environment of power. One's very being was subject to this flux. Thus one's self-identity was at stake.

Foucault did not associate freedom with the modern liberal doctrine of individual rights. He believed that the complexity and experience of power/freedom could not be fully accommodated by a rights-based approach. He criticized liberalism because it lacked a politics of the self and failed to grasp the operation of power. He maintained that legal rights do not provide us with a good defense against the workings of disciplinary power. As John Ransom puts it, rights "tend to formalize and legitimate yesterday's battle lines at the expense of the search for new frontiers."[26] Furthermore, while rights are "presented as covering the whole ground of human freedom," they "represent only a thin strip of human experience."[27]

Foucault did not maintain that human rights should be disposed of. For people to experience freedom and democracy, there must be agreements and guarantees about the configuration of personal and public space. Yet rights need to be redescribed. They need to be understood as conventional agreements on spatial relations that reflect negotiated power settlements. Liberal legalists construct space as a neutral, stable, and legally demarcated ground of negative and positive freedom. Foucauldian space is the product of power dynamics that cannot be easily contained, stabilized, or juridically demarcated. Liberal liberty, both negative and positive, seeks to displace contingency, ambiguity, and conflict. Foucauldian freedom does the exact opposite. It is about the struggle for self-creation within a complex mosaic of public and private hybrid spaces. Furthermore, freedom is more about our trangressive obligations than about our protective rights.

Lawrence Hatab has defined rights "as functional and practical relationships that are conferred upon human beings in the social order, and not as something 'natural,' as individual possessions that stem from certain truths about human beings."[28] We should therefore speak of 'civil rights' as those guarantees necessary for the operation of a democratic culture, society, and polity. And we should speak of 'existential rights' as "includ[ing] pursuits and settings that are distinct or separate from political practice, and that therefore are to be protected from politics, in the sense of restricting governmental power and interference in citizens' lives."[29] Rights should also be understood as the manifestation of conflictual power relations. Thus rights claims will always be in conflict. Hatab's recommendation is that we adopt "a more pragmatic and contextual approach" and employ a "nondogmatic method of 'ad hoc interest balancing' when it comes to the enactment of rights."[30]

In this sense we are back to Nietzsche's definition of rights as "recognized and guaranteed degrees of power."[31] Foucault would have agreed with this definition. He would have further defined rights as a governmental product. That is, rights are part of the apparatus of modern governmentality. Foucault would have agreed with those who contend that rights are integral to modern governance. Yet he would have added that freedom is integral to the art of self-care and the practice of self-creation. I would conclude that while rights are indeed integral to democratic governance, freedom is integral to the *demos*.

Local Resistance

Consistent with his understanding of the workings of modern and contemporary power and the resistance within power configurations, Foucault called upon us to "turn away from all projects that claim to be global or radical."[32] Power networks should be contested through local struggles oriented toward "very specific transformations."[33] Strategies of humanist liberation, seeking control over the state or capitalism, and mobilizing mass emancipatory movements were not the focus of Foucault's oppositional politics. He regarded grand plans for revolution and radical change as largely counterproductive. Too often, he said, they have "only led to the return of the most dangerous traditions."[34]

Foucault politicized everyday life and advocated appropriate local and microlevel strategies of resistance. Local struggles are the manifestation of communities of revolt, resistance, and democratic action that crystallize at specific nodal points in power networks. That is why Foucault could not specify the form that communities would take. They would be forged in response to particular correlations of power relations.

Resistance is specific to the "we" formed at a particular time-space-power conjuncture and around a specific issue. Struggles over clean water, toxic waste sites, endangered species, depressed neighborhoods, business fraud, domestic violence, and many other issues shape the politics of local resistance. The "we" that is constructed around these diverse issues can neither be predicted nor necessarily sustained. The voices of local resistance are the product of multiple subjects and narratives that intersect relative to specific power/issue formations.

This reflects the dynamics of our late modern/postmodern transition. It has produced a new postmodern layer of associational life. It is a complex, multilayered network of diverse social and cultural spaces. The construction of local communities of resistance occurs within this context. Just as the self is the product of plural narratives reflexively organized into a relational unity, local resistance communities are the product of plural narratives forged into civic associational identities by particular power/issue formations.

The result is a postmodern civic pluralism that exhibits both associational and agonistic features. Many of us are involved in multiple and overlapping social, workplace, and civic settings and associations. Local associational networks carry out the ordinary day-to-day activities that sustain our civic infrastructure. They often involve voluntary cooperation in the midst of cultural difference. Cooperation in local ventures, designed to build stronger social and civic networks that promote voluntary action, self-governance, and mutual aid, takes place despite the diversity of individual and group identities and interests. Yet this civic associational dynamic is forged in reaction to a particular power/issue formation that fuels a spirit of resistance. In other words, many civic associations operating are the product of specific power/resistance formations.

Strategies of Democracy

The strategies profiled here were endorsed by Foucault as types of human agency that could contest the normalizing effects of disciplinary governance. He believed that we could modify power/knowledge regimes to create spaces of freedom and thereby exercise some creative control over our lives. I contend that these primarily defensive strategies of resistance can also be employed as more affirmative strategies of democratic action if they are implemented at the local and microlevels, which is what they were designed for. We can alter the rules of existing power games if we learn how complex power networks operate and apply our strategies at appropriate points or junctures in the system.

Yet at the same time we must acknowledge the risks and limitations of a local strategic approach to democracy. A strategic approach tends to define democracy largely in terms of the art of war. The focus is on favorable positionings, planning movements, devising tactics, and disorganizing and demoralizing one's enemies. While this is an important feature of politics and the practice of democracy, politics and democracy are not exclusively about means. They are equally about ends and conditions. In short, strategies are not enough: what is needed is an ethos of democracy. An ethical sensibility and ethical types of relationships need to be articulated, and the conditions required to nurture and sustain this way of life must be created. This is different from a teleology, a set of goals that takes on the character of a developmental sequence or unfolding process moving toward an identified and justified end point.

Furthermore, Foucault's focus on the local and his suspicion of the global as the context for both interpretation and action should be recast in favor of the "glocal." The image of global power frameworks being resisted by local strategies and practices should be replaced by a more updated image of the complex interplay between global and local forces and practices. Major technological innovations such as the Internet have dissolved time-space distances and reconfigured economic, social, cultural, and political relationships so that events are shaped and changes occur at the point where global power frameworks and local circumstances intersect. Therefore, the portrait painted by Foucault of power/knowledge and resistance in terms of a global-local opposition should be reconceived as a glocal dialectical dynamic. We can retain Foucault's emphasis on the context or positionality of power, knowledge, subjectivity, and action, yet we should phrase this in terms of glocality rather than locality.

The Challenge of a Critical Postmodern Democratic Politics

The idea of a critical postmodern democratic politics is different from that of a modern democratic politics. It does not appeal to a universal human nature, free will, natural rights, individualism, a common good, egalitarian justice, rational consensus, electoral representation, or emancipatory action. It appeals to a different constellation of ideas and practices. They include grasping our social condition as a late modern/postmodern transition of complex glocality, articulating the need for a perspectival pluralism, defining freedom in terms of creative engagement, revisioning civil society as a postmodern associational space, shifting from a work to a leisure ethic, and focusing on local and microlevel strategies of resistance and adaptation to government.

In the course of presenting the case for critical postmodernism and democracy, I have examined the ideas of a late modern/postmodern transition, complex glocality, a perspectival pluralism, freedom as creative engagement, and local and microlevel democratic strategies. Yet revisioning civil society as a postmodern associational space and shifting from a work to a leisure ethic require further explanation.

Civil society has become a complex network of diverse and overlapping social spaces more local and global, culturally pluralized, and associational. It is an archipelago of those human activities of work, recreation, consumption, intimacy, and civic life that intersect, recombine, and reconnect in faster and more complex ways. Therefore, civil society should be conceived less as a communitarian space of "civic virtue" or a deliberative "public sphere" and more as a postmodern space of diverse sociocultural identities linked by multiple networks of work, recreation, consumption, intimacy, sociality, and civic association.

In this postmodern milieu, new types of individual and collective behaviors have emerged. They are shaped by greater global/local references and commitments, the cultivation of specific lifestyles, mass media, imaginary taste communities, recreational consumption, and a more pluralized and transitory associational environment. We are more individualistic, more tribal, and more massified. That is, we are highly focused on our own selves and the pursuit of distinct lifestyles. At the same time, we are members of microsocial affinity groups that share similar lifestyles. These "neo-tribes" include youth subcultures, hobbyists, sports enthusiasts, restaurant and night-club regulars, TV show fans, and Internet discussion groups.[35] Yet at the same time, we share a common "imaginary" world of global popular culture provided by our mass media and consumer industries.

This complex, multilayered, postmodern social realm is still driven by a compulsive work/consumption ethic. And this is the challenge we face. It involves moving beyond this ethic toward that of a more leisured civic ethos. This in turn requires a revaluation of the activities of work or labor, recreation, consumption, intimacy, civic engagement, and leisure.

"Work" is an invention of modern Protestant-capitalist culture. It was forged out of the connection established between one's salvation ("calling") and the disciplined, dutiful pursuit of mundane worldly tasks ("labor"). This Puritan ethic was economically rationalized into a male social role bound up with one's identity as a member of a paid labor force and workplace community. Modern capitalism also separated "work time" as an economic activity from "recreation" or "pastime."[36] "Consumption" is the ethos of a mature capitalism driven by the logic of consumerism or recreation turned into consumption. Yet work continues to be the central defining and disciplinary norm of our society. It determines how we organize and give meaning to our nonwork time. We work hard to recreate and consume.

Today, high-tech, fast-paced, productive consumption is rapidly consuming time and space itself. We live in a world where time rushes forward in advance of itself, pulled along by the accelerating forces of complexity, variety, novelty, and opportunity. Freedom, leisure, and a rich associational life seem to elude most of us. Technology and expert systems are advertised as the means by which we can experience more freedom, more leisure, and more meaningful relationships with others. Yet this is not to be. We are baffled, frustrated, and driven. Productive power networks demand more of our time and energy, and at the same time promise us even greater rewards in the future. We are both disciplined and seduced. The future never becomes the present. Yet if we are to experience a democratic culture that is critically postmodern, the conditions of freedom, leisure, and a rich associational life must be in place and in play.

The most difficult change we face is cultural and deep seated. We need to reorient our "free time" away from complete immersion in the seductive and addictive world of modern (commodity acquisition) and postmodern (simulated pleasure) consumption. This is the world of television watching, shopping malls, blockbuster movies, fast food, video gaming, Internet surfing, fantasy theme parks, and credit card debt. Despite all the talk of consumer choice, diversity, and synergy, this world is one-dimensional. What is needed is a revaluation of "the American Dream" (which has become globalized) from a story about ordinary people striving for fast-track material success, comfortable conformity, and cultural adolescence ("the pursuit of happiness") to a story about ordinary people striving for leisure time to cultivate creative engagement ("the pursuit of freedom").

This cultural shift seeks to replace "recreational consumption" with "free leisure time" as the critical value that guides our lives. Leisure needs to be distinguished from work (one's occupation), recreational consumption, and amusement (childlike play). It is neither production nor consumption. It is creation. Leisure is the condition of creative agency. It is free time for cultural creation, the cultivation of the mind and the body, intimate relations, meditation, civic association, critical agonistics, and serious play.[37] The pursuit of leisure thus requires a revaluation of values. Yet it must also be accompanied by alterations in the power networks and structures of everyday life. An infrastructure needs to be created and sustained by which people can gain the experience, confidence, and skills needed to make the transition from a predominantly work-consumer culture to a more civic-leisure culture.

Several reforms should be considered to facilitate this transition. Among those would be the active promotion of the "living wage" movement, with the goal of instituting minimum wage laws at the municipal level higher than the federal minimum wage. A negative income tax (NIT) could become part of the income tax system. A certain level of income would be designated as a basic guaranteed annual income (GAI) and those households that fell below this level would receive a positive income transfer from the government.[38] Steps should also be taken to reduce the standard work week from five days and forty hours to four days and thirty-two hours.[39]

Both health care and child care should be elevated to the same level as Social Security; that is, they should become universal entitlement programs that include flexible options, such as vouchers for purchasing private care and tax credits for home caretaking. A college education should be tuition-free if a very good to excellent grade level is maintained, and "leisure studies" as well as "civic service" should be integrated into the core curriculum. The idea of "retirement" also requires radical rethinking. Indeed, it should be replaced by the idea of leisure. A new model of life planning should be promoted that strives to integrate work, recreation, leisure, civic, and private time all along an individual's lifespan and this model should be guided by an ethos of lifelong learning and an openness to threshold experiences.

We must also confront the power of the transnational corporation and its neofeudal vision of a universal capitalist commonwealth.[40] Corporate capitalist governmentalities today exert enormous influence over weakened national governments, international institutions, highly disciplined workers, and seduced consumers. Their reach is both global and personal. They have adopted the strategies of "reengineering," "lean production," "downsizing," "outsourcing," "compressed workweeks," and "modular manufacturing" to increase productivity and profitability in a now globally competitive marketplace. Yet these strategies have resulted in an accelerated work pace, greater employee monitoring and survelliance, and a larger contingent workforce of part-time and temporary workers.

Counterstrategies need to be in place and in play to deal with late modern/postmodern corporate capitalism. Workers should continue to do what they have always done, that is, cultivate strategies of workplace resistance. Consumers should cultivate strategies of resistance to corporate advertising propaganda, telemarketing harassment, and the ideology of consumerism. And governmental, worker, consumer, and stakeholder alliances should pressure shareholders and CEOs to implement new corporate governance arrangements. Their model should be that of the "collaborative corporation."[41]

The model of the collaborative corporation is dedicated to expanding democracy within the economic firm. It is based on the strategy of building cooperative, incentive-based relations among owners, managers, shareholders, and workers. Collaborative work arrangements include the following elements: (1) greater worker responsibility and control over their jobs; (2) participation in teams; (3) extensive job training and information sharing; (4) job rotation; (5) flex time; (6) assurances that layoffs will be used as a last resort; (7) health insurance; (8) child-care services; (9) profit-sharing plans; (10) employee stock-ownership plans; (11) greater protections for whistle-blowers; (12) worker representation on the board of directors; and (13) having the firm's board of directors elected by several different stakeholder constituencies, rather than by the shareholders exclusively.

Various strategies of "relocalization" should also be pursued.[42] These include making more capital available to local citizens through community-based banks, the promotion of "buy local" campaigns, establishing local "tool-lending libraries" where people can share agricultural, home repair, and gardening tools and equipment, and fostering both farmers' markets and the Community Supported Agriculture (CSA) movement, which connects consumers directly with local farmers.

These practical proposals for reform do not constitute a programmatic agenda. Rather, they sketch out a perspective of how we might create an infrastructure that allows people more opportunity to pursue democratic lifestyles that value the concrete practices of freedom, civic association, critical agonism, and leisure. More "free time" does not necessarily translate into an ethos whose central values are civic and creative engagement. The reigning culture of compulsive work, consumption, and media spectacle is better positioned to take advantage of people with more time on their hands. Yet at the same time, it is also vulnerable to critique and resistance as the juggernaut of late modern/postmodern American consumerism places more demands on its subjects to keep pace with its machinery of discipline/seduction.

One must also face the reality that these changes will surely require greater entanglement with modern frameworks and relations of power. More governmentalities delivering more goods and services carry with them the risk of entwining us in more disciplinary networks and matrices. In creating conditions that could nurture a more leisured and associational civic culture, we run the risk of trapping ourselves in new disciplinary technologies. On the one hand, we must be prepared to admit that there are many problems that local and microlevel democratic strategies cannot negotiate effectively. On the other hand, we must realize that in undertaking such endeavors, we need to adopt modern governmental strategies and thus face the consequences of operating within their boundaries.

Foucault wrestled with this paradox in his later work on governance and freedom. In the essay "What Is Enlightenment?" he indicated that we need to focus our studies on "the paradox of the relations of capacity and power."[43] We must confront the question, "How can the growth of capabilities be disconnected from the intensification of power relations?"[44] That is, how can we increase our capabilities for freedom in a world where our technological way of doing things carries with it procedures and techniques of social regulation and normalization?

He concluded that in today's world the freedom with which we act is shaped within the boundaries of "practical systems" conveyed by complex technologies.[45] These complex systems determine the rules of the game. Yet we can modify the rules of the game "up to a certain point" by learning how these practical systems operate.[46] Foucault realized that human capacities and relations are inescapably technologized. To escape from technology is a futile project. Therefore, the analysis of techniques and strategies is needed. From this we can better distinguish between technologies and strategies of domination and those of power/freedom. I would also contend that we would reach the conclusion that politics in general and democracy in particular are driven by the necessary tension between governance and resistance, power and freedom.

It is this tension between governance and resistance, and its negotiation in our late modern/postmodern time, that best defines my idea of a critical postmodern democratic politics. It is a democratic politics that will never be hegemonic or part of a mass movement. It does not aspire to be a majoritarian voice "of the people." It does not share the ethos, values, and attitudes of the dominant political culture. Nor does it seek to institutionalize its ethos within the framework of our representative-bureaucratic political system.

Critical postmodern democracy does not locate meaningful politics in the struggle to acquire governmental power. Rather, it aims to create social spaces and networks where creative engagement, civic association, cultural interaction, critical agonistics, and leisure can be more freely experienced. These values and practices largely thrive in the interstices of, and in opposition to, the dominant culture, society, and government. This does not mean that critical postmodern democrats will not participate in modern politics — they will. Yet critical postmodern democrats will always be self-consciously part of a subculture. A critical postmodern democratic culture will always be subaltern.

Conclusion
Negotiating the Late Modern/
Postmodern Transition

> *I tramp a perpetual journey (come listen all!)*
> *My signs are a rain-proof coat, good shoes,*
> *and a staff cut from the woods,*
> *No friend of mine takes his ease in my chair,*
> *I have no chair, no church, no philosophy,*
> *I lead no man to a dinner-table, library, exchange,*
> *But each man and each woman of you I will lead*
> *upon a knoll,*
> *My left hand hooking you round the waist,*
> *My right hand pointing to landscapes of*
> *continents and the public road.*
> *Not I, not any one else can travel that road for you,*
> *You must travel it for yourself.*
> — Walt Whitman, "Song of Myself"

Marx's analysis of modernity in *The Communist Manifesto*, which uses the metaphor "all that is solid melts into air," still rings true today.[1] Ours is a time of ever accelerating high-tech innovations, information accumulation, global time-space compression, cultural effervescence, ecological foreboding, and millenarian temptations. It is a time that offers diverse opportunities for adventure, travel, life stylization, civic involvement, and self-reflection. It is also a time of capitalist creative destruction, neotribalism, terrorism, overpopulation, unprecedented human migration, imploding selves, environmental risks, and instantaneous bread and circuses. It is a time whose mood is both heavy and light. Whether one characterizes this mood as bearable or unbearable depends on one's location in all of this, as well as one's sense of self.

Our time is also a transitional one, a passage from one set of circumstances to another. In the many ways described and analyzed in this study, our present condition is both modern and postmodern. It is indeed late modern/postmodern. To be modern is to be rational, humanistic, progressive, and reformist. To be postmodern is to be skeptical, perspectivist, presentist, and ironic. To be critically postmodern is to see the present as a more complex and precarious intertwinement of late modern and postmodern features and forces pulling us in different directions. Perceived in this way, we can better appreciate the complexity and contingency that defines our tensional and transitional time and negotiate our way accordingly.

Yet if the nature of our present is transitional, then what lies beyond postmodernity? This we cannot know for sure, as it should be. Yet the temptation to know the future remains strong. For is not the modern imperative bound up with controlling the future? To resist this temptation, to embrace the present and negotiate its fortunes in a lighthearted manner is to embrace a postmodern sensibility. Yet can't we steer a more prudent course between these two extremes — between the modern cognitive compulsion to control the future and the postmodern aesthetic disposition to enjoy the present? Is there not a sensibility worthy of cultivation that lies somewhere between compulsive purposiveness and anxiety-free play?

This is how a good Aristotelian would negotiate our late modern/postmodern transition. We should seek a moderate course between two extremes. We should locate the mean and cultivate practical wisdom (*phronesis*) and temperance (*sophrosune*). Foucault, however, would urge us to ride the tension between modernity and postmodernity. The transgressive testing of these modalities and moods is more in keeping with Foucault's critical ethos and understanding of the lived practice of freedom.

I conclude that Michel de Montaigne's Renaissance skepticism is best suited for our late modern/postmodern time. What I mean is a kind of critical postmodern modesty. In Montaigne's *Essays* one encounters a skeptical tolerance in a transitional time of conflict and intolerance, a sixteenth-century Europe torn apart by the theological-political wars between Protestants and Catholics.[2] His skepticism combined a mood of doubt with a pragmatic experimental approach to the art of daily living. The portrait that he painted of himself in his *Essays,* journals, and letters exemplifies Foucault's ethic of self-care. Both implicit and explicit in the writings and disposition of Montaigne are certain Renaissance ideals that have been reinvented by our postmodern sensibility and its critical postmodern offspring. Among these are an affirmative skepticism linked to lifestyle experimentation, an appeal to local practical knowledge, a pragmatic (from the Greek word *pragma,* meaning act or deed) conception of truth, and the cultivation of an unpremeditated philosophical outlook on life.

Montaigne's affirmative skepticism was a prudent response to a time of dogmatism and fanaticism, as was his preference for private over public life. Doubt was the best means in the pursuit of happiness. It was the antidote to the dangerous excesses of the rational mind, the clever trickster that causes us to rise above all other animals in the fervent pursuit of solutions to our self-imposed riddles of the universe. With Montaigne's modest doubt comes the positive affirmation of the experience of living. With modest doubt comes tolerance and civility. With modest doubt comes "the heightened awareness of insistent variety."[3]

Noel O'Sullivan asks us to consider the idea of a postmodern philosophy of modesty. Consider the postmodern self as "a wholly unpretentious character."[4] "The main feature of this deconstructed creature is, as has been noticed, its sense of contingency."[5] At the turn of the twenty-first century, "postmodernism marks the final abandonment of the yearning for a cosmic setting, and the contingency of existence is accepted as part of the natural order of human life."[6] The modesty of the postmodern self can be found in its acceptance of a decentered existence, in its rejection of absolute and universalist foundations, in its perspectivism, and its location of the sublime in the daily details of living. Above all, concludes O'Sullivan, "the only solid basis for moral and political thought now available is one which rests on a concept of self-limitation, and simultaneously acknowledges that the self in question is a specifically Western self, rather than man as such."[7]

Marx's famous eleventh thesis on Feuerbach calls on us not only to interpret the world, but to change it.[8] There is much debate today concerning whether or not it is the task of Homo sapiens to shape the course of events human and nonhuman. I would assert that it is surely our fate to illuminate and intervene in the stuff of this world. Therefore, Lenin's famous political question "What is to be done?" continues to be relevant.[9] Critical postmodern thinkers should acknowledge this. Yet how do we

answer Lenin's compelling question? I would submit that all human ideologies, teleologies, revolutionary practices, and detailed blueprints designed to change the world should be given strict scrutiny.

Our late modern/postmodern condition is best negotiated by cultivating a critical postmodern sensibility. It is an ethos that generates a
modest skepticism toward things. It further calls upon us to rethink the
meaning of human freedom and association, how we relate our experience of self-identity to the experience of others, both human and nonhuman. And it should continuously remind us that a democratic existence
is concerned first and foremost with the struggles of ordinary people to
create a free way of life.

Montaigne wrote that on reflecting upon the human condition, the
ancient Greek philosopher Democritus "never went out in public but
with a mocking and laughing face," while his contemporary Heraclitus
"wore a face perpetually sad, and eyes filled with tears."[10] He preferred
the disposition of Democritus. Montaigne's studies of himself, others,
and the nature of his present led him to the following conclusion: "Our
own specific property is to be equally laughable and able to laugh."[11]

Notes

Introduction

1. Immanuel Kant, "An Answer to the Question: 'What Is Enlightenment?' " in *Kant: Political Writings,* ed. Hans Reiss and trans. H. B. Nisbet (Cambridge: Cambridge University Press, 1991), 54–60.

1. The Modern-Postmodern Debate and Its Legacy

1. The idea of an "Enlightenment project" is not a single, unitary entity. It refers instead to a constellation of thinkers, ideas, and social and political doctrines that emerged and interacted during the eighteenth century to give shape to a modern worldview committed to rational humanism. It has been invoked in the past few decades as the key pivot of the modern-postmodern debate. See Peter Gay's social history of the European Enlightenment in *The Enlightenment: The Science of Freedom* (New York and London: W. W. Norton, 1977). See also John Gray, *Enlightenment's Wake: Politics and Culture at the Close of the Modern Age* (New York and London: Routledge, 1995); Dorina Outram, *The Enlightenment* (Cambridge: Cambridge University Press, 1995); and James Schmidt, ed., *What Is Enlightenment? Eighteenth-Century Answers and Twentieth-Century Questions* (Berkeley and Los Angeles: University of California Press, 1996).

2. On the competing conceptions of modernity and postmodernity, see Bryan S. Turner, ed., *Theories of Modernity and Postmodernity* (London: Sage Publications, 1990); and Peter Brooker, ed., *Modernism/Postmodernism* (New York and London: Longman, 1992).

3. See Stanley Trachtenberg, ed., *The Postmodern Moment: A Handbook of Contemporary Innovation in the Arts* (Westport, Conn.: Greenwood Press, 1985); Andreas Huyssen, *After the Great Divide: Modernism, Mass Culture, and Postmodernism* (Bloomington: Indiana University Press, 1986); Silvio Gaggi, *Modern/Postmodern: A Study in Twentieth-Century Arts and Ideas* (Philadelphia: University of Pennsylvania

Press, 1989); and Paul Crowther, *Critical Aesthetics and Postmodernism* (Oxford: Clarendon Press, 1993).

4. Charles Jencks, *The Language of Post-Modern Architecture* (New York: Pantheon, 1977); *Late-Modern Architecture and Other Essays* (New York: Rizzoli, 1980); *What Is Post-Modernism?* (New York: St. Martin's Press, 1990); and *Post-Modern Triumphs in London* (New York: St. Martin's Press, 1991). See also Heinrich Klotz, *The History of Postmodern Architecture*, trans. Radka Donnell (Cambridge: MIT Press, 1988).

5. See Ihab Hassan, *The Dismemberment of Orpheus: Toward a Postmodern Literature* (New York: Oxford University Press, 1971); "The Culture of Postmodernism," *Theory, Culture, and Society* 2, no. 3 (1985): 119–31; and *The Postmodern Turn: Essays in Postmodern Theory and Culture* (Columbus: Ohio State University Press, 1987).

6. See Mark Poster, *Existentialist Marxism in Postwar France: From Sartre to Althusser* (Princeton: Princeton University Press, 1975); Vincent Descombes, *Modern French Philosophy*, trans. L. Scott-Fox and J. M. Harding (Cambridge: Cambridge University Press, 1980); and Luc Ferry and Alain Renaut, *French Philosophy of the Sixties: An Essay on Antihumanism*, trans. Mary H. S. Cattani (Amherst: University of Massachusetts Press, 1990).

7. Ferdinand de Saussure, *Course in General Linguistics*, trans. Wade Baskin (New York: McGraw-Hill, 1966).

8. On structuralist thought and the structuralist movement, see Fredric Jameson, *The Prison-House of Language: A Critical Account of Structuralism and Russian Formalism* (Princeton: Princeton University Press, 1972); Edith Kurzweil, *The Age of Structuralism: Lévi-Strauss to Foucault* (New York: Columbia University Press, 1980); and John Fekete, ed., *The Structural Allegory: Reconstructive Encounters with the New French Thought* (Minneapolis: University of Minnesota Press, 1984).

9. See Peter Dews, *Logics of Disintegration: Post-Structuralist Thought and the Claims of Critical Theory* (London: Verso, 1987); Richard Harland, *Superstructuralism: The Philosophy of Structuralism and Post-Structuralism* (London and New York: Methuen, 1987); and Manfred Frank, *What Is Neo-Structuralism?* (Minneapolis: University of Minnesota Press, 1989).

10. See Scott Lash, ed., *Post-Structuralist and Post-Modernist Sociology* (Northampton, Mass.: Elgar Publishing, 1991).

11. See Georges Bataille, *Visions of Excess* (Minneapolis: University of Minnesota Press, 1985); and *The Accursed Share*, 3 vols., trans. Robert Hurley (New York: Zone Books, 1991). See also Susan Sontag, "The Pornographic Imagination," in *Styles of Radical Will* (New York: Farrar, Straus and Giroux, 1966); Michel Foucault, "A Preface to Transgression," in *Language, Counter-Memory, Practice: Selected Essays and Interviews* (Ithaca: Cornell University Press, 1977); Jacques Derrida, "From Restricted to General Economy: A Hegelianism without Reserve," in *Writing and Difference* (Chicago: University of Chicago Press, 1978), 251–77; and Shadia B.

Drury, "Bataille's Revolt," chap. 8 in *Alexandre Kojeve: The Roots of Postmodern Politics* (New York: St. Martin's Press, 1994), 103–23.

12. Gilles Deleuze, *Nietzsche and Philosophy,* trans. Hugh Tomlinson (New York: Columbia University Press, 1983).

13. See Gilles Deleuze and Felix Guattari, *Anti-Oedipus: Capitalism and Schizophrenia,* trans. Robert Hurley, Mark Seem, and Helen R. Lane (Minneapolis: University of Minnesota Press, 1983).

14. See Bill Readings, *Introducing Lyotard: Art and Politics* (London and New York: Routledge, 1991).

15. Jacques Derrida, "Structure, Sign, and Play in the Discourse of the Human Sciences," in *Writing and Difference,* trans. Alan Bass (Chicago: University of Chicago Press, 1978), 278–93.

16. For an explanation of the theoretical and interpretive strategy of deconstruction, see Rodolphe Gasché, "Deconstruction as Criticism," chap. 1 in *Inventions of Difference: On Jacques Derrida* (Cambridge: Harvard University Press, 1994), 22–57.

17. Jacques Derrida, "Différance," in *Margins of Philosophy,* trans. Alan Bass (Chicago: University of Chicago Press, 1982), 1–27. Also by Derrida, *Positions,* trans. Alan Bass (Chicago: University of Chicago Press), 37–96.

18. See Derrida, "Violence and Metaphysics: An Essay on the Thought of Emmanuel Levinas," in *Writing and Difference,* 79–153.

19. On the implications of Derridean deconstruction for social and political theory, see Catherine Zuckert, "The Politics of Derridean Deconstruction," in *Polity* 23, no. 3 (spring 1991): 335–56; Bill Martin, *Matrix and Line: Derrida and the Possibilities of Postmodern Social Theory* (Albany: State University of New York Press, 1992); and Richard Beardsworth, *Derrida and the Political* (London and New York: Routledge, 1996).

20. See Michel Foucault's first major works: *Madness and Civilization: A History of Insanity in the Age of Reason,* trans. Richard Howard (New York: Random House, 1965); *The Birth of the Clinic: An Archaeology of Medical Perception,* trans. A. M. Sheridan Smith (New York: Pantheon Books, 1973); and *The Order of Things: An Archaeology of the Human Sciences* (New York: Vintage Books, 1973).

21. Foucault, "The Human Sciences," chap. 10 in *The Order of Things,* 386–87.

22. Jane Flax, "Postmodernism and Gender Relations in Feminist Theory," *Signs: Journal of Women in Culture and Society* 12, no. 4 (1987): 621–43.

23. Daniel Bell, *The Cultural Contradictions of Capitalism* (New York: Basic Books, 1976).

24. For historical and theoretical treatments of Frankfurt School critical theory and its theorists, see Martin Jay, *The Dialectical Imagination* (Boston: Little, Brown and Company, 1973); Zoltan Tar, *The Frankfurt School* (New York and London: John Wiley and Sons, 1977); Seyla Benhabib, *Critique, Norm, and Utopia* (New York: Columbia University Press, 1986); and Douglas Kellner, *Critical Theory, Marxism, and Modernity* (Baltimore: Johns Hopkins University Press, 1989).

25. On the thought of Jürgen Habermas, see Thomas McCarthy, *The Critical Theory of Jürgen Habermas* (Cambridge and London: MIT Press, 1978); *Habermas and Modernity,* ed. Richard Bernstein (Cambridge: MIT Press, 1985); David Ingram, *Habermas and the Dialectic of Reason* (New Haven: Yale University Press, 1987); David M. Rasmussen, *Reading Habermas* (Oxford: Basil Blackwell, 1990); and Stephen K. White, ed., *The Cambridge Companion to Habermas* (New York: Cambridge University Press, 1995).

26. See Jürgen Habermas, "Three Perspectives: Left Hegelians, Right Hegelians, and Nietzsche," in *The Philosophical Discourse of Modernity: Twelve Lectures,* trans. Frederick Lawrence (Cambridge: MIT Press, 1987), 51–74.

27. See Habermas, "The Entry into Postmodernity: Nietzsche as a Turning Point," in *The Philosophical Discourse of Modernity,* 83–105.

28. See Habermas, "The Undermining of Western Rationalism through the Critique of Metaphysics: Martin Heidegger," in *The Philosophical Discourse of Modernity,* 131–160.

29. See Habermas, "Between Eroticism and General Economics: Georges Bataille" and "The Critique of Reason as the Unmasking of the Human Sciences: Michel Foucault," in *The Philosophical Discourse of Modernity,* 211–65.

30. See David M. Rasmussen, "Reading Habermas: Modernity vs. Postmodernity," chap. 6 in *Reading Habermas* (Oxford: Basil Blackwell, 1990), 94–113.

31. See Habermas, "An Alternative Way Out of the Philosophy of the Subject: Communicative Versus Subject-Centered Reason," in *The Philosophical Discourse of Modernity,* 294–326.

32. Jürgen Habermas, "What Is Universal Pragmatics?" in *Communication and the Evolution of Society,* trans. Thomas McCarthy (Boston: Beacon Press, 1979), 1–68.

33. See Habermas's essays in *Moral Consciousness and Communicative Action,* trans. Christian Lenhardt and Shierry Weber Nicholsen (Cambridge: MIT Press, 1990); and *Justification and Application: Remarks on Discourse Ethics,* trans. Ciaran Cronin (Cambridge: MIT Press, 1993).

34. See Simone Chambers, "Proceduralism without Metaphysics," part 1 in *Reasonable Democracy: Jürgen Habermas and the Politics of Discourse* (Ithaca: Cornell University Press, 1996), 17–56; and "Discourse and Modernity," part 3 in ibid., 109–52.

35. Habermas developed his sociological analysis of crisis tendencies in advanced capitalism in *Legitimation Crisis,* trans. Thomas McCarthy (Boston: Beacon Press, 1975).

36. Ernesto Laclau and Chantal Mouffe, introduction to *Hegemony and Socialist Strategy: Towards a Radical Democratic Politics* (London: Verso, 1985), 1–5.

37. Their genealogy of the concept of hegemony, traced from Rosa Luxemburg to "the Gramscian watershed," is presented in chapters 1 and 2 of *Hegemony and Socialist Strategy.*

38. "Hegemony and Radical Democracy," chap. 4 in ibid., 149–94.

39. "Beyond the Positivity of the Social: Antagonisms and Hegemony," chap. 3 in ibid., 93–97, 105–14.

40. William E. Connolly, *Political Theory and Modernity* (Oxford: Basil Blackwell, 1993). See especially chapter 1, "The Order of Modernity," and "Modernity, Territorial Democracy, and the Problem of Evil," epilogue to the 1993 edition.

41. See Connolly's essays in *Identity\Difference: Democratic Negotiations of Political Paradox* (Ithaca: Cornell University Press, 1991).

42. See Richard Rorty, introduction to *Contingency, Irony, and Solidarity* (Cambridge: Cambridge University Press, 1989), xiii–xvi.

43. Ibid., 53.

44. "Private Irony and Liberal Hope," chap. 4 in ibid., 73–95.

45. "Self-Creation and Affiliation: Proust, Nietzsche, and Heidegger," chap. 5 in ibid., 96–121.

46. "The Last Intellectual in Europe: Orwell on Cruelty," chap. 8 in ibid., 169–88.

47. See Rosemarie Tong, "Postmodern Feminism," chap. 8 in *Feminist Thought: A Comprehensive Introduction* (Boulder: Westview Press, 1989); Linda J. Nicholson, ed., *Feminism/Postmodernism* (New York and London: Routledge, 1990); and Judith Butler and Joan W. Scott, *Feminists Theorize the Political* (New York and London: Routledge, 1992); and Margaret Ferguson and Jennifer Wicke, eds., *Feminism and Postmodernism* (Durham, N.C.: Duke University Press, 1994).

48. Luce Irigaray, *Speculum of the Other Woman,* trans. Gillian C. Gill (Ithaca: Cornell University Press, 1985); and *This Sex Which Is Not One,* trans. Catherine Porter with Carolyn Burke (Ithaca: Cornell University Press, 1985).

49. Helene Cixous, "Sorties," in *New French Feminisms,* ed. Elaine Marks and Isabelle de Courtivron (New York: Schocken Books, 1971), 90–98; and "Castration or Decapitation?" *Signs: Journal of Women in Culture and Society* 7, no. 1, (1981): 41–55.

50. Julia Kristeva, *Revolution in Poetic Language,* trans. Margaret Waller (New York: Columbia University Press, 1984). Also see Toril Moi, ed., *The Kristeva Reader* (New York: Columbia University Press, 1986).

51. See Jane Flax, *Thinking Fragments: Psychoanalysis, Feminism, and Postmodernism in the Contemporary West* (Berkeley and Los Angeles: University of California Press, 1990), and *Disputed Subjects: Essays on Psychoanalysis, Politics and Philosophy* (New York and London: Routledge, 1993); Judith Butler, *Gender Trouble: Feminism and the Subversion of Identity* (New York: Routledge, 1990); Susan Hekman, *Gender and Knowledge: Elements of a Postmodern Feminism* (Boston: Northeastern University Press, 1990); Jana Sawicki, *Disciplining Foucault: Feminism, Power, and the Body* (New York and London: Routledge, 1991); and Lois McNay, *Foucault and Feminism* (Boston: Northeastern University Press, 1993).

52. On the influence of Foucault on the second wave of postmodern feminism, see all of the previously cited work as well as Kathy Ferguson, *The Feminist*

Case against Bureaucracy (Philadelphia: Temple University Press, 1984); Irene Diamond and Lee Quinby, eds., *Feminism and Foucault: Reflections on Resistance* (Boston: Northeastern University Press, 1988); and Sandra Lee Bartky, *Femininity and Domination: Studies in the Phenomenology of Oppression* (New York and London: Routledge, 1990).

53. See Douglas Kellner, "Techno-Capitalism," chap. 7 in *Critical Theory, Marxism, and Modernity* (Baltimore: Johns Hopkins University Press, 1989), 176–203; and "Theory and Practice: The Politics of Critical Theory," chap. 8 in ibid., 204–33.

54. Steven Best and Douglas Kellner, *Postmodern Theory: Critical Interrogations* (New York: Guilford Press, 1991), 257.

55. Ibid., 261.

56. Ibid.

57. "Towards the Reconstruction of Critical Social Theory," chap. 8 in ibid., 263–74.

58. Ben Agger, "Postmodernism: Ideology or Critical Theory?" chap. 15 in *The Discourse of Domination: From the Frankfurt School to Postmodernism* (Evanston, Ill.: Northwestern University Press, 1992), 278–306; and *Fast Capitalism: A Critical Theory of Significance* (Urbana: University of Illinois Press, 1989).

59. Michael E. Zimmerman, *Contesting Earth's Future: Radical Ecology and Postmodernity* (Berkeley and Los Angeles: University of California Press, 1994), 16.

60. Ibid., 91.

2. A Society in Transition

1. On the debate between modern and postmodern sociological theory, see Steven Seidman, ed., *The Postmodern Turn: New Perspectives in Social Theory* (Cambridge: Cambridge University Press, 1994); David R. Dickens and Andrea Fontana, eds., *Postmodernism and Social Inquiry* (New York: Guilford Press, 1994); Robert Hollinger, *Postmodernism and the Social Sciences: A Thematic Approach* (Thousand Oaks, Calif.: Sage Publications, 1994); and George Pavlich, "Contemplating a Postmodern Sociology: Genealogy, Limits, and Critique," *The Sociological Review* 43, no. 3 (1995): 548–72.

2. I define the modern sociological agenda in terms of four major pursuits: (1) the construction of a foundational theory that provides epistemological justification for social-scientific frameworks of analysis; (2) the theorization of society as a totality; (3) the ongoing refinement of the dialogue between micro (agency) and macro (structure) levels of analysis; and (4) the continued relevance and upgrading of the modernization paradigm.

3. Jean-François Lyotard, "Postmodern Science as the Search for Instabilities," chap. 13 in *The Postmodern Condition: A Report on Knowledge,* trans. Geoff Bennington and Brian Massumi (Minneapolis: University of Minnesota Press, 1984), 53–59; and "Legitimation by Paralogy," chap. 14 in ibid., 60–67. Lyotard's criticism of contemporary science is much closer to Paul Feyerabend than to Thomas Kuhn.

See Richard Rorty, "Habermas and Lyotard on Postmodernity," in *Habermas and Modernity*, ed. Richard J. Bernstein (Cambridge: MIT Press, 1985), 161–75.

4. Ibid., xxiii; and "The Narrative Function and the Legitimation of Knowledge," chap. 8 in ibid., 27–31.

5. "The Nature of the Social Bond: The Postmodern Perspective," chap. 5 in ibid., 14–17.

6. Zygmunt Bauman, *Intimations of Postmodernity* (New York and London: Routledge, 1992), 187–88.

7. "The Re-enchantment of the World; or, How Can One Narrate Postmodernity?" introduction to ibid., vii–xxviii.

8. See "Consumer Society," chap. 2 in *Jean Baudrillard: Selected Writings*, ed. Mark Poster (Stanford: Stanford University Press, 1988), 29–56. Originally published as *La Societe de Consommation* (Paris: Gallimard, 1970).

9. Baudrillard, "The System of Objects," chap. 1 in *Selected Writings*, 10–28. Originally published as *Le Système des Objets* (Paris: Denoel-Gontheir, 1968).

10. Baudrillard, "For a Critique of the Political Economy of the Sign," chap. 3 in *Selected Writings*, 57–97. Originally published as *Pour une Critique de l'Economie Politique du Signe* (Paris: Gallimard, 1972).

11. See Mark Gottdiener, "The System of Objects and the Commodification of Everyday Life: The Early Baudrillard," in *Baudrillard: A Critical Reader*, ed., Douglas Kellner (Oxford: Blackwell, 1994), 25–40.

12. Baudrillard, "Simulacra and Simulations," chap. 7 in *Selected Writings*, 166–84. Originally published as *Simulacres et Simulation* (Paris: Galilee, 1981).

13. Baudrillard, "The Implosion of Meaning in the Media," in *In the Shadow of the Silent Majorities... Or the End of the Social and Other Essays*, trans. Paul Foss, Paul Patton, and John Johnston (New York: Semiotext(e) Inc., 1983), 95–110.

14. See Jean-François Lyotard and Jean-Loup Thebaud, *Just Gaming*, trans. Wlad Godzich (Minneapolis: University of Minnesota Press, 1985).

15. For a more in-depth analysis of Lyotard's postmodern rethinking of justice, judgment, and their interrelationship, see Andrew Benjamin, ed., *Judging Lyotard* (New York and London: Routledge, 1992).

16. Lyotard's fully developed philosophy of justice as difference appears in *The Differend: Phrases in Dispute*, trans. Georges Van Den Abbeele (Minneapolis: University of Minnesota Press, 1988).

17. See Zygmunt Bauman, "On Communitarianism and Human Freedom; Or, How to Square the Circle," *Theory, Culture and Society* 13, no. 2 (May 1996): 79–90.

18. Zygmunt Bauman, "Moral Responsibilities, Ethical Rules," chap. 1 in *Postmodern Ethics* (Oxford: Basil Blackwell, 1991), 31–36.

19. "Morality in Modern and Postmodern Perspective," introduction to ibid., 1–15.

20. "The Elusive Universality," chap. 2 in 47–53; "The Elusive Foundations," chap. 3 in ibid., 69–81; and "The Moral Party of Two," chap. 4 in ibid., 82–109.

21. "Private Morals, Public Risks," chap. 7 in ibid., 199–209.

22. See Zygmunt Bauman, *Life in Fragments: Essays in Postmodern Morality* (Oxford: Blackwell, 1995).

23. Bauman, "Philosophical Affinities of Postmodern Sociology," in *Intimations of Postmodernity*, 114–48.

24. See Max Weber, *From Max Weber: Essays in Sociology*, trans. J. H. Gerth and C. Wright Mills (New York: Oxford University Press, 1958); *The Protestant Ethic and the Spirit of Capitalism*, trans. Talcott Parsons (New York: Charles Scribners and Sons, 1958); and *Economy and Society*, ed. Guenther Roth and Claus Wittich (Berkeley and Los Angeles: University of California Press, 1978). Also see Anthony Giddens, *Capitalism and Modern Social Theory: An Analysis of the Writings of Marx, Durkheim, and Max Weber* (Cambridge: Cambridge University Press, 1971).

25. Habermas's social theory of modernity is grounded in an integration of systems and action sociological theories. As an action theorist, Habermas has drawn upon phenomenological sociology (lifeworld theory), the social psychology of George Herbert Mead, and the speech-act theory of Austin, Searle, and Strawson. As a systems theorist, he has incorporated the work of Talcott Parsons, Niklas Luhmann, and Claus Offe. His system/lifeworld model of social action is in turn embedded in a theory of human social evolution indebted to Max Weber's theory of societal rationalization. Habermas's social theory is fully elaborated in *The Theory of Communicative Action*, vol. 1, *Reason and the Rationalization of Society*, trans. Thomas McCarthy (Boston: Beacon Press, 1984) and vol. 2, *Lifeworld and System: A Critique of Functionalist Reason*, trans. Thomas McCarthy (Boston: Beacon Press, 1987).

26. In chapter 2 of *Reason and the Rationalization of Society*, Habermas makes the case that Weber "allows himself to be guided by the restricted use of purposive rationality" (143). Weber argued that the motor force of Western modernization was to be found in the unique character of Occidental rationalism, which maintained a strong distinction between purposive-rational (utilitarian) and value-rational action. Habermas concludes that for Weber "the real reason for the dialectic of rationalization is not an unbalanced institutional embodiment of available cognitive potentials; he locates the seeds of destruction of the rationalization of the world in the very differentiation of independent cultural value spheres that released that potential and made that rationalization possible" (241).

27. Ibid., 237–40. See also Thomas McCarthy, "Reflections on Rationalization in *The Theory of Communicative Action*," in *Habermas and Modernity*, ed. Richard J. Bernstein (Cambridge: MIT Press, 1985), 176–91.

28. Habermas's defense of a new modern culture based on communicative ethics can be found in "The Normative Content of Modernity," in Habermas, *The Philosophical Discourse of Modernity*, 336–67.

29. David Harvey, *The Condition of Postmodernity: An Enquiry into the Origins of Cultural Change* (Oxford: Basil Blackwell, 1989), vii.

30. Ibid., 121–24.

31. "Modernity and Modernism," chap. 2 in ibid., 10–38.

32. "Postmodernism," chap. 3 in ibid., 39–65.

33. "Fordism" and "From Fordism to Flexible Accumulation," chaps. 8 and 9 in ibid., 125–72.

34. "The Time and Space of the Enlightenment Project," chap. 15 in ibid., 240–59.

35. Ibid., 240.

36. "Time-Space Compression and the Rise of Modernism as a Cultural Force," chap. 16 in ibid., 260–83.

37. "Time-Space Compression and the Postmodern Condition," chap. 17 in ibid., 284–307.

38. "Theorizing the Transition," chap. 10 in ibid., 173–88; and "The Crisis of Historical Materialism," chap. 26 in ibid., 353–55.

39. "Responses to Time-Space Compression," chap. 25 in ibid., 350–52.

40. "Cracks in the Mirrors, Fusions at the Edges," chap. 27 in ibid., 356–59.

41. Giddens's thesis of "radicalized modernity" was first introduced in *The Consequences of Modernity* (Stanford: Stanford University Press, 1990).

42. See Ulrich Beck, *Risk Society: Towards a New Modernity* (London: Sage Publications, 1992) and *Ecological Politics in the Age of Risk* (Cambridge: Polity Press, 1994). Also by Beck, "World Risk Society as Cosmopolitan Society? Ecological Questions in a Framework of Manufactured Uncertainties," *Theory, Culture and Society* 13, no. 4 (November 1996): 1–32.

43. Ulrich Beck, "The Reinvention of Politics: Towards a Theory of Reflexive Modernization," in Beck, Anthony Giddens, and Scott Lash, *Reflexive Modernization: Politics, Tradition and Aesthetics in the Modern Social Order* (Stanford: Stanford University Press, 1994), 5.

44. See Anthony Giddens, "The Social Revolutions of Our Time," chap. 3 in *Beyond Left and Right: The Future of Radical Politics,* 78–103.

45. Ibid., 86.

46. See Anthony Giddens, "The Contours of High Modernity," chap. 1 in *Modernity and Self-Identity: Self and Society in the Late Modern Age,* 21.

47. Giddens, "Conservatism: Radicalism Embraced," chap. 1 in 45–50; and "Modernity under a Negative Sign: Ecological Issues and Life Politics," chap. 8 in ibid., 202–208.

48. Giddens, "The Emergence of Life Politics," chap. 7 in *Modernity and Self-Identity,* 209–31.

49. Giddens, "A Comparison of Conceptions of Post-Modernity (PM) and Radicalized Modernity (RM)," table 2 in *The Consequences of Modernity,* 150.

50. Giddens, *Beyond Left and Right,* 252.

51. Giddens's social theory of modernity is most fully elaborated in *The Constitution of Society: Outline of the Theory of Structuration* (Berkeley and Los Angeles: University of California Press, 1984); *The Nation-State and Violence,* vol. 2 of *A Con-*

temporary Critique of Historical Materialism (Berkeley and Los Angeles: University of California Press, 1985); and *The Consequences of Modernity* (1990). See also David Held and John B. Thompson, eds., *Social Theory of Modern Societies: Anthony Giddens and His Critics* (Cambridge: Cambridge University Press, 1989).

52. See Giddens, *The Consequences of Modernity,* 151–73. See also Giddens, "The Social Revolutions of Our Time," chap. 3 in *Beyond Left and Right,* 97–103.

53. Giddens, *Beyond Left and Right,* 78–79.

54. In the late 1960s, Baudrillard produced a series of Marxist structuralist analyses of consumer society. In the mid-1970s he broke with Marxism and semiotics (the structuralist method of analyzing cultural forms as symbolic systems), shifted to cybernetics and postmodernism, proclaimed the arrival of the simulated society, and became the first postmodern social theorist. In the 1980s he proclaimed the arrival of the hypersimulated society and abandoned the project of postmodern social theory for radical postmodern cultural critique.

Baudrillard's later works include *Seduction* (New York: St. Martin's Press, 1980), originally published as *De la Seduction* (Paris: Denoel-Gonthier, 1979); *Fatal Strategies* (New York: Semiotext(e), 1990), originally published as *Les Strategies Fatales* (Paris: Bernard Grasset, 1983); *America,* trans. Chris Turner (London: Verso, 1988); and *The Illusion of the End,* trans. Chris Turner (Stanford: Stanford University Press, 1994). See also William Stearns and William Chaloupka, eds., *Jean Baudrillard: The Disappearance of Art and Politics* (New York: St. Martin's Press, 1992).

55. On Immanuel Kant's political philosophy, see Susan M. Shell, *The Rights of Reason: A Study of Kant's Philosophy and Politics* (Toronto: University of Toronto Press, 1980); Patrick Riley, *Kant's Political Philosophy* (Totowa, N.J.: Rowan and Littlefield, 1983); and William James Booth, *Interpreting the World: Kant's Philosophy of History and Politics* (Toronto: University of Toronto Press, 1986).

56. See Douglas Kellner, "Zygmunt Bauman's Postmodern Turn," in *Theory, Culture and Society* 15, no. 1 (1998): 73–86.

57. For a well-developed critique of Habermas's conception of rationality and his understanding of the relationship between reason and the lifeworld, or the worldly context of human thought and action, see Fred Dallmayr, *Between Freiburg and Frankfurt: Toward a Critical Ontology* (Amherst: University of Massachusetts Press, 1991), chaps. 1, 4, and 5.

58. Giddens's social theory remains thoroughly modern in its dedication to the powers of the individual as a knowledgeable agent and constitutive subject. This individual reflexive agent is a purposive rational actor capable of shaping the social environments of action in which she or he is embedded. My reading of Giddens leads me to conclude that his social ontology of reflexive action is grounded in a largely ahistorical philosophical anthropology of universal psychological needs. For a more detailed examination of Giddens's theorization of reflexive action, see "Elements of the Theory of Structuration" and "Consciousness, Self, and Social Encounters," chaps. 1 and 2 in *The Constitution of Society,* 41–109; *The Consequences of*

Modernity, 92–100; and "The Self: Ontological Security and Existential Anxiety," chap. 2 in *Modernity and Self-Identity,* 35–69.

For critiques of Giddens's social theory from a postmodern perspective, see Zygmunt Bauman, "Hermeneutics and Modern Social Theory," in *Social Theory of Modern Societies: Anthony Giddens and His Critics,* ed., David Held and John B. Thompson (Cambridge: Cambridge University Press, 1989), 34–55; Roy Boyne, "Power-Knowledge and Social Theory: The Systematic Misrepresentation of Contemporary French Social Theory in the Work of Anthony Giddens," in *Giddens' Theory of Structuration: A Critical Appreciation,* ed. Christopher G. A. Bryant and David Jary (New York and London: Routledge, 1991), 52–73; and Kenneth H. Tucker Jr., "Aesthetics, Play, and Cultural Memory: Giddens and Habermas on the Postmodern Challenge," *Sociological Theory* 11, no. 2 (July 1993): 194–211.

59. In *Beyond Left and Right,* Giddens develops these solutions in response to the challenges he sees facing the inhabitants of advanced Western societies living under conditions of radicalized modernity. They are (1) to repair damaged solidarities; (2) to recognize the increasing centrality of lifestyle issues to politics; (3) to develop and extend dialogic democracy both globally and in areas of personal life; (4) to fundamentally rethink the welfare state; and (5) to confront the pervasive influence of violence in human affairs. See the introduction, 1–21.

60. Ibid., 249–50.

61. Giddens concludes *Beyond Left and Right* with the following statement: "An ethics of a globalizing post-traditional society implies recognition of the sanctity of human life and the universal right to happiness and self-actualization — coupled to the obligation to promote cosmopolitan solidarity and an attitude of respect towards non-human agencies, present and future. Far from seeing the disappearance of universal values, this is perhaps the first time in humanity's history when such values have real purchase" (253).

62. Edward W. Soja, "Postmodern Geographies and the Critique of Historicism," in *Postmodern Contentions: Epochs, Politics, Space,* ed. John Paul Jones III, Wolfgang Natter, and Theodore R. Schatzki (New York: Guilford Press, 1993), 113.

63. Ibid., 118.

64. Ibid., 121.

65. See Mike Featherstone, *Undoing Culture: Globalization, Postmodernism and Identity* (London: Sage Publications, 1995).

66. Roland Robertson, "Glocalization: Time-Space and Homogeneity-Heterogeneity," in *Global Modernities,* ed. Mike Featherstone, Scott Lash, and Roland Robertson (London: Sage Publications, 1995), 25–44.

67. Arjun Appadurai, "Disjuncture and Difference in the Global Political Economy," in *Global Culture: Nationalism, Globalization and Modernity,* ed. Mike Featherstone (London: Sage Publications, 1990), 295–310. Appadurai identifies five major global cultural flows: (1) ethnoscapes of migrating and globally mobile people, such as immigrants, refugees, tourists, professionals, expatriates, and guestworkers;

(2) technoscapes of technologies with a global scope; (3) finanscapes involving global financial markets; (4) mediascapes of globalized, telecommunicational image production and dissemination; and (5) ideoscapes of transnational ideas and ideologies. See also Appadurai's recent essays in *Modernity at Large: Cultural Dimensions of Globalization* (Minneapolis: University of Minnesota Press, 1996).

68. Jan Nederveen Pieterse, "Globalization as Hybridization," in Featherstone, Lash, and Robertson, *Global Modernities,* 45–68.

69. Homi K. Bhabha, *The Location of Culture* (London and New York: Routledge, 1994), 2.

70. See Michael Mann, "Societies as Organized Power Networks," chap. 1 in *The Sources of Social Power,* vol. 1, *A History of Power from the Beginning to A.D. 1760* (Cambridge: Cambridge University Press, 1986), 1–33. Also, on the recent emphasis on spatiality in contemporary social theory, see Ilana Friedrich Silber, "Space, Fields, Boundaries: The Rise of Spatial Metaphors in Contemporary Sociological Theory," in *Social Research* 62, no. 2 (summer 1995): 323–55.

71. Stewart R. Clegg, *Frameworks of Power* (London: Sage Publications, 1989), 186.

72. "Frameworks of Power: An Overview of the Argument," chap. 1 in ibid., 1–20.

73. "Circuits of Power: A Framework for Analysis," chap. 8 in ibid., 187–98.

74. Ibid., 198–207.

75. Ibid., 223–39.

76. Ibid., 199.

77. See Clegg's circuits of power diagram, 214.

78. See Scott Lash and John Urry, *The End of Organized Capitalism* (Madison: University of Wisconsin Press, 1987); Scott Lash, *Sociology of Postmodernism* (London and New York: Routledge, 1990); Scott Lash, "Reflexive Modernization: The Aesthetic Dimension," in *Theory, Culture and Society* 10 (1993): 1–23; Scott Lash and John Urry, *Economies of Signs and Space* (London: Sage Publications, 1994); and Scott Lash, "Reflexivity and its Doubles: Structure, Aesthetics, and Community," in Beck, Giddens, and Lash, *Reflexive Modernization,* 110–73.

79. In *The End of Organized Capitalism,* Lash and Urry advanced the thesis that "organized capitalism" is being replaced by a new form of "disorganized capitalism." By disorganization, they meant the "spatial scattering or deconcentration" of organized capitalism's institutional structures "in terms of a decline of not just the city, but of the region and the nation-state." See chap. 1, "Introduction," 1–16.

In *Economies of Signs and Space,* Lash and Urry explain how their new reflexive modernization approach supercedes their earlier thesis of disorganized capitalism. While this earlier study was a comparative analysis of Western political economies still wedded to a nation-state, "society-centric" frame of reference, their subsequent approach is a transnational analysis of social and cultural flows and reflexive individualization, which rejects the modern concepts of "society" and the "nation-state." This global-local sociology of cultural economies takes as its primary analytic concern the increased "semioticization" (informational and aesthetic signs) and "spatialization" (globalized, high-speed flows) of both subjects and objects. It is, therefore, a sociology of both flows and of reflexivity. See the introduction and conclusion, 1–11 and 314–326.

80. Lash and Urry, "Mobile Objects," chap. 2 in *Economies of Signs and Space*, 15.

81. Ibid., 5.

82. Ibid., 5–8; "Reflexive Subjects," chap. 3 in ibid., 44–59; and "Accumulating Signs: The Culture Industries," chap. 5 in ibid., 112–43.

83. Ibid., 17–30.

84. On the role of the new global city in high-tech capitalism, see Manuel Castells, *The Informational City* (Oxford: Basil Blackwell, 1989); and Saskia Sasson, *The Global City: New York, London, Tokyo* (Princeton: Princeton University Press, 1991).

85. See Edward W. Soja, "It All Comes Together in Los Angeles," chap. 8 in *Postmodern Geographies: The Reassertion of Space in Critical Social Theory* (London: Verso, 1989); and "Taking Los Angeles Apart: Towards a Postmodern Geography," chap. 9 in ibid.

86. Lash and Urry, *Economies of Signs and Space*, 64.

87. Ibid., 67.

88. Ibid., "Discursive Reflexivity: Information-Rich Production Systems," 94–107.

89. Ibid., 109.

90. Scott Lash, "Expert-systems or Situated Interpretation? Culture and Institutions in Disorganized Capitalism," in Beck, Giddens, and Lash, *Reflexive Modernization*, 207–9.

91. Lash and Urry, "Ungovernable Spaces: The Underclass and Impacted Ghettoes," chap. 6 in *Economies of Signs and Space*, 145–70.

3. The Idea of Critical Postmodernism

1. See Michel Foucault, "What Is Enlightenment?" in *The Foucault Reader*, ed. Paul Rabinow (New York: Pantheon Books, 1984), 39.

2. See Anthony Giddens, "The Self: Ontological Security and Existential Anxiety," chap. 2 in *Modernity and Self-Identity: Self and Society in the Late Modern Age* (Stanford: Stanford University Press, 1991), 47–55.

3. Zygmunt Bauman, *Intimations of Postmodernity* (London and New York: Routledge, 1992), 129.

4. Ibid., 132.

5. Leslie Paul Thiele, *Thinking Politics: Perspectives in Ancient, Modern, and Postmodern Political Theory* (Chatham, N. J.: Chatham House Publishers, 1997), 14.

6. Jürgen Habermas contends that philosophical thinking today is "postmetaphysical" rather than postmodern. He regards the postmodern privileging of ontology over epistemology as one of the major drawbacks of contemporary phi-

losophy. Habermas defines postmetaphysical thinking as "the procedural rationality of the scientific process" and limits interpretive reasoning to a mediating function between expert knowledge (communicative rationality) and everyday practices (lifeworld). Critical postmodernism asserts the primacy of critical ontology. See "The Horizon of Modernity Is Shifting" and "Themes in Postmetaphysical Thinking" in Jürgen Habermas, *Postmetaphysical Thinking: Philosophical Essays,* trans. William Mark Hohengarten (Cambridge: MIT Press, 1992), 3–9 and 28–53.

7. Fred Dallmayr, *Between Freiburg and Frankfurt: Toward a Critical Ontology* (Amherst: University of Massachusetts Press, 1991), vii.

8. Ibid., vii–viii.

9. Ibid., 1–12. Dallmayr's commitment to the idea of a "critical ontology" has been consistent throughout his career. His philosophical interrogation of the time we live in has been principally influenced by the work of Martin Heidegger, Theodor Adorno, and Maurice Merleau-Ponty. Dallmayr's other major works include *Twilight of Subjectivity: Contributions to a Post-Individualist Theory of Politics* (Amherst: University of Massachusetts Press, 1981); *Polis and Praxis: Exercises in Contemporary Political Theory* (Cambridge: MIT Press, 1984); *Critical Encounters: Between Philosophy and Politics* (Notre Dame, Ind.: University of Notre Dame Press, 1987); *Margins of Political Discourse* (Albany: SUNY Press, 1989); and *The Other Heidegger* (Ithaca: Cornell University Press, 1993).

10. William E. Connolly, "Nothing Is Fundamental . . ." in *The Ethos of Pluralization* (Minneapolis: University of Minnesota Press, 1995), 1. See also William E. Connolly, "Beyond Good and Evil: The Ethical Sensibility of Michel Foucault," in *Political Theory* 21, no. 3 (August 1993): 365–89.

11. Connolly, "Nothing Is Fundamental . . . ," 1–9.

12. Ibid., 1.

13. Ibid., 32–40.

14. Ibid., 36.

15. There exists a substantial recent literature on the life, work, and ideas of German philosopher Martin Heidegger (1889–1976). On the connection between Heidegger, political philosophy, and postmodern thought, see Fred Dallmayr, "Ontology of Freedom: Heidegger and Political Philosophy," *Political Theory* 12, no. 2 (May 1984): 204–34; "Rethinking the Political: Some Heideggerian Contributions," *The Review of Politics* 52, no. 4 (fall 1990): 524–52; and *The Other Heidegger* (Ithaca: Cornell University Press, 1993). See also Leslie Paul Thiele, *Timely Meditations: Martin Heidegger and Postmodern Politics* (Princeton: Princeton University Press, 1995); and Dana R. Villa, *Arendt and Heidegger: The Fate of the Political* (Princeton: Princeton University Press, 1996).

16. See Dallmayr, "Life-World and Critique," in *Between Freiburg and Frankfurt,* 13–43.

17. On the critical theory of Theodor Adorno, see Susan Buck-Morss, *The Origin of Negative Dialectics* (New York: The Free Press, 1977); Gillian Rose, *The*

Melancholy Science (New York: Columbia University Press, 1978); Martin Jay, *Adorno* (Cambridge: Harvard University Press, 1984); Fred Dallmayr, "Phenomenology and Critique: Adorno," in *Critical Encounters*, 39–72; Terry Eagleton, "Art after Auschwitz: Theodor Adorno," chap. 13 in *The Ideology of the Aesthetic* (Oxford: Basil Blackwell, 1990), 341–65; and Shane Phelan, "Interpretation and Domination: Adorno and the Habermas-Lyotard Debate," *Polity* 25, no. 4 (summer 1993): 597–616.

18. See Theodor Adorno, *Negative Dialectics* (London: Routledge, 1973) and *Against Epistemology* (Cambridge: MIT Press, 1983).

19. Dallmayr, *Between Freiburg and Frankfurt*, 37.

20. Dallmayr, "Adorno and Heidegger," chap. 2 in ibid., 44–71.

21. Ibid., 109–110.

22. Ibid., 132–33.

23. See Jürgen Habermas, *Moral Consciousness and Communicative Action*, trans. Christian Lenhardt and Shierry Weber Nicholson (Cambridge: MIT Press, 1990).

24. Thomas McCarthy, introduction to ibid., vii–xiii.

25. Dallmayr, *Between Freiburg and Frankfurt*, 150–51.

26. Richard Bernstein, *The New Constellation: The Ethical-Political Horizons of Modernity/Postmodernity* (Cambridge: MIT Press, 1992), 1–14.

27. Ibid., 338.

28. "Heidegger's Silence: Ethos and Technology," chap. 4 in ibid., 79–141.

29. "Serious Play: The Ethical-Political Horizon of Derrida," chap. 6 in ibid., 172–198.

30. "Rorty's Liberal Utopia," chap. 9 in ibid., 258–92.

31. Stephen K. White, "Understanding the Modern-Postmodern Tension," chap. 2 in *Political Theory and Postmodernism* (Cambridge: Cambridge University Press, 1991): 13–30.

32. Ibid., 33.

33. Ibid., "Heidegger and Responsibility to Otherness," chap. 4 in ibid., 55–74.

34. Ibid., "From/After This Laughter and This Dance . . . ," chap. 5 in ibid., 85–94.

35. Ibid., 116–17.

36. Ibid., 73.

37. Ibid., "Difference Feminism and Responsibility to Otherness," 95–113.

38. Ibid., "Rethinking Justice," chap. 7 in ibid., 143.

39. Martin J. Matustik, *Postnational Identity: Critical Theory and Existential Philosophy in Habermas, Kierkegaard, and Havel* (New York: Guilford Press, 1993). See especially chap. 5, "The Performative Mode of Identity," 107–26. Also see my review of Matustik in the *Canadian Journal of Political Science* 27, no. 2 (June 1994): 407–8.

40. White calls this kind of feminist thought "difference feminism" and defines it as that "wing of feminism that has focused most closely on the idea of care and its ethical-political implications" (95). The best representatives of this approach include Carol Gilligan, Sara Ruddick, Jean Bethke Elshtain, and Kathy Ferguson.

41. See Bonnie Honig, "Toward an Agonistic Feminism: Hannah Arendt and the Politics of Identity," in *Feminist Interpretations of Hannah Arendt*, ed. Bonnie Honig (University Park, Penn.: Pennsylvania State University Press, 1995), 135–66; and Chantal Mouffe, "Feminism, Citizenship, and Radical Democratic Politics," in *The Return of the Political* (London: Verso, 1993), 74–89.

42. White writes: "As for the notions of 'care of the self' and an 'aesthetics of existence,' I do not mean to imply that they are of no interest to ethics; rather, I simply see no evidence that they produce any substantial insights into the broad range of ethical-political issues upon which I am focusing in the present context." See *Political Theory and Postmodernism*, 91 n. 49.

43. Hannah Arendt's major works include *The Origins of Totalitarianism* (New York: Harcourt Brace and Company, 1951); *The Human Condition* (Chicago: University of Chicago Press, 1958); *On Revolution* (New York: Viking Press, 1963); *Between Past and Future* (New York: Viking Press, 1968); *Crises of the Republic* (New York: Harcourt Brace Jovanovich, 1972); *Eichmann in Jerusalem* (New York: Penguin Books, 1977); *The Life of the Mind*, 2 vols. (New York: Harcourt Brace Jovanovich, 1978); and *Lectures on Kant's Political Philosophy*, ed. Ronald Beiner (Chicago: University of Chicago Press, 1982). Also see George Kateb, *Hannah Arendt: Politics, Conscience, Evil* (Totowa, N.J.: Rowman and Allanheld, 1983); Dana R. Villa, *Arendt and Heidegger* (1996); and Seyla Benhabib, *The Reluctant Modernism of Hannah Arendt* (Thousand Oaks, Calif.: Sage Publications, 1996).

44. Bonnie Honig, *Political Theory and the Displacement of Politics* (Ithaca: Cornell University Press, 1993), 2.

45. Ibid.

46. Ibid., 3.

47. Ibid.

48. Ibid., 4.

49. Honig's interpretation of Nietszche centers on his deconstruction of the morally responsible individual that is constructed in response to the self's encounter with contingency and otherness. The "virtuous" response to the experience of contingency and otherness is to both legislate and conform to disciplinary moral codes. The "virtù" response is to experience the tension between contingency, otherness, and the self's need for autonomy and identity through existential stylization. See "Nietzsche and the Recovery of Responsibility," chap. 3 in ibid., 42–75.

50. Arendt's reading of Aristotle is explained in Dana Villa, "Arendt, Aristotle, and Action," chap. 1 in *Arendt and Heidegger*, 17–41.

51. "Arendt, Nietzsche, and the 'Aestheticization' of Political Action," chap. 3 in ibid., 80–109.

52. Honig, "Arendt's Accounts of Action and Authority," chap. 4 in *Political Theory and the Displacement of Politics*, 77–84.

53. Ibid., 111–13.

54. Villa, "The Heideggerian Roots of Arendt's Political Theory," chap. 4 in *Arendt and Heidegger,* 113–29.

55. Ibid., 130–43.

56. "The Critique of Modernity," chap. 6 in ibid., 188–201.

57. "Arendt, Heidegger, and the Oblivion of *Praxis,*" chap. 7 in ibid., 211–30.

58. Ibid., 230–40; and "Heidegger, *Poiesis,* and Politics," chap. 8 in ibid., 241–70.

59. Ibid., 270.

60. Honig, *Political Theory and the Displacement of Politics,* 118–19.

61. Ibid., 120.

62. Ibid., 120–22.

63. In the concluding section of chapter 4, Honig argues that Arendt's own theoretical framework, as well as our current cultural and political situation, "mandates a radicalization of her account of action" (119). Yet Honig's radicalization of Arendt reads more like Foucault. This is evident in her commentary on the collapse of the public-private distinction; the dispersal and spatial reconfiguration of public space today; of politics going underground and relocating itself "in the rifts and fractures of identities, both personal and institutional" (122); of action as resistance; of "a politics of performativity situated in the self-evidences of the private realm" (123); and of politics understood in terms of "spaces of performative freedom" (124). By the end of her radicalization of Arendt we have moved beyond Arendt. See "Making Space for Arendt's *Virtù* Theory of Politics," 115–25.

64. Villa, *Arendt and Heidegger,* 206.

65. See Stewart R. Clegg, *Frameworks of Power* (London: Sage Publications, 1989), 15–16; and "Post-Structuralism, Sovereign Power and Disciplinary Power," chap. 7 in ibid., 149–86.

66. William E. Connolly, *The Ethos of Pluralization* (Minneapolis: University of Minnesota Press, 1995), 13.

67. Ibid., 20–21.

68. Ibid., 13.

69. Ibid., 14.

70. Ibid., 24.

71. Ibid.

72. Ibid., 22.

73. Ibid.

74. Ibid., 38.

75. William E. Connolly, "Beyond Good and Evil: The Ethical Sensibility of Michel Foucault," *Political Theory* 21, no. 3 (August 1993): 365–89.

76. Connolly, *The Ethos of Pluralization,* xii.

77. Ibid., xiii–xv.

78. Ibid., xv–xix.

79. Ibid., xxi.

80. Jeffrey C. Isaac, *Arendt, Camus, and Modern Rebellion* (New Haven: Yale University Press, 1992), 228.

81. Ibid., 228–29.

82. Ibid., 248–49.

83. See Brent Pickett, "Foucault and the Politics of Resistance," *Polity* 28, no. 4 (summer 1996): 445–66. I agree with Pickett that the idea of resistance was evident throughout Foucault's career and evolved through different periods. I disagree, however, with his assertion that Foucault celebrated a resistance without limits. His final work on the ethics of self-care as a practice of freedom refutes this claim. Pickett's reconstruction of Foucauldian resistance is focused on the Foucault of the 1960s and 1970s, with minimal treatment of the 1980s and his work on ethics, self-identity, the Enlightenment, and governmentality.

84. See David Macey, "Dissident," chap. 15 in *The Lives of Michel Foucault* (New York: Pantheon Books, 1993), 378–414.

85. Isaac, *Arendt, Camus, and Modern Rebellion,* 307 n. 6.

86. For a more in-depth account of Foucault's "heterotopian" conceptualization of space and its relation to his conception of freedom, see Thomas L. Dumm, "Freedom and Space," chap. 2 in *Michel Foucault and the Politics of Freedom* (Thousand Oaks: Sage Publications, 1996), 29–68.

4. Foucault's Presence

1. James Miller, *The Passion of Michel Foucault* (New York: Doubleday: 1993).

2. David Macey, *The Lives of Michel Foucault: A Biography* (New York: Pantheon Books, 1993), xi–xxiii.

3. On the relationship between Foucault and the discipline of philosophy, as well as the philosophical significance of his work, see Jitendra Mohanty, "Foucault as a Philosopher," in *Foucault and the Critique of Institutions,* ed. John Caputo and Mark Yount (University Park: Pennsylvania State University Press, 1993), 27–40. On Foucault the historian, see Thomas Flynn, "Foucault's Mapping of History," in *The Cambridge Companion to Foucault,* ed. Gary Gutting (Cambridge: Cambridge University Press, 1994), 28–46.

4. In his interview with Gerard Raulet, Foucault stated, "I have never been a Freudian, I have never been a Marxist and I have never been a structuralist" (198). He further maintained "I do not understand what kind of problem is common to the people we call post-modern or post-structuralist" (205). See "Structuralism and Post-Structuralism: An Interview with Michel Foucault," in *Telos* 55 (spring 1983): 195–211.

5. While acknowledging the relevance of this interpretive schema, David Macey also points out: "It makes no allowance for the trajectory that took Foucault from membership of the Parti Communiste Français, through a period of political quietism to a period of full-blooded leftist militancy and then to a concern for human rights. Nor does it take account of the important literary phase in Foucault's ca-

reer." See Macey, *The Lives of Michel Foucault*, xii. Gary Gutting interprets Foucault's work in terms of three types of intellectual artifacts: histories, theories, and myths. See "Introduction to Michel Foucault: A User's Manual," in Gutting, *The Cambridge Companion to Foucault*, 1–27.

6. On Foucault's archaeological histories, see Gary Gutting, *Michel Foucault's Archaeology of Scientific Reason* (Cambridge: Cambridge University Press, 1989).

7. On the movement from archaeology to genealogy, see Hubert L. Dreyfus and Paul Rabinow, *Michel Foucault: Beyond Structuralism and Hermeneutics* (Chicago: University of Chicago Press, 1983), especially chap. 5, "Interpretive Analytics," 104–125. See also C. G. Prado, *Starting with Foucault: An Introduction to Genealogy* (Boulder, Colo.: Westview Press, 1995).

8. See Michel Foucault, *Discipline and Punish: The Birth of the Prison*, trans. Alan Sheridan (New York: Vintage Books, 1975); *The History of Sexuality: An Introduction*, trans. Robert Hurley (New York: Vintage Books, 1978); and *Power/Knowledge: Selected Interviews and Other Writings, 1972–1977*, ed. Colin Gordon (New York: Pantheon, 1980).

9. A number of Foucault's critics define his project in terms of his archaeological and genealogical periods and ignore or downplay his final work in the late 1970s and 1980s on the self, ethics, governmentality, and resistance. Habermas portrays Foucault this way in *The Philosophical Discourse on Modernity*, as does Axel Honneth in *The Critique of Power: Reflective Stages in a Critical Social Theory*, trans. Kenneth Baynes (Cambridge: MIT Press, 1991). See also Jean L. Cohen and Andrew Arato, "The Genealogical Critique: Michel Foucault," chap. 6 in *Civil Society and Political Theory* (Cambridge: MIT Press, 1992), 255–98; and Shadia B. Drury, "Foucault's Folie," chap. 9 in *Alexandre Kojeve: The Roots of Postmodern Politics* (New York: St. Martin's Press, 1994), 125–40. I further disagree with Christopher Norris when he characterizes Foucault's work in the 1980s on ethics as "a shift in rhetorical strategy" rather than a rethinking of his earlier work. See " 'What Is Enlightenment?': Kant According to Foucault," in Gutting, *The Cambridge Companion to Foucault*, 159–96.

10. See Michel Foucault, "What Is Enlightenment?" in *The Foucault Reader*, ed. Paul Rabinow (New York: Pantheon Books, 1984), 45.

11. Jon Simons interprets Foucault's life and intellectual project in terms of the analysis of limits (the limits of discourse, power, knowledge, subjects, and government) and their transgression (through art, critical thought, practices of the self, and politics). See *Foucault and the Political* (London and New York: Routledge, 1995).

12. See "Critical Theory/Intellectual History," Foucault's 1983 interview with Gerard Raulet, in *Michel Foucault: Politics, Philosophy, Culture: Interviews and Other Writings 1977–1984*, ed. Lawrence D. Kritzman (New York and London: Routledge, 1988), 37.

13. Rabinow, *The Foucault Reader*, 76.

14. Foucault identified and examined the operation of these three types of modern power in *Discipline and Punish* and the first volume of *The History of Sexuality*. Closer to Nietzsche and Weber than to Marx and Freud, Foucault's ideas about power and its deployment challenged the Marxist analytic model of capital/labor as well as Freudian and Freudian-Marxist accounts of repression in decoding the dynamics and forces of modern social control.

15. See John Ransom, "Genealogy in the Disciplinary Age," chap. 4 in *Foucault's Discipline: The Politics of Subjectivity* (Durham: Duke University Press, 1997), 85–100.

16. Ibid., 88.

17. Ibid., 95.

18. Ibid.

19. Ibid., 96.

20. Ibid.

21. Ibid., 97.

22. Ibid., 98.

23. Foucault, "What Is Enlightenment?" 42.

24. This is also the way Foucault believed Kant defined Enlightenment. See ibid., 34.

25. See Foucault's other lecture/essay on Kant, "The Art of Telling the Truth," in *Michel Foucault: Politics, Philosophy, Culture,* ed. Lawrence D. Kritzman, 86–95.

26. See Immanuel Kant, "An Answer to the Question: 'What Is Enlightenment?' in *Kant: Political Writings,* ed. Hans Reiss and trans. H. B. Nisbet (Cambridge: Cambridge University Press, 1991), 54–60.

27. Foucault, "What Is Enlightenment?" 39–42.

28. Ibid., 45–46.

29. Ibid., 47.

30. Ibid., 48.

31. Ibid., 50.

32. Ibid.

33. Ibid.

34. Foucault, *The History of Sexuality: An Introduction,* 92–95.

35. Ibid., 96.

36. Ibid., 95–96.

37. Ibid., 96.

38. Foucault, "The Subject and Power," afterword to Dreyfus and Rabinow, *Michel Foucault: Beyond Structuralism and Hermeneutics,* 211.

39. Ibid., 211–12.

40. Ibid., 212.

41. Ibid., 213.

42. Giddens, *Modernity and Self-Identity: Self and Society in the Late Modern Age* (Stanford: Stanford University Press, 1991), 209.

43. Ibid., 215.

44. Ibid., 211.

45. See Andrew Cutrofello, *Discipline and Critique: Kant, Poststructuralism, and the Problem of Resistance* (Albany: State University of New York Press, 1994).

46. Michel Foucault, "Morality and Practice of the Self," chap. 3 in *The Use of Pleasure*, vol. 2 of *The History of Sexuality*, trans. Robert Hurley (New York: Pantheon Books, 1985), 25–32.

47. Ibid. The "arts of existence" are defined on pages 10–11 and *askesis* on pages 72–77.

48. Ibid., 10–11.

49. Michel Foucault, "An Aesthetics of Existence," in *Foucault Live (Interviews 1966–84)*, trans. John Johnston, ed. Sylvere Lotringer (New York: Semiotext(e), 1989), 311.

50. Foucault, *The Use of Pleasure*, 26–28. See also Paul Rabinow, "The History of Systems of Thought," introduction to *The Essential Works of Michel Foucault 1954–1984*, vol. 1, *Ethics: Subjectivity and Truth*, ed. Paul Rabinow, trans. Robert Hurley et al. (New York: The New Press, 1997), xxvii–xl.

51. Foucault, "The Ethic of Care for the Self as a Practice of Freedom: An Interview with Michel Foucault on January 29, 1984," interview by Raul Fornet-Betancourt, Helmut Becker, and Alfredo Gomez-Muller, trans. J. D. Gauthier, in *The Final Foucault*, ed. James Bernauer and David Rasmussen (Cambridge: MIT Press, 1988), 4.

52. Ibid., 6.

53. Ibid., 7.

54. Ibid., 3 and 11–12.

55. Ibid., 20.

56. On the Foucault-Habermas debate, see Michael Kelly, ed., *Critique and Power: Recasting the Foucault/Habermas Debate* (Cambridge: MIT Press, 1994).

57. Thomas McCarthy, "The Critique of Impure Reason: Foucault and the Frankfurt School," 243–82.

58. Richard Bernstein, "Foucault: Critique as a Philosophical Ethos," in ibid., 211–41.

59. See Terry Eagleton, "From the Polis to Postmodernism," chap. 14 in *The Ideology of the Aesthetic* (Oxford: Basil Blackwell, 1990), 366–417; Alex Callinicos, "The Aporias of Poststructuralism," chap. 3 in *Against Postmodernism: A Marxist Critique* (New York: St. Martin's Press, 1990), 62–91; Richard Wolin, "Foucault's Aesthetic Decisionism," *Telos* 67 (1986): 71–86, and "Michel Foucault and the Search for the Other of Reason," chap. 8 in *The Terms of Cultural Criticism: The Frankfurt School, Existentialism, Poststructuralism* (New York: Columbia University Press, 1992), 170–93; and David Harvey, "Postmodernism," chap. 3 in *The Condition of Postmodernity*, 39–65.

60. Leslie Paul Thiele, "Nietzsche's Legacy," chap. 1 in *Timely Meditations: Martin Heidegger and Postmodern Politics* (Princeton: Princeton University Press, 1995), 13–22.

61. Ibid., 27–34.

62. Ibid., 71.

63. Michael Kelly, "Foucault, Habermas, and the Self-Referentiality of Critique," in Kelly, *Critique and Power*, 382.

64. Susan J. Hekman, *Gender and Knowledge: Elements of a Postmodern Feminism* (Boston: Northeastern University Press, 1990), 185.

65. Ibid.

66. Jane Bennett, " 'How Is It, Then, That We Still Remain Barbarians?': Foucault, Schiller, and the Aestheticization of Politics," in *Political Theory* 24, no. 4 (November 1996): 665.

67. On the "plebian aspect" of Foucault's thought, see John Ransom, "The 'Plebian Aspect,' " chap. 5 in *Foucault's Discipline: The Politics of Subjectivity*, 101–53.

68. See Foucault's course summaries, "Security, Territory, and Population," "The Birth of Biopolitics," and "On the Government of the Living," reprinted in *The Essential Works of Michel Foucault 1954–1984*, ed. Paul Rabiinow, vol. 1, *Ethics: Subjectivity and Truth*, 67–85.

69. See Michel Foucault, "Politics and Reason," in *Michel Foucault: Politics, Philosophy, Culture: Interviews and Other Writings, 1977–1984*, 57–85.

70. See Foucault's 1978 lecture on governmentality in "Governmentality," chap. 4 in *The Foucault Effect: Studies in Governmentality*, ed. Graham Burchell, Colin Gordon, and Peter Miller (Chicago: University of Chicago Press, 1991), 87–104.

71. See Foucault's course summary, "On the Government of the Living," in Rabinow, *The Essential Works of Michel Foucault*, 81.

72. See Foucault's course summary, "The Birth of Biopolitics," in Rabinow, *The Essential Works of Michel Foucault*, 74.

73. Foucault, "Governmentality," in Burchell, Gordon, and Miller, *The Foucault Effect: Studies in Governmentality*, 101–104.

74. Foucault, "Politics and Reason," in Kritzman, *Michel Foucault: Politics, Philosophy, Culture: Interviews and Other Writings, 1977–1984*, 60–63.

75. Ibid., 63–67.

76. Ibid., 67–71.

77. Ibid., 74.

78. Ibid.

79. Ibid., 74–77.

80. Ibid., 77–83.

81. Ibid., 84–85.

82. On Foucault's analysis of modern liberal government, see Colin Gordon, "Governmental Rationality: An Introduction," in Burchell, Gordon, and Miller, *The Foucault Effect*, 14–27.

83. Ibid., 27–36.

84. On Foucault and neoliberalism, see Nikolas Rose, Governing 'Advanced' Liberal Democracies," in *Foucault and Political Reason: Liberalism, Neo-Liberalism,*

and Rationalities of Government, ed. Andrew Barry, Thomas Osborne, and Nikolas Rose (Chicago: University of Chicago Press, 1996), 37–64.

85. Foucault, "Governmentality," in Burchell, Gordon, and Miller, *The Foucault Effect,* 102.

86. See Thomas L. Dumm, "Freedom and Seduction," chap. 4 in *Michel Foucault and the Politics of Freedom* (London: Sage Publications, 1996), 123–58.

87. On the relevance of "perspectivism" as an epistemological standpoint, see Brian Fay, *Contemporary Philosophy of Social Science: A Multicultural Approach* (Oxford: Blackwell, 1996).

88. C. G. Prado, *Starting with Foucault: An Introduction to Genealogy* (Boulder, Colo.: Westview Press, 1995), 126.

89. Fay, *Contemporary Philosophy of Social Science,* 90.

90. Steven Best and Douglas Kellner, *Postmodern Theory* (New York: Guilford Press, 1991), 265.

91. See Foucault, "Nietzsche, Genealogy, History," in Rabinow, *The Foucault Reader,* 83.

92. See Richard Dawkins, *The Selfish Gene* (Oxford: Oxford University Press, 1989).

93. Leslie Paul Thiele, *Thinking Politics: Perspectives in Ancient, Modern, and Postmodern Political Theory* (Chatham, N.J.: Chatham House Publishers, 1997), 42.

5. Complexity, Governmentality, and the Fate of Democracy

1. See Chantal Mouffe, *The Return of the Political* (London and New York: Verso, 1993); Fred Dallmayr, "Rethinking the Political: Some Heideggerian Contributions," in *The Review of Politics* 52, no. 4 (fall 1990): 524–52; Dana R. Villa, *Arendt and Heidegger: The Fate of the Political* (Princeton: Princeton University Press, 1996); and Seyla Benhabib, ed., *Democracy and Difference: Contesting the Boundaries of the Political* (Princeton: Princeton University Press, 1996).

2. Claude Lefort, *Democracy and Political Theory,* trans. David Macey (Minneapolis: University of Minnesota Press, 1988), 10–11 and 216–18.

3. Ibid., 10–11.

4. Ibid., 11–12.

5. Ibid., 19.

6. Ibid., 17.

7. Ibid., 13.

8. Ibid., 12–14.

9. See Chantal Mouffe, "Radical Democracy: Modern or Postmodern?" in *The Return of the Political,* 9–22; Fred Dallmayr, "Postmetaphysics and Democracy," in *Political Theory* 21, no. 1 (February 1993): 101–127; and Patrick F. McKinlay, "Postmodernism and Democracy: Learning from Lyotard and Lefort," in *The Journal of Politics* 60, no. 2 (May 1998): 481–502.

10. Sheldon Wolin, "The Liberal/Democratic Divide: On Rawls's *Political Liberalism*," *Political Theory* 24, no. 1 (February 1996): 97–119.

11. G. J. Mulgan, *Politics in an Antipolitical Age* (Williston, Vt.: Blackwell, 1994), 18.

12. See Edward S. Herman and Robert W. McChesney, *The Global Media: The New Missionaries of Corporate Capitalism* (London: Cassell, 1997).

13. "Main Players in the Global Media System," chap. 3 in ibid., 70–105.

14. See Benjamin R. Barber, "Who Owns McWorld?: The Media Merger Frenzy," chap. 9 in *Jihad vs. McWorld: How Globalism and Tribalism are Reshaping the World* (New York: Ballantine Books, 1996), 137–51.

15. See Anthony Giddens, *Modernity and Self-Identity* (Stanford: Stanford University Press, 1991), 26, 84.

16. Danilo Zolo, *Democracy and Complexity: A Realist Approach,* trans. David McKie (University Park: Pennsylvania State University Press, 1992), 157–60.

17. Ibid., 157–58.

18. Ibid., 159.

19. Ibid.

20. Ibid., 160.

21. Ibid., 165–66.

22. Ibid., 163.

23. Ibid., 163–64.

24. For a good survey of the new ideological landscape of neoliberalism, which includes libertarianism, public choice theory, neoconservatism, and communitarianism, see Vernon Van Dyke, *Ideology and Political Choice: The Search for Freedom, Justice, and Virtue* (Chatham, N.J.: Chatham House Publishers, 1995). See also Giddens, "Conservatism: Radicalism Embraced," chap. 1 in *Beyond Left and Right,* 22–50.

25. Nikolas Rose, "Governing 'Advanced' Liberal Democracies," in *Foucault and Political Reason: Liberalism, Neo-Liberalism, and Rationalities of Government,* ed., Andrew Barry, Thomas Osborne, and Nikolas Rose (Chicago: University of Chicago Press, 1996), 37–64.

26. Ibid., 52.

27. Ibid., 54.

28. Ibid.

29. Ibid., 43.

30. Ibid., 56.

31. Ibid.

32. Ibid., 57.

33. Ibid.

34. Ibid., 57–58.

35. Ibid., 58.

36. Ibid.

37. Ibid., 58–59.

38. Ibid., 61.

39. Ibid.

40. In describing these alternative normative theories of democracy as "models," I am deliberately referring to the work of democratic theorists C. B. Macpherson and David Held. In *The Life and Times of Liberal Democracy* (Oxford: Oxford University Press, 1977), Macpherson employed the idea of "models of democracy" to explain the different adaptation of liberal democracy in the nineteenth and twentieth centuries. They were protective (the model of Jeremy Bentham and James Mill), developmental (John Stuart Mill's model), equilibrium (developed by Joseph Schumpeter and modified into the American pluralist model), and participatory democracy (developed by Macpherson and Carole Pateman). A model of democracy was "a theoretical construction intended to exhibit and explain the real relations, underlying the appearances, between or within the phenomena under study"; "to explain the probability or possibility of future changes in those relations"; and with "a concern for what is desirable or good or right" (2–4).

In *Models of Democracy* (Stanford: Stanford University Press, 1987, 1996), David Held employed Macpherson's approach. His models consisted of a principle of justification, key political features, and "assumptions about the nature of the society in which democracy is or might be embedded" (1987, 7). Held kept Macpherson's four models of liberal democracy and added seven more: classical Athenian democracy, civic republicanism, Marx's model of direct democracy, a model of technocratic competitive elitism based on the thought of Max Weber and Joseph Schumpeter, the New Right model of "legal democracy" indebted to the laissez-faire and libertarian thought of Friedrich Hayek and Robert Nozick, and his own contemporary models of democratic autonomy (1987) and cosmopolitan democracy (1996). This resulting grand history spanned the development of Western democracy from the ancient Athenian constitution of Kleistenes in 507 B.C. to the present-day circumstances of globalization (1996).

41. See Benjamin Barber, *Strong Democracy* (Berkeley and Los Angeles: University of California Press, 1984); Daniel Bell, *Communitarianism and Its Critics* (Oxford: Clarendon, 1993); Robert Bellah et al., *Habits of the Heart: Individualism and Commitment in American Life* (Berkeley and Los Angeles: University of California Press, 1985); Amitai Etzioni, *The Spirit of Community: The Reinvention of American Society* (New York: Simon and Schuster, 1993) and Etzioni, *The New Golden Rule: Community and Morality in a Democratic Society* (New York: Basic Books, 1996); William Galston, *Liberal Purposes* (Cambridge: Cambridge University Press, 1991); Michael Sandel, *Liberalism and the Limits of Justice* (New York: Cambridge University Press, 1982); Thomas Spragens, *Reason and Democracy* (Durham, N.C.: Duke University Press, 1990); and Charles Taylor, *Sources of the Self: The Making of Modern Identity* (Cambridge: Cambridge University Press, 1989). See also Stephen Mulhall and Adam Swift, *Liberals and Communitarians* (Oxford: Blackwell, 1992);

and Amitai Etzioni, ed., *The Essential Communitarian Reader* (Rowman and Little-field, 1998).

42. See John Rawls, *A Theory of Justice* (Cambridge: Harvard University Press, 1971).

43. In 1991, the quarterly journal *The Responsive Community* was founded and "The Responsive Communitarian Platform" was issued. As the movement's leader, Etzioni envisions communitarianism as the equivalent of the late nineteenth-century Progressive movement.

44. Due to the influence of William Galston, who was White House domestic policy advisor in Clinton's first term, communitarianism became part of the Clinton administration's policy agenda as evident in the Family Leave Act and the Ameri-Corps national service program. Galston is Director of the Institute for Philosophy and Public Policy at the University of Maryland School of Public Affairs. See also by Galston, "Clinton and the Promise of Communitarianism," *Chronicle of Higher Education,* 2 December 1991), A52.

45. See Michael Sandel, "The Procedural Republic and the Unencumbered Self," in *Political Theory* 12, no. 1 (February 1984): 81–96.

46. Amitai Etzioni, "A Moderate Communitarian Proposal," in *Political Theory* 24, no. 2 (May 1996): 157.

47. Ibid., 166.

48. Ibid., 167.

49. See Amitai Etzioni, "On Restoring the Moral Voice," in *Rights and the Common Good: The Communitarian Perspective,* ed. Etzioni (New York: St. Martin's Press, 1995), 274.

50. Etzioni, *The New Golden Rule,* xvii.

51. Ibid., 3–12.

52. See Etzioni, *Rights and the Common Good,* 13.

53. See Seyla Benhabib, ed., *Democracy and Difference: Contesting the Boundaries of the Political* (Princeton: Princeton University Press, 1996); James Bohman, *Public Deliberation: Pluralism, Complexity, and Democracy* (Cambridge: MIT Press, 1996); John Dryzek, *Discursive Democracy: Politics, Policy, and Political Science* (Cambridge: Cambridge University Press, 1990); James Fishkin, *Democracy and Deliberation: New Directions for Democratic Reform* (New Haven: Yale University Press, 1991); Jürgen Habermas, *Between Facts and Norms: Contributions to a Discourse Theory of Law and Democracy,* trans. William Rehg (Cambridge: MIT Press, 1996); and Mark Warren, "What Should We Expect from More Democracy?: Radically Democratic Responses to Politics," in *Political Theory* 24, no. 2 (May 1996): 241–70.

54. See Seyla Benhabib, "Toward a Deliberative Model of Democratic Legitimacy," in *Democracy and Difference,* 67–94.

55. On the concept and history of the public sphere, see Joan Landes, *Women and the Public Sphere in the Age of the French Revolution* (Ithaca: Cornell University Press, 1988); Jürgen Habermas, *The Structural Transformation of the Public Sphere*

(Cambridge: MIT Press, 1989); Craig Calhoun, ed., *Habermas and the Public Sphere* (Cambridge, Mass.: MIT Press, 1992); the Black Public Sphere Collective, *The Black Public Sphere* (Chicago: University of Chicago Press, 1995); and Nancy Fraser, *Justice Interruptus: Critical Reflections on the "Postsocialist" Condition* (New York and London: Routledge, 1997), 69–120.

56. Jürgen Habermas, "Three Normative Models of Democracy," *Constellations* 1, no. 1 (1994): 7.

57. Ibid., 6.

58. On the idea of a "postconventional" moral consciousness, see Habermas, "Moral Consciousness and Communicative Action," *Moral Consciousness and Communicative Action* (Cambridge: MIT Press, 1990), 116–94.

59. Habermas, "Three Normative Models of Democracy," 7.

60. Ibid., 9–10.

61. Ibid., 8.

62. Ibid.

63. Also known as "radical democracy," this model is strongly influenced by postmodern thought and the cultural politics of the post-Marxist Left. See David Trend, ed., *Radical Democracy: Identity, Citizenship, and the State* (London and New York: Routledge, 1996).

64. See Connolly's essays in *The Ethos of Pluralization* (Minneapolis: University of Minnesota Press, 1995).

65. William E. Connolly, *Identity\Difference: Democratic Negotiations of Political Paradox* (Ithaca: Cornell University Press, 1991), x.

66. Chantal Mouffe, *The Return of the Political* (London and New York: Verso, 1993), 150.

67. Chantal Mouffe, ed., *Dimensions of Radical Democracy: Pluralism, Citizenship, Community* (London: Verso, 1992), 14.

68. Mouffe, *The Return of the Political,* 9–13.

69. Ibid., 12.

70. Ibid., 84.

71. Mouffe, "For an Agonistic Pluralism," introduction to *The Return of the Political,* 1–8.

72. Ibid., 70.

73. See Paul Hirst, *Associative Democracy: New Forms of Economic and Social Governance* (Amherst: University of Massachusetts Press, 1994), 15.

74. See Joshua Cohen and Joel Rogers, "Secondary Associations and Democratic Governance," *Politics and Society* 20, no. 4 (December 1992): 393–472.

75. Ibid., "The Idea of Associative Democracy," 416–22.

76. Ibid.

77. Hirst, *Associative Democracy,* 20.

78. "An Associational and Confederal Welfare State," chap. 7 in ibid., 176–202.

79. Cohen and Rogers, "Secondary Associations and Democratic Governance," 416–17.

80. See Etzioni's policy proposals in *The Spirit of Community: The Reinvention of American Society* (New York: Simon and Schuster, 1993).

81. See Iris Marion Young, "Communication and the Other: Beyond Deliberative Democracy," in Benhabib, *Democracy and Difference,* 120–35; and Lynn M. Sanders, "Against Deliberation," *Political Theory* 25, no. 3 (June 1997): 347–76.

82. On the emergence of local social justice movements, see Andrew Szasz, *Ecopopulism: Toxic Waste and the Movement for Environmental Justice* (Minneapolis: University of Minnesota Press, 1994); John Anner, ed., *Beyond Identity Politics: Emerging Social Justice Movements in Communities of Color* (Boston: South End Press, 1996); and David Schlosberg, *Environmental Justice and the New Pluralism* (Oxford: Oxford University Press, 1999).

83. Cohen and Rogers, "Secondary Associations and Democratic Governance," 453.

84. I agree with Paul Hirst's critique of the Cohen and Rogers model. See his "Comments on 'Secondary Associations and Democratic Governance,'" in *Politics and Society* 20, no. 4 (December 1992): 473–80.

85. The concept of "social capital" has been used by social scientists to describe the social networks in civil society that generate norms of trust and mutual aid, which in turn produce an ethos of civic voluntarism and engagement. See the work of Robert Putnam, *Making Democracy Work: Civic Traditions in Modern Italy* (Princeton: Princeton University Press, 1993); and "The Prosperous Community: Social Capital and Public Life," in the *American Prospect* (spring 1993): 35–42.

86. Danilo Zolo, *Democracy and Complexity: A Realist Approach* (University Park: Pennsylvania State University Press, 1992), 1.

87. Ibid., 3.

88. Ibid.

89. Ibid., 38.

90. "The Evolutionary Risks of Democracy," chap. 4 in ibid., 115–35.

91. Ibid., 99–109.

92. Ibid., "Complexity and Democratic Theory," 65–73.

93. Ibid., 82–88.

94. Ibid., 109–14.

95. Ibid., 70.

96. Ibid., 181–82.

97. See Francis Fukuyama, *The End of History and the Last Man* (New York: Free Press, 1992).

98. Zolo, *Democracy and Complexity,* 184.

99. Ibid., ix, 180–81.

100. Ibid., 35–45.

101. Ibid., 39.

6. Postmodern Strategies and Democratic Politics

1. Sheldon Wolin, "Fugitive Democracy," in Benhabib, *Democracy and Difference*, 31.

2. Ibid., 33.

3. Ibid.

4. Ibid.

5. Ibid.

6. Ibid., 31.

7. Ibid., 36.

8. Ibid., 43–44.

9. Ibid., 43.

10. On Foucault's discussion of "universal" and "specific" intellectuals, see his interview "Truth and Power," in Rabinow, *The Foucault Reader*, 51–75.

11. More precisely, it was a major defining theme of Foucault's early thought. See his essays and interviews in *Language, Counter-Memory, Practice: Selected Essays and Interviews,* trans. Donald Bouchard (Ithaca: Cornell University Press, 1977). See also Brent L. Pickett, "Foucault and the Politics of Resistance," *Polity* 28, no. 4 (summer 1996): 445–66.

12. Here Foucault was influenced by his reading of the work of Georges Bataille and Maurice Blanchot.

13. See Jon Simons, *Foucault and the Political* (London and New York: Routledge, 1995), 68–104.

14. See Foucault, *Language, Counter-Memory, Practice*, 35.

15. Foucault's early identification with the thought of Bataille and Blanchot and the practice of "transgression" gave way to his later identification with Baudelaire and his idea of "transfiguration."

16. The modern liberal causal model of agency and power runs from the early modern thought of Hobbes, Locke, and Hume through the behavioralism of Robert Dahl in the 1950s to the development of the "rational choice" or "public choice" models on the logic of individual and collective action.

17. See Jessica J. Kulynych, "Performing Politics: Foucault, Habermas, and Postmodern Participation," *Polity* 30, no. 2 (winter 1997): 315–46.

18. See Friedrich Nietzsche, "Homer on Competition," in *On the Genealogy of Morality,* ed. Keith Ansell-Pearson, trans. Carol Diethe (Cambridge: Cambridge University Press, 1994), 187–94.

19. See Leslie Paul Thiele, "The Agony of Politics: The Nietzschean Roots of Foucault's Thought," *American Political Science Review* 84, no. 3 (September 1990): 923.

20. See Lawrence J. Hatab, "Agonistic Democracy" and "Democracy, Excellence, and Merit," chaps. 4 and 5 in *A Nietzschean Defense of Democracy: An Experiment in Postmodern Politics* (Chicago and La Salle, Ill.: Open Court, 1995), 78–144.

21. Foucault gave a seminar at the University of California at Berkeley in 1983 titled "Discourse and Truth: The Problemization of 'Parrhesia.'" He also delivered lectures on this topic while at Berkeley.

22. See R. Bracht Branham and Marie-Odile Goulet-Caze, eds., *The Cynics: The Cynic Movement in Antiquity and Its Legacy* (Berkeley and Los Angeles: University of California Press, 1996).

23. James Miller writes that Foucault's "last five lectures of his life" delivered at the College de France "between February 29 and March 28, 1984" were on the topics of parrhesia, the ancient Cynics, and Diogenes. See *The Passion of Michel Foucault* (New York: Anchor Books, 1993), 360.

24. See S. Sara Monoson, "Frank Speech, Democracy, and Philosophy: Plato's Debt to a Democratic Strategy of Civic Discourse," in *Athenian Political Thought and the Reconstruction of American Democracy,* ed. J. Peter Euben, John R. Wallach, and Josiah Ober (Ithaca: Cornell University Press, 1994), 172–97.

25. See John S. Ransom, "Politics, Norms, and the Self," chap. 6 in *Foucault's Discipline: The Politics of Subjectivity* (Durham: Duke University Press, 1997), 155–67.

26. Ibid., 159–60.

27. Ibid., 160.

28. Lawrence J. Hatab, *A Nietzschean Defense of Democracy,* 214.

29. Ibid., 215.

30. Ibid., 216.

31. Ibid., 215.

32. Foucault, "What Is Enlightenment?" in Rabinow, *The Foucault Reader,* 46.

33. Ibid.

34. Ibid.

35. See Michel Maffesoli, *The Time of Tribes: The Decline of Individualism in Mass Society,* trans. Don Smith (Thousand Oaks, Calif.: Sage Publications, 1996).

36. See E. P. Thompson, *The Making of the English Working Class* (New York: Vintage, 1963); and "Time, Work-Discipline, and Industrial Capitalism," *Past and Present* 38 (1967): 56–97.

37. See *The Politics of Aristotle,* ed. and trans. Ernest Barker, book 7, "Political Ideals and Educational Principles," (Oxford: Oxford University Press, 1958), 321–324; Sebastian de Grazia, *Of Time, Work and Leisure* (New York: Anchor Books, 1962); and Raghavan Iyer, "An Unfinished Dream," chap. 16 in *Parapolitics: Toward the City of Man* (Oxford: Oxford University Press, 1979), 299–331.

38. See Fred L. Block, "The Road Forward," chap. 28 in *The Vampire State: And Other Myths and Fallacies about the U.S. Economy* (New York: The New Press, 1996), 259–75.

39. See Jeremy Rifkin, "The Dawn of the Post-Market Era," part 5 in *The End of Work: The Decline of the Global Labor Force and the Dawn of the Post-Market Era* (New York: G. P. Putnam's Sons, 1995), 221–93; and Stanley Aronowitz and William

DiFazio, *The Jobless Future: Sci-Tech and the Dogma of Work* (Minneapolis: University of Minnesota Press, 1994).

40. See William Greider, *One World, Ready or Not: The Manic Logic of Global Capitalism* (New York: Simon and Schuster, 1997).

41. See Roger E. Alcaly, "Reinventing the Corporation," in *The New York Review of Books,* 10 April 1997, 38–45.

42. See Helena Norberg-Hodge, "Shifting Direction: From Global Dependence to Local Interdependence," in *The Case Against the Global Economy: And for a Turn Toward the Local,* ed. Jerry Mander and Edward Goldsmith (San Francisco: Sierra Club Books, 1996), 393–406.

43. Michel Foucault, "What Is Enlightenment?" in *The Foucault Reader,* 47.

44. Ibid., 48.

45. Ibid.

46. Ibid.

Conclusion

1. Karl Marx and Friedrich Engels, "Manifesto of the Communist Party," in *The Marx-Engels Reader,* ed. Robert C. Tucker (New York: W. W. Norton, 1978), 476. Marx and Engels describe how the modern bourgeoisie "cannot exist without constantly revolutionising the instruments of production" and thus modern capitalism sweeps away all fixed relationships in its wake.

2. See Philip P. Hallie, *The Scar of Montaigne: An Essay in Personal Philosophy* (Middletown, Conn.: Wesleyan University Press, 1966); and Ermanno Bencivenga, *The Discipline of Subjectivity: An Essay on Montaigne* (Princeton: Princeton University Press, 1990).

3. Philip P. Hallie, *The Scar of Montaigne,* 37.

4. Noel O'Sullivan, "Political Integration, the Limited State, and the Philosophy of Postmodernism," *Political Studies* 41 (1993): 31.

5. Ibid.

6. Ibid.

7. Ibid., 34–35.

8. Karl Marx, "Theses on Feuerbach," in *The Marx-Engels Reader,* ed. Robert C. Tucker, 145. The eleventh thesis reads, "The philosophers have only interpreted the world, in various ways; the point, however, is to change it."

9. V. I. Lenin, "What Is to Be Done? Burning Questions of Our Movement," vol. 5 of *V. I. Lenin: Collected Works* (Moscow: Progress Publishers, 1961), 347–567.

10. Michel de Montaigne, "On Democritus and Heraclitus," in *The Essays of Michel de Montaigne,* ed. and trans. by M. A. Screech (London: Penguin Press, 1991), 339.

11. Ibid., 340.

Index

Wayne Gabardi is associate professor of political science at Idaho State University, where he teaches political philosophy and theory. His areas of expertise and interest include Western political philosophy, contemporary social and political theory, democratic thought, and politics and literature.